The Chronological Word Truth Life

BIBLE

IN THE BEGINNING

Genesis to Deuteronomy

With Selected Text From 1 Chronicles

C. Austin Tucker

ROUTE 66 MINISTRIES

The Chronological Word Truth Life Bible
In the Beginning ~ Genesis to Deuteronomy
With Selected Text From 1 Chronicles
Copyright © 2016 by Route 66 Ministries
All rights reserved.

Any use of The Chronological Word Truth Life Bible text
must include proper acknowledgment, as follows:
Scripture is taken from The Chronological Word Truth Life Bible.
Copyright © 2016 by Route 66 Ministries. Used by permission.

Printed in the United States of America
First Printing: 2016
ISBN 978-0-9890381-1-9

www.WordTruthLifeBible.com
www.Route66Ministries.com

Table of Contents

Scripture Index

Introduction to The Chronological Word Truth Life Bible

The Chronological Word Truth Life Bible is published by Route 66 Ministries, which is so named in reference to the 66 books of the Bible. The ministry is dedicated to teaching people to encounter God through reading and understanding the Bible in chronological order.

Two scriptures in the Gospel of John inspired the "Word Truth Life" series title. John the disciple identifies Jesus as *the Word* (**John 1:1, John 1:14**), and Jesus identified himself as *the Way, the Truth, and the Life* (**John 14:6**). These adjectives not only apply to Jesus himself, but to the book that illuminates him, the Bible.

The Word Truth Life Bible (WTLB) was born of the desire to provide a Bible version that's easier to read and understand. Many Christians know the Bible's familiar stories, but for many reasons they don't read the entire Bible to learn how everything fits together. Some of the most common reasons for this are:

- The Bible is big.
- The Bible is confusing.
- The Bible is boring.

The WTLB solves these issues. Although there will be many differences in comparison with traditional Bibles, Route 66 Ministries is committed not only to acknowledging the full and complete authority of scripture, but also remaining true to its entire message. Therefore, despite its different packaging, unique formatting, and shorter length, none of the Bible's content is missing. This has been the main concern in undertaking such a project.

Here are just a few benefits of The Word Truth Life Bible:

It's chronological – Events are placed in the order that they occurred, as far as could be determined.

It's harmonized – Harmonization is one of the main features that makes this Bible unique. It means scriptures that provide the same information are merged into one narrative. Most people are familiar with harmonies of the Gospels, but once this Bible is complete, it will harmonize scripture from Genesis to Revelation.

It's shorter – Because of the harmonization feature, the entire Bible is shorter, but no information is lost. This eliminates the intimidation of reading such a huge book. For example, all four Gospels can be read in half the time it would normally take.

It's uniquely formatted – For example:

- ❧ Chapters and verses have been removed from within the narratives to prevent unnatural breaks in the story line. However, scripture references are present in the heading of each section for those who prefer them.

- ❧ Scripture references are aligned right instead of left; this makes it easier to read the Bible like a novel, as the headings don't interfere with or interrupt the reading flow.

- ❧ Tables and bullets are used to break up text, making the information easier to understand.

- ❧ Dialogue is formatted as is common in novels, making it easier to follow the speaker.

Because of the vastness of such a project, each portion of the Bible is being published as it is completed. Old Testament volumes will continue to be published in the coming year, as well as Acts in the New Testament.

Connect with us to follow the publication progress of future installments and receive Bible-reading tips:

Websites: WordTruthLifeBible.com and Route66Ministries.com

Facebook: Facebook.com/WordTruthLifeBible

Twitter: Twitter.com/Word_Truth_Life

We look forward to accompanying you on this journey as you experience the Bible in a new and exciting way. And please let us know what you think. You can ask questions about this translation or report errors or concerns by visiting: *wordtruthlifebible.com/contact/* or emailing *wtlb@ wordtruthlifebible.com.*

KJV, NIV, ESV – A Word About Bible Translations

Walk into any Christian bookstore and you'll find countless Bibles in various translations and for different groups of people. What exactly does translation mean? It's simply the process of taking words from one language and expressing them in a different language. So American Bibles translate the original Hebrew, Aramaic, and Greek texts into English. Many people view multiple translations as a bad thing, but translations aren't evil; they're necessary. Without them, only people who know the original languages could read the Bible, but God intended that all people be able to read and understand its riches.

But why so many translations? Because of the complexity of language, one can write a concept or phrase in many different ways; there's more than one way to skin a cat! (Notice how those last two sentences state the same thing in two completely different ways.)

Some people choose certain translations based on how well they understand them, some choose based on the beauty and style of the language, while others choose based on word-for-word translation accuracy. All translations have their benefits, and there's no need to choose sides. Everyone is entitled to his preference. Each Bible translation serves a different function, depending on your purpose for reading it.

The King James Version

Many of us grew up reading the King James Version (KJV), and it remains one of the most beautiful translations ever penned. It's truly a literary masterpiece! Now, the KJV is also known as the "authorized version," but that title doesn't make it superior to other Bibles. It simply means that King James of England authorized its publication. But many people believe that the KJV is the only true Bible translation and that all other translations "change" the true word of God. This simply isn't true.

Despite the beauty of the old English language, the KJV isn't as accurate as more modern translations like the English Standard Version (ESV) or the New International Version (NIV). The reason for this has to do with the source text used for translation.

Here's an overview: The term "manuscripts" refers to the Greek and Hebrew documents containing the text of the Bible. Now the manuscripts available when the KJV was published were flawed, and knowledge of the languages — particularly Hebrew — was not as advanced as it is today. The scholars did an excellent job with what they had. However, more accurate manuscripts were found after the KJV was published, and subsequent Bible translations use them as their underlying text. So that's the reason for the differences between the KJV and other translations. No conspiracy involved! :-)

Because we speak English, it's easy to forget that we don't have a monopoly on the perfect Bible translation. People in other countries need to read the Bible too. So there are German translations, Spanish translations, Italian translations, etc. No single translation is inspired in the same way the original documents were; therefore none deserves to be put on a pedestal to the exclusion of the others.

It's fine to embrace our own traditions but it's not fair to insist that everyone else embrace them too. Many translations were published before the KJV, many were published afterward, and many will be published in the future. Instead of making the KJV the standard by which all other translations are judged, we must evaluate it along with every other translation to determine whether it most accurately reflects the author's intent and meaning as written in the original language.

Reading the KJV today is difficult simply because we don't speak the way they spoke back then. There's a barrier between our language and theirs. The people who lived in the 1600s spoke the same English in which the KJV was written, but we don't speak the King's English anymore. As language changes and words take on different meanings, new translations are necessary. Just as they had a Bible in the 1600s that reflected the way they actually spoke, people today need the same. It's not necessary to struggle over archaic words meant for a different time when translations with more modern phrasing are available.

The Word Truth Life Bible is different from other Bibles because of its goal: To provide a Bible that will aid people in reading and understanding all that God has to say, without the hindrances of the traditional Bible format.

The Bible's message remains intact — no content is missing. All stories include the same details that were originally present. The WTLB is not intended to take the place of traditional Bibles, which will always be necessary for use in church services and for in-depth Bible study. Nor is this Bible intended to replace your favorite translation. Everyone should have multiple translations available for different tasks and for the insight gained in noting the differences between them. This Bible is simply an addition to your library. It's for reading the Bible chronologically, like a novel, and gaining a true understanding of its overall story. It's perfect for those new to the Bible, those who want to introduce others to the Bible, and those who simply want a fresh new way to read it.

In the Beginning:
An Introduction to This Book

The first five books of the Old Testament — Genesis, Exodus, Leviticus, Numbers, and Deuteronomy — are commonly known either as the Torah (which means "law or teachings" and is primarily a Jewish designation) or the Pentateuch (which comes from two Greek words meaning "five books").

The Pentateuch is perhaps the most attacked portion of the Bible. Are the stories in Genesis true? Did Moses really write all five books? Did Abraham really exist? Did the Israelites really spend 400 years as slaves in Egypt? The answer to all these questions is yes because we believe the Bible is the very Word of God — God-Breathed! (2 Timothy 3:16)

In addition to being the most attacked, the Pentateuch may be the hardest to read through completely. We make it through Genesis and the first part of Exodus pretty well. The creation, Noah, Abraham, Moses, and the Exodus are all very familiar and interesting stories. But then somewhere around the middle of Exodus, things begin to go downhill. Exodus has a long section on the building of the Tabernacle; Leviticus has all those uncomfortable laws; Numbers records the Israelites wandering in the desert, with some odd laws mixed in; and Deuteronomy seems to randomly cover information already covered in Genesis through Numbers.

While the Pentateuch is largely chronological, there are some elements that are out of order. This Bible helps by placing events in a logical order, combining many repetitive laws, and merging repetitive passages.

It's essential to understand that it's not as important *when* events occurred, only that they *did* occur. This rendition of the Pentateuch seeks to provide a possible sequence of events, without omitting any of the information that each book uniquely provides. But it doesn't presume to be the final authority — it is only one interpretation among many. It's not meant to be a replacement for reading and studying the Pentateuch in full for yourself.

Explore the Word, Embrace the Truth, and Experience Life!

C. Austin Tucker

CHAPTER 1
Creation to Noah

God Creates Everything
GN 1:1-31|GN 2:1-25|GN 3:20|GN 3:25

Creation Introduction
GN 1:1-2

In the beginning, God created the heavens and the earth. Now at that time, the earth was shapeless and empty, darkness covered the deep waters, and the Spirit of God hovered over the surface of the waters.

DAY 1 – Day and Night
GN 1:3-5

Then God said, "Let there be light."

Light appeared and God was pleased with it. He separated the light from the darkness and called the light "day" and the darkness "night." Evening passed and morning came; this was the first day.

DAY 2 – Sky
GN 1:6-8

And God said, "Let there be a huge space between the waters to separate them."

And it was so. He separated the water beneath the space from the water above it, and he called the space "sky." That evening and the next morning was the second day.

DAY 3 – Earth, Seas, and Plant Life
GN 1:9-13

And God said, "Let the waters under the sky gather in one place and let dry land appear."

And it was so. He called the dry land "earth" and the gathered waters "seas." And he was pleased with them.

1

Then God said, "Let the land produce vegetation: seed-bearing plants and trees that bear seed-bearing fruit, each according to its own type."

It was so and God was pleased. That evening and the next morning was the third day.

DAY 4 – Sun, Moon, and Stars
GN 1:14-19

And God said, "Let there be lights in the sky to separate the day from the night and give light to the earth. Let them serve as signs to mark the beginning of seasons, days, and years."

It was so and God was pleased with them. The sun was the largest and it governed the day; the moon was smaller and it governed the night. The smallest lights were stars. That evening and the next morning was the fourth day.

DAY 5 – Birds and Sea Life
GN 1:20-23

Then God said, "Let the water be filled with living creatures, and let birds of every kind fly above the earth and across the sky."

So God created the great sea creatures, all water creatures that move and swarm, and various types of birds. And he was pleased. He blessed them and said, "Be fruitful and multiply. Let the sea creatures fill the seas and let the birds increase on the earth."

That evening and the next morning was the fifth day.

DAY 6 – Humans and Animals
GN 1:24-31|GN 2:4-25

And God said, "Let the land produce livestock, crawling creatures, and wild animals, each according to its kind."

It was so and God was pleased.

Now wild bushes and plants hadn't yet grown, because there was no one to cultivate the soil and the Lord God hadn't yet sent rain on the earth. Instead, streams beneath the earth's surface watered the ground.

So God said, "Let us make humans in our own image and likeness." He formed a man from the earth's soil and breathed life-giving breath into his nostrils, and the man became a living person.

The Lord God had planted a garden in the east, in Eden, and he placed the man, Adam, in it. He made various trees grow that were visually pleasing and produced delicious fruit. The tree of life and the tree of the knowledge of good and evil stood in the middle of the garden.

A river watering the garden flowed from Eden and divided into four rivers:

- The Pishon, which flows through the entire land of Havilah, where there is pure gold, aromatic resin, and onyx
- The Gihon, which flows through the entire land of Cush
- The Tigris, which flows along the east side of Ashur
- The Euphrates

The Lord God put Adam in the Garden of Eden to work it and take care of it and commanded him, "You are free to eat from any tree in the garden, but you must not eat from the tree of the knowledge of good and evil. When you eat from it, you will certainly die."

Now the Lord brought all the livestock, wild animals, and birds to Adam so he could name them, and whatever he called each one was its name.

But there was no companion for Adam.

Then the Lord God said, "It's not good for the man to be alone, so I'll make a suitable helper for him."

He put Adam into a deep sleep, took one of his ribs, and closed up the flesh. He created a woman from the rib and then brought her to Adam.

Then Adam proclaimed, "This is now bone of my bones and flesh of my flesh; she will be called 'woman,' because she was taken out of man."

For this reason, a man leaves his father and mother and unites with his wife, and they become one flesh.

Adam named his wife "Eve" because she would become the mother of all the living. Now they were both naked but they felt no shame.

After God created humans in his own image, male and female, he blessed them and said, "Be fruitful and multiply; fill the earth and rule over it. Reign over the fish in the sea and the birds in the sky, the wild animals, and every living creature that moves on the ground. For food, I'm giving you every seed-bearing plant on earth and every tree with seed-bearing fruit. I'm giving all the green plants to the wild animals, the birds in the sky, and the crawling creatures — everything that has the breath of life in it."

So God was pleased with everything he had made. And that evening and the next morning was the sixth day.

DAY 7 – God Rests and Initiates the Sabbath
GN 2:1-3

By the seventh day, the heavens, the earth, and everything in them were completed, and God stopped working. He blessed the seventh day and made it holy because on it he rested from all his work.

Now the serpent was more cunning than any of the wild animals the Lord God had made. He said to Eve, "Did God really say you must not eat from any tree in the garden?"

"We may eat fruit from the trees in the garden," Eve replied, "but God did say we would die if we eat fruit from or even touch the tree in the middle of the garden."

"You won't die," the serpent said. "God knows that when you eat from it, your eyes will be opened and you'll be like him, knowing good and evil."

Eve saw that the tree was beautiful and its fruit looked delicious, and now she was convinced it would make her wise, so she ate it. She gave some to her husband, who was with her, and he ate it too. Then both their eyes were opened and they realized they were naked, so they sewed fig leaves together to cover themselves.

As the Lord God walked in the garden in the cool of the day, Adam and Eve heard him and hid among the trees.

"Where are you?" the Lord God called to Adam.

"I heard you in the garden and I was afraid because I was naked, so I hid."

"Who told you that you were naked? Did you eat of the tree from which I commanded you not to eat?"

"The woman you put here with me gave me some fruit from the tree, and I ate it."

"What have you done?" the Lord God asked Eve.

"The serpent deceived me," she said, "so I ate it."

So the Lord God said to the serpent, "Because you did this, you are cursed above all livestock and wild animals. You will crawl on your belly and eat dust all the days of your life. I will cause hostility between you and the woman, and between your descendants and her descendants; her seed will crush your head and you will strike his heel."

To Eve he said, "I will increase your pain and labor when you give birth. You will desire control over your husband, but he will rule over you."

To Adam he said, "Because you listened to your wife and ate fruit from the forbidden tree, the ground is now cursed. You will struggle to produce food from it all your life. It will produce thorns and thistles, and you'll eat the plants of the field. By the sweat of your brow you will eat your food until you return to the ground, because from it you were taken; for dust you are and to dust you will return."

The Lord God made clothing from animal skins for Adam and Eve, and he dressed them.

Then he said, "The humans are now like one of us, knowing good and evil. They must not be allowed to eat from the tree of life and live forever."

So the Lord God banished Adam and Eve from the Garden of Eden, and he made Adam work the ground from which he came. Then he placed cherubim on the east side of the Garden, and a flaming sword that flashed back and forth, to guard the tree of life.

Cain Kills Abel
GN 4:1-16

Adam made love to Eve and she gave birth to a son. "The Lord helped me bring forth a man," she said, so she named him Cain. Later she gave birth to his brother, Abel.

Now Abel was a shepherd and Cain was a farmer. After a while, Cain brought some produce from the land as an offering to the Lord. Abel brought the firstborn of his flock and their fat portions as an offering. The Lord approved of Abel and his offering, but he didn't approve of Cain and his offering. So Cain was very angry and looked miserable.

"Why are you angry?" God asked Cain. "Why do you look so unhappy? You'll be accepted if you do what is right. But if you don't, sin is crouching at your door waiting to control you. You must master it."

But one day Cain said to Abel, "Let's go out to the field." And then Cain attacked Abel and killed him.

So the Lord asked Cain, "Where is your brother, Abel?"

"I don't know," he replied. "Am I responsible for my brother?"

"What have you done?" the Lord asked. "You spilled your brother's blood. Listen! It cries out to me from the very ground that soaked it up. Now you are cursed and alienated from the ground, and it will no longer yield crops for you. You will wander restlessly on the earth."

"My punishment is more than I can bear," Cain said. "You're driving me from the land and from your presence today, and I'll be a restless wanderer. Anyone who finds me will kill me!"

"No," the Lord said, "anyone who kills you will be punished seven times over."

Then he put a mark on Cain to prevent anyone from killing him.

So Cain left the Lord's presence and lived in the land of Nod, which was east of Eden.

Cain's Descendants
GN 4:17-24

Cain made love to his wife and she gave birth to Enoch, so Cain named the city he was building after his son. Enoch fathered Irad, Irad fathered Mehujael, Mehujael fathered Methushael, and Methushael fathered Lamech.

Lamech married two women, Adah and Zillah. Adah gave birth to Jabal, who was the first of those who live in tents and raise livestock. His brother's name was Jubal, who was the first of those who play the harp and flute. Zillah gave birth to Tubal-Cain, who made all kinds of bronze and iron tools. He had a sister named Naamah.

Lamech said to his wives, "Adah and Zillah, listen to me; wives of Lamech, heed my words. I killed a man for wounding me, a young man for injuring me. If Cain is avenged 7 times, then Lamech 77 times."

From Seth to Noah
GN 4:25-26|GN 5:1-31|1 CHR 1:1-3

This is the account of Adam's family line: God created male and female in his own likeness, and he blessed them and called them "humans."

Adam made love to his wife again. She gave birth to a son and named him Seth, saying, "God has granted me another child to replace Abel, who Cain killed."

Adam was 130 years old when he had Seth, a son in his own likeness and image. Afterward Adam lived 800 years and had other sons and daughters. He died at age 930.

Seth was 105 years old when he fathered Enosh. At that time people began to worship the Lord. Afterward Seth lived 807 years and had other sons and daughters. He died at age 912.

Enosh was 90 years old when he fathered Kenan. Afterward Enosh lived 815 years and had other sons and daughters. He died at age 905.

Kenan was 70 years old when he fathered Mahalalel. Afterward Kenan lived 840 years and had other sons and daughters. He died at age 910.

Mahalalel was 65 years old when he fathered Jared. Afterward Mahalalel lived 830 years and had other sons and daughters. He died at age 895.

Jared was 162 years old when he fathered Enoch. Afterward Jared lived 800 years and had other sons and daughters. He died at age 962.

Enoch was 65 years old when he fathered Methuselah. Afterward Enoch lived 300 years and had other sons and daughters. He walked faithfully with God for 365 years, but then he disappeared because God took him.

Methuselah was 187 years old when fathered Lamech. Afterward Methuselah lived 782 years and had other sons and daughters. He died at age 969.

Lamech was 182 years old when fathered a son. He named him Noah and said, "He will bring us relief from the painful labor of working this ground that the Lord has cursed." Afterward Lamech lived 595 years and had other sons and daughters. He died at age 777.

CHAPTER 2
Noah and the Ark

The World Becomes Wicked
GN 6:1-8|GN 6:11-12

When humans began to populate the earth, the sons of God noticed that the women were beautiful, and they married whoever they wanted.

Then the Lord said, "My Spirit won't remain with humans forever, for they are mortal; from now on their life span will be limited to 120 years."

In those days and for some time after, the Nephilim lived on the earth. They were the offspring of the sons of God and the daughters of humans; they were heroes and mighty warriors of ancient times.

The Lord saw how wicked everyone on earth had become and that their thoughts were continually evil, and his heart was grieved. So he said, "I'm sorry I ever created these humans; I will wipe them from the face of the earth, as well as all the animals and birds."

But the Lord was pleased with Noah.

God Commissions Noah to Build an Ark
GN 5:32|GN 6:9-10|GN 6:13-22|GN 7:2-3|GN 7:5|1 CHR 1:4

This is the account of Noah and his family. He was 500 years old when he fathered Shem, Ham, and Japheth. Noah was righteous — the only blameless man among the people of his time — and he walked with God.

God said to Noah, "I'm going to send a flood to destroy the earth and all living creatures because they've filled the earth with their violence. Build an ark of cypress wood, filled with rooms. Coat it with tar inside and out. Make it 450 feet long, 75 feet wide, and 45 feet high. Leave below the roof an 18-inch opening all around and build a door on the side of the ark. Build a lower, middle, and upper deck.

"I'm going to destroy all life under the heavens, every creature that has the breath of life in it. But I'll establish my covenant with you, and you'll take your wife, your sons, and their wives into the ark. Also take with you seven pairs of every kind of clean animal and bird and two of every kind of unclean animal and bird. Each pair must include a male and female, and all of them will come to you to be kept alive so they can reproduce again. Gather various types of food and store it away for yourselves and for the animals."

So Noah did everything God commanded him.

God Sends the Flood
GN 7:1|GN 7:4|GN 7:6-16

Then the Lord said to Noah, "Seven days from now I will send rain upon the earth for 40 days and 40 nights, and I will wipe every living creature I created from the face of the earth. But I have found you righteous in this generation, so take your whole family and enter the ark."

So Noah, his wife, his sons — Shem, Ham, and Japheth — and their wives entered the ark to escape the waters of the flood. And pairs of male and female, clean and unclean animals and birds arrived and entered the ark, as God had commanded. There were wild animals, livestock, small animals, and birds of every kind. Then the Lord shut the door behind them.

Seven days later the rain began to flood the earth. It was the 17th day of the 2nd month, and Noah was 600 years old. All the springs burst forth from the earth. The windows of heaven opened and rain fell for 40 days and 40 nights. The water rose and spread across the earth, rising to more than 20 feet and covering the highest mountaintops. It lifted the ark high above the ground and caused it to float on the water's surface. Everything that had life perished — all the animals, birds, and humans. Only Noah and those with him in the ark were left.

The waters flooded the earth for 150 days.

God Ends the Flood
GN 8:1-14

At the end of the 150 days, God remembered Noah and all the animals with him in the ark. He had closed the springs beneath the earth and closed the windows of heaven, so the rain had stopped falling. Then he sent wind to blow over the earth, and the waters began to recede. The ark rested on the mountains of Ararat on the 17th day of the 7th month. The waters continued to recede until the 1st day of the 10th month, when the mountaintops became visible.

Forty days later, Noah wanted to determine whether the water had receded. So he opened a window and sent out a raven, which kept flying back and forth, waiting for the water to dry up. Later Noah sent out a dove but it could find nowhere to land. So the dove returned and Noah brought it back into the ark. He sent the dove out again 7 days later and it returned that evening with a freshly plucked olive leaf in its beak. So Noah knew that the water was almost gone. He sent the dove out again 7 days later and this time it didn't return.

The water was gone by the 1st day of the 1st month, and Noah was 601 years old. He removed the ark's cover and saw that the ground was drying. The earth was completely dry by the 27th day of the 2nd month.

Noah's Family Exits the Ark
GN 8:15-22

Then God said to Noah, "You and your family come out of the ark. Bring out the birds and animals so they can reproduce and repopulate the earth."

So Noah and his family exited the ark. All the animals and birds left the ark in groups, according to their species.

Then Noah built an altar to the Lord and sacrificed on it every kind of clean animal and bird as a burnt offering. The Lord smelled the pleasing aroma and vowed to himself, *I'll never again curse the ground because of humans, even though their thoughts are evil from childhood. And I'll never again destroy all living beings. As long as the earth remains, there will seedtime and harvest, cold and heat, summer and winter, day and night.*

God Makes a Covenant With Noah
GN 9:1-17

God blessed Noah and his sons and said, "I'm placing all the animals, birds, and fish under your authority; therefore they will be afraid of you. They will all be food for you. Just as I gave you grain and vegetables, I now give you everything. But you must not eat meat with the blood still in it, because that is the source that gave it life. And I'll require the life of every animal and every man who takes a human life. Whoever sheds human blood will have his blood shed by humans, because I made humans in my own image.

"Be fruitful and repopulate the earth. I'm establishing my covenant with you, your descendants, and every living creature that came out of the ark with you. Never again will I destroy all living beings or the earth with a flood. I've placed my rainbow in the clouds as a sign of the covenant between me and the earth and between me, you, and every living creature. It's a covenant for all generations to come. Whenever I bring clouds over the earth and the rainbow appears, I'll remember the eternal covenant I have established."

Noah Curses and Blesses His Sons
GN 9:18-28

Noah's three sons who came out of the ark with him were Shem, Ham, and Japheth. Through them the whole earth was repopulated.

Now Noah was a farmer and he was the first person to plant a vineyard. One day he got drunk on the wine he had made from the grapes, and he slept naked in his tent. Ham saw him and went outside to tell his two brothers. But Shem and Japheth laid a cloth across their shoulders, walked in backward, and covered their father, turning their faces away so they wouldn't see him naked.

When Noah was sober again, he found out what his youngest son had done to him.

"Your son Canaan and his descendants are cursed!" he said to Ham. "They will be the lowest of slaves to their relatives. Praise the Lord, the God of Shem! May Canaan be the slaves of Shem's descendants. May God extend the territory of Japheth's descendants and let them live in peace with Shem's descendants, and may Canaan be his slave."

Noah lived 350 years after the flood, a total of 950 years, and then he died.

Noah's Descendants
GN 10:1-32

Introduction
GN 10:1

This is the account of Noah's sons — Shem, Ham, and Japheth — who had sons after the flood.

Japheth's Descendants
GN 10:2-5|1 CHR 1:5-7

Japheth's sons: **Gomer**, Magog, Madai, **Javan**, Tubal, Meshek, and Tiras.

Gomer's descendants: The people of Ashkenaz, Riphath, and Togarmah.

Javan's descendants: The people of Elishah, Tarshish, Cyprus, and Rhodes. They were the ancestors of those who live along the coast. They spread out to various lands clan by clan, each with its own language and national identity.

Ham's Descendants
GN 10:6-20|1 CHR 1:8-16

Ham's sons: Cush, Egypt, Put, and **Canaan.**

Cush's descendants: Seba, Havilah, Sabtah, **Raamah**, Sabteka, and **Nimrod**.

Raamah's descendants: Sheba and Dedan.

Nimrod became a mighty warrior and hunter before the Lord. His name became famous and others like him were said to be *like Nimrod, the mighty hunter*. His kingdom began with Babylon, Uruk, and Accad — all three cities were in Babylonia. He then expanded to Assyria, where he built Nineveh, Rehoboth-Ir, Calah, and Resen, which is between Nineveh and Calah — the great city.

Egypt was the father of the Ludites, Anamites, Lehabites, Naphtuhites, Pathrusites, Kasluhites, and the Caphtorites (from Crete) — from whom the Philistines descended.

Canaan fathered Sidon (his firstborn) and Heth (the ancestor of the Hittites). Canaan was also the ancestor of the Jebusites, Amorites, Girgashites, Hivites, Arkites, Sinites, Arvadites, Zemarites, and Hamathites. Later the Canaanite clans scattered, and the borders of Canaan stretched from Sidon toward Gerar — as far as Gaza — and then toward Sodom, Gomorrah, Admah, and Zeboyim — as far as Lasha.

These are the descendants of Ham clan by clan, each with its own language and national identity.

Shem's Descendants
GN 10:21-32|1 CHR 1:17-23

Shem's older brother was Japheth. Shem was the ancestor of all the sons of **Eber**.

Shem's sons: Elam, Ashur, **Arphaxad**, Lud, and **Aram**.

Aram's descendants: Uz, Hul, Gether, and Meshek.

Arphaxad was the father of **Shelah**.

Shelah was the father of **Eber**.

Eber had two sons: One was named Peleg because during his time people were scattered throughout the earth; his brother's name was **Joktan**.

Joktan's descendants: Almodad, Sheleph, Hazarmaveth, Jerah, Hadoram, Uzal, Diklah, Obal, Abimael, Sheba, Ophir, Havilah, and Jobab. The region where they lived stretched from Mesha toward Sephar, in the eastern hill country.

These are Shem's descendants, identified by their regions and clans, each with its own language and national identity.

All of these families descended from Noah's sons, nation by nation, according to their lines of descent. All these nations spread out over the earth after the flood.

The Tower of Babel
GN 11:1-9

At that time, people spoke the same language and had the same vocabulary. As they migrated eastward, they settled on a plain in Shinar.

"Let's make bricks and harden them with fire," they said. "Then we can build a city with a tower that reaches the sky and make a name for ourselves. Otherwise we'll be scattered across the whole earth!"

So they used bricks instead of stone, and tar to hold the bricks together.

But the Lord came down, saw the city and tower they were building, and said, "The people are united, and if they succeed nothing they plan will be impossible. Let's confuse them with different languages so they won't understand each other."

In this way the Lord stopped them from building the city and scattered them all over the earth. The city was called *Babel* because the Lord confused their language there.

From Shem to Tereh
GN 11:10-25|1 CHR 1:24-26

This is the account of Shem's descendants. Two years after the flood, when Shem was 100 years old, he fathered Arphaxad. Afterward he lived another 500 years and had other sons and daughters.

Arphaxad was 35 years old when he fathered Shelah. Afterward he lived another 403 years and had other sons and daughters.

Shelah was 30 years old when he fathered Eber. Afterward he lived another 403 years and had other sons and daughters.

Eber was 34 years old when he fathered Peleg. Afterward he lived another 430 years and had other sons and daughters.

Peleg was 30 years old when he fathered Reu. Afterward he lived another 209 years and had other sons and daughters.

Reu was 32 years old when he fathered Serug. Afterward he lived another 207 years and had other sons and daughters.

Serug was 30 years old when he fathered Nahor. Afterward he lived another 200 years and had other sons and daughters.

Nahor was 29 years old when he fathered Terah. Afterward he lived another 119 years and had other sons and daughters.

CHAPTER 3
Abraham and Lot

Terah's Family
GN 11:26-32|1 CHR 1:27

This is the account of Terah's descendants. He was 70 years old when he fathered **Abram**, **Nahor**, and **Haran**.

Haran fathered Lot and his sisters, Milcah and Iskah. But Haran died before his father in Ur of the Chaldeans, where he was born.

Nahor married Haran's daughter Milcah.

Abram married Sarai, but she was childless because she was unable to conceive.

Terah left Ur of the Chaldeans with his son Abram, his grandson Lot, and his daughter-in-law Sarai to travel to Canaan. But when they arrived at the city of Haran, they settled there.

And Terah died in Haran at age 205.

God Calls Abram in Haran
GN 12:1-9|GN 13:7b|GN 28:19b

Now the Lord told Abram, "Leave your country, your people, and your father's household and go to the land I will show you. I'll make you into a great nation and make your name famous. I'll bless you and you'll be a blessing, because everyone on earth will be blessed through you. I'll bless those who bless you and curse those who dishonor you."

Abram was 75 years old when he left Haran as the Lord instructed, taking with him his wife Sarai, his nephew Lot, and all the people and possessions they had acquired in Haran. They started for Canaan, where the Canaanites and Perizzites lived, traveling through the land as far as Shechem, near the great tree of Moreh.

The Lord appeared to Abram and said, "I'm giving this land to your descendants."

So Abram built an altar there to the Lord. Then he traveled toward the hill country east of Luz (later known as Bethel) and camped there, with Luz on the west and Ai on the east. He built another altar there and worshiped the Lord. Abram continued traveling from place to place until he reached the Negev.

Abram Goes to Egypt
GN 12:10-20

Now there was a severe famine in the land and there was no food, so Abram went down to Egypt to live there for a while. Right before they entered, he said to Sarai, "You're a beautiful woman. When the Egyptians find out you're my wife, they'll kill me and let you live. Say you're my sister so they'll treat me well and spare my life because of you."

When they arrived, the Egyptians did notice that Sarai was very beautiful. Some officials told Pharaoh, the king of Egypt, about her and she was taken to his palace. He treated Abram well because of her, giving him sheep and cattle, donkeys, servants, and camels.

But the Lord afflicted Pharaoh and his household with terrible diseases because of Sarai.

So Pharaoh summoned Abram. "What have you done to me?" he asked. "I took her as my wife because I didn't know you were married! Why did you tell me she's your sister? Take her and leave!"

So Pharaoh's men sent them away, as he had ordered.

Abram and Lot Separate
GN 13:1-7a|GN 13:8-10a|GN 13:11-18

Abram left Egypt and went up to the Negev with his wife, Lot, and everything he had. He went to the Negev and then traveled from place to place until he arrived at the place between Luz and Ai, where he had camped earlier and built an altar. And he worshiped the Lord.

Abram had become very wealthy with livestock, silver, and gold. Lot also had sheep, goats, cattle, and a large family and household. Now Abram and Lot's herdsmen began to argue because the land wasn't big enough for them both. Their possessions were so numerous that they could no longer stay together.

So Abram said to Lot, "We're family; let's not argue or allow our herdsmen to argue. The whole land is open to you. Let's separate. If you go left then I'll go right; if you go right then I'll go left."

So Lot looked around. When he looked toward Zoar, he saw that the whole Jordan Valley had plenty of water, like the Lord's garden or the land of Egypt. So Lot chose it for himself and journeyed east to live among the cities of the valley, camping near Sodom. Now the people of Sodom were wicked and constantly sinned against the Lord.

Abram settled in Canaan and the Lord said, "Look to the north and the south, to the east and the west. Go walk through the entire land; I'm giving it to you and your descendants as a permanent possession, as far as you can see. I'll give you so many descendants that, like the dust of the earth, they cannot be counted!"

Then Abram moved his camp to Hebron near the great trees of Mamre, where he camped and built an altar to the Lord.

Abram Rescues Lot
GN 14:1-24

Now there was war in the land at that time. For 12 years King Bera of Sodom, King Birsha of Gomorrah, King Shinab of Admah, King Shemeber of Zeboyim, and the king of Bela (also called Zoar) had been forced to pay tribute to King Kedorlaomer. But in the 13th year, these 5 kings rebelled, joining forces in the Valley of Siddim (also called the Dead Sea Valley). There they prepared to fight against King Kedorlaomer and his 3 allies: King Amraphel of Shinar, King Arioch of Ellasar, and King Tidal of Goyim — 4 kings in all.

So Kedorlaomer and his alliance of kings headed toward the Valley of Siddim, but first they defeated the Rephaites in Ashteroth-Karnaim, the Zuzites in Ham, the Emites in Shaveh-Kiriathaim, and the Horites in the hill country of Seir — as far as El-Paran, near the desert. Then they turned back and went to En-Mishpat (also called Kadesh) and conquered the whole territory of the Amalekites, as well as the Amorites who were living in Hazezon-Tamar.

In the 14th year, they finally arrived at the Valley of Siddim to battle the alliance of 5 kings — so it was 4 kings against 5 kings. The kings of Sodom and Gomorrah realized they were losing the battle and tried to escape, but they fell into one of the valley's many tar pits. The rest of the kings escaped and hid in the mountains. After Kedorlaomer and his alliance won the war, they went to Sodom and Gomorrah and seized all of their possessions and food. Since Abram's nephew Lot was living in Sodom, the kings also captured him and took his possessions. Then they left.

Now Abram the Hebrew was living near the great trees that belonged to Mamre the Amorite and his brothers, Eshkol and Aner. All three were allied with Abram. A man who had escaped capture came and told Abram that Lot had been taken, so Abram assembled the 318 trained men born in his household and pursued the alliance of 4 kings as far as Laish (later known as Dan). During the night, Abram divided his men into groups for the attack. They defeated the kings, pursuing them as far as Hobah, north of Damascus. He recovered all the goods that had been taken and brought Lot and his possessions back to his camp, along with the women and other captives.

After Abram returned from defeating Kedorlaomer and his alliance, the king of Sodom went to meet Abram in the Shaveh Valley (also called the King's Valley). Then King Melchizedek of Salem, priest of God Most High, brought bread and wine. He said to Abram, "Blessed be Abram by God Most High, Creator of heaven and earth. And praise God Most High, who delivered your enemies into your hand."

Then Abram gave him a tenth of the recovered goods.

Then the king of Sodom said to Abram, "Give me back my people and keep the goods for yourself."

Abram replied, "I've solemnly sworn to the Lord, God Most High, Creator of heaven and earth, that I'll accept nothing belonging to you, not even a thread or the strap of a sandal. That way you'll never be able to say that you made me rich. I'll accept only what my men ate and the share that belongs to my allies — Aner, Eshkol, and Mamre."

The Lord Makes a Covenant With Abram
GN 15:1-21

Then the Lord said to Abram in a vision, "Don't be afraid; I am your shield and will give you a great reward."

"Sovereign Lord," Abram said, "What good is a reward since you've given me no children? Now my servant Eliezer of Damascus will inherit my estate."

"No he won't," God said. "I'll give you a son to be your heir — your own flesh and blood."

He took Abram outside and said, "Look up at the sky and count the stars, if you can. That's how numerous your descendants will be."

Abram believed the Lord and the Lord counted him as righteous.

"I am the Lord, who brought you out of Ur of the Chaldeans to take possession of this land I've given you."

"Sovereign Lord," Abram said, "how can I be sure that I'll possess it?"

"Bring me a female cow, a female goat, and a ram, each three years old. Also bring a dove and a young pigeon."

Abram brought all these to him, cut them in two, and laid the halves side by side; he didn't cut up the birds. Vultures descended on the carcasses, but Abram drove them away. As the sun was setting, Abram fell into a deep sleep and great fear and terror fell upon him. When the sun set and darkness fell, a smoking firepot with a flaming torch passed between the carcasses Abram had cut up.

The Lord made a covenant with Abram that day and said, "Know for certain that your descendants will live as foreigners in a land not their own, where they will be mistreated as slaves for 400 years. I'll punish the nation that enslaves them and they will leave with numerous possessions. But you'll die in peace and be buried at a ripe old age. When it's time for the sins of the Amorites to be punished, your descendants will return to this land in the fourth generation.

"I'm giving your descendants this land from the border of Egypt to the great Euphrates river — the land of the Kenites, Kenizzites, Kadmonites, Hittites, Perizzites, Rephaites, Amorites, Canaanites, Girgashites, and the Jebusites."

Hagar Conceives Ishmael
GN 16:1-16

Abram had been living in Canaan 10 years and Sarai was still unable to give him any children. So she said to Abram, "The Lord has kept me from having children. Sleep with my servant and maybe I can have children through her."

Abram agreed, so Sarai gave him her Egyptian servant Hagar as his concubine, and he slept with her. When she found out she was pregnant, she treated Sarai with contempt.

So Sarai said to Abram, "I gave my servant to you and now that she's pregnant, she hates me. This is your fault. May the Lord show which of us is right!"

"Look, your servant is your responsibility," Abram said. "Deal with her as you wish."

And Sarai treated Hagar so cruelly that she ran away.

The angel of the Lord found Hagar near a spring of water in the desert, on the road to Shur. "Hagar, Sarai's servant, where did you come from and where are you going?"

"I'm running away from my mistress," she replied.

"Go back and submit to her and I'll give you descendants too numerous to count. You are going to have a son and you'll name him *Ishmael* (which means *God hears*) because the Lord has heard your cry of distress.

19

He will live like a wild donkey; he will be against everyone and everyone will be against him. And he will live in hostility toward all his relatives."

Hagar said, "Have I really seen God and lived to tell about it?" So she called the Lord *The God Who Sees*. That's why the well was called *Beer-lahai-roi* (which means *well of the Living One who sees me*). It's located between Kadesh and Bered.

Abram was 86 years old when Hagar gave birth to his son, and he named him Ishmael.

God Initiates the Covenant of Circumcision
GN 17:1-27

When Abram was 99 years old, the Lord appeared to him and said, "I am God Almighty; serve me faithfully and be blameless, and I'll make a covenant with you and give you many descendants."

Abram bowed with his face to the ground.

"This is my covenant with you," the Lord said. "Your name will no longer be Abram, but Abraham, for I'll make you the father of many nations. Kings will come from you and I'll establish an eternal covenant with you and your descendants for the generations to come. I'll give the whole land of Canaan, where you now reside as a foreigner, to your descendants as an eternal possession, and I will be their God.

"This will be the sign of the covenant, which you must keep for the generations to come: Every male 8 days old or more must be circumcised by cutting off the foreskin of his male organ. This includes not only your family members but also anyone born in your household or purchased from a foreigner. They must all be circumcised. In this way your bodies will be marked as a symbol of my eternal covenant. Any male who hasn't been circumcised will be cut off from his people, because he has broken my covenant.

"And now you must no longer call your wife Sarai, but Sarah. I will bless her and certainly give you a son through her. She will be the mother of nations, and kings of nations will descend from her."

Abraham bowed with his face to the ground again. And then he laughed and said to himself, *Can I have a son when I'm 100 years old? Will Sarah have a child at the age of 90?* Then he said to God, "If only Ishmael could be the one to inherit your blessing!"

"No," God replied. "Sarah will bear you a son and you'll name him Isaac. I'll establish an eternal covenant with him and his descendants. As for your request regarding Ishmael, I'll certainly bless him and give him numerous descendants. He will be the father of 12 princes and I'll make

20

him a great nation. But I'll establish my covenant with Isaac, whom Sarah will bear to you by this time next year."

Then God left Abraham.

That same day Abraham circumcised Ishmael, the men born in his household, and the men purchased from foreigners, as God had instructed. Abraham was 99 years old when he was circumcised and Ishmael was 13.

The Lord Visits Abraham
GN 18:1-15

One day Abraham was sitting at the entrance to his tent near Mamre's oak trees. It was the hottest time of the day. He looked up and saw three men standing nearby, so he ran to meet them and bowed to the ground. "If I've found favor in your eyes, my lord, please stay for a while," he said. "I'll bring water so you can wash your feet and rest under the tree. And since you've honored your servant with this visit, allow me to prepare some food to refresh you before you continue your journey."

"Yes, we'll stay," they answered."

So Abraham ran into the tent and told Sarah, "Hurry! Knead three gallons of our best flour and bake some bread."

Then he ran and selected a choice, tender calf from the cattle and gave it to a servant, who quickly prepared it. Then Abraham served the men yogurt, milk, and meat beneath the tree.

"Where's your wife Sarah?" they asked.

"In the tent."

One of the visitors was actually the Lord, and he said, "I will certainly return to you about this time next year, and Sarah will have a son."

Now Abraham and Sarah were very old, and she was past childbearing age. Sarah was listening at the entrance to the tent behind them, and she laughed to herself and thought, *I'm worn out and my lord is old; will I now have such pleasure?*

Then the Lord said to Abraham, "Why did Sarah laugh and say, 'Can an old woman like me really have a child?' Is anything too hard for the Lord? I'll return at the appointed time next year and she will have a son."

Sarah was afraid so she lied and said, "I didn't laugh."

"Yes, you did," the Lord said.

Abraham Pleads for Sodom
GN 18:16-33

The men got up and went to a place where they could look down on Sodom. Abraham walked with them to see them off. The Lord thought, *I won't hide what I'm going to do from Abraham. His descendants will certainly become a great and powerful nation, and all the nations on earth will be blessed through him. He will command his children and his descendants to obey me and do what's right, and then I'll fulfill my promise to him.*

The other two men, who were angels, left and headed toward Sodom, but the Lord stayed with Abraham and said, "The accusations against Sodom and Gomorrah are great, and their sin is very serious. I'm going down to find out if their actions are as evil as I've heard."

Abraham approached him and said, "Will you spare the city if there are 50 righteous people there? Surely you'd never kill the righteous with the wicked, punishing the innocent along with the guilty! You wouldn't do such a thing! The Judge of the whole earth must do the right thing."

The Lord said, "If I find 50 righteous people in Sodom, I'll spare the entire city for their sake."

I'm only dust and ashes," Abraham said, "but since I've begun to speak, allow me to continue. What if there were only 45 righteous people? Will you destroy the whole city for lack of five people?"

"If I find 45 there, I won't destroy it."

"What if you find only 40?"

"I won't destroy it if there are 40."

"Lord, please don't be angry but I must speak again. What if you find only 30?"

"I won't do it if I find 30."

"Forgive my boldness in continuing to speak, Lord. What if only 20 are found there?"

"If there are 20, I won't destroy it."

"Lord please don't be angry, but let me speak just once more. What if there are only 10?"

"I won't destroy it if I find 10 righteous people."

Then the Lord left and Abraham returned home.

God Destroys Sodom and Gomorrah
GN 13:10b|GN 19:1-29

The two angels arrived in Sodom that evening. Lot was sitting at the city gate and he got up to meet them. Then he bowed with his face to the ground and said, "My lords, please come to your servant's house so you can wash your feet and spend the night. You can continue your travels early in the morning."

"No," they answered, "we'll spend the night in the city square."

But Lot kept insisting, so they went with him. He prepared a feast and baked bread without yeast, and they ate.

Before they went to bed, all the men of Sodom — both young and old — surrounded the house. They shouted to Lot, "Bring out the men visiting you so we can have sex with them!"

Lot went outside and closed the door behind him. "No, my friends, don't do such a wicked thing. Look, I have two virgin daughters. I'll bring them out and you can do what you want with them. But leave these men alone; they're my guests and are under my protection."

"Get out of our way," they replied. "You're a foreigner here and now you want to judge us! We'll treat you worse than them!"

They pushed against Lot to try to break down the door, but the angels inside reached out, pulled him back into the house, and closed the door. Then they struck all the men outside with blindness, so they gave up trying to find the door.

Then the angels said to Lot, "Get your family out of here — your sons, daughters, sons-in-law, or any other relatives. The outcry to the Lord against this city is so great that he sent us to destroy it."

So Lot said to his daughters' fiancés, "Hurry! We've got to get out of here because the Lord is going to destroy the city!"

But they thought he was joking.

At dawn the angels urged Lot, saying, "Hurry now with your wife and your two daughters, or you'll die when the city is destroyed."

When Lot hesitated, the men grabbed his hand and the hands of his wife and two daughters, and led them safely out of the city, for the Lord was merciful. Then one of the angels said, "Run for your lives! Don't look back and don't stop anywhere in the valley! Run to the mountains or you'll be killed!"

"Oh no, my lords," Lot begged. "You've shown me favor and great kindness in sparing my life, but I can't run to the mountains; the disaster will overtake me and I'll die before I get there. Look, here's a city close enough. Let me go there and I'll be safe — it's only a small place."

"Very well, I'll grant your request and spare this city. But hurry, because I can't do anything until you reach it."

That city was called *Zoar* because Lot had called it *small.*

The sun had risen by the time Lot reached Zoar, and then the Lord rained burning sulfur on Sodom and Gomorrah. He destroyed the entire valley — all the people and the land's vegetation. But Lot's wife looked back and she became a pillar of salt.

Early the next morning, Abraham got up and returned to the place where he'd spoken with the Lord. He looked out across the valley toward Sodom and Gomorrah and watched as the smoke rose, as if from a furnace.

So God destroyed the cities of the valley where Lot had lived, but he remembered Abraham and rescued Lot from the catastrophe.

Lot's Daughters Deceive Him
GN 19:30-38

Lot was afraid to stay in Zoar, so he and his two daughters left and settled in a cave in the mountains.

One day the older daughter said to her sister, "There's no man here to give us children like everyone else has. Before our father gets too old, let's get him drunk and sleep with him to preserve our family line."

That night they got their father drunk, and the older daughter went in and had intercourse with him. But he was so drunk that he didn't realize it.

The next day the older daughter said to her sister, "Let's get our father drunk again tonight and this time you sleep with him."

They got their father drunk that night also and the younger daughter went in and had intercourse with him. Again, he wasn't aware of it.

So both of Lot's daughters became pregnant by their father. The oldest had a son and she named him Moab; he would be the ancestor of the Moabites. The younger daughter also had a son and she named him Ben-Ammi; he would be the ancestor of the Ammonites.

Abraham Encounters Abimelech at Gerar
GN 20:1-18

Now Abraham moved into the region of the Negev and lived between Kadesh and Shur. Later while he was staying in Gerar, he introduced Sarah as his sister, so Abimelech sent for her.

But God appeared to Abimelech in a dream one night and said, "You're as good as dead; the woman you took is married."

Abimelech hadn't touched her yet, so he said, "Lord, would you destroy an innocent nation? Didn't they both claim to be brother and sister? My conscience is clear! I've done nothing wrong."

"Yes, I know," God said. "I kept you from sinning against me by preventing you from touching her. Now return her to Abraham. He's a prophet; he'll pray for you and you'll live. But if you don't return her, you and all your people will certainly die."

Early the next morning, Abimelech summoned his officials and told them everything that had happened, and they were terrified. Then Abimelech summoned Abraham and said, "What have you done to us? What did I do to cause you to bring such great guilt upon me and my kingdom? No one should ever do what you've done to me. Why did you do it?"

Abraham replied, "I thought no one here would fear God and that they would kill me because of her. She's my wife, but she really is my sister. We have the same father but not the same mother. When God sent me from my father's house into foreign lands, I said to her, 'Show your love for me everywhere we go by saying I'm your brother.'"

Abimelech returned Sarah to Abraham and gave him sheep, cattle, and slaves. "Take your pick of the land and live wherever you like," he said.

He also told Sarah, "I'm giving your brother 1,000 pieces of silver in front of everyone as proof of your innocence; you are completely blameless."

Then Abraham prayed and God healed Abimelech, his wife, and his female slaves so they could have children again. The Lord had kept them all from conceiving because of Abraham's wife.

CHAPTER 4
Isaac and Rebekah

Isaac Is Born
GN 21:1-7

When Abraham was 100 years old, the Lord did what he had promised for Sarah. She became pregnant and gave birth to a son exactly when God had said she would. Abraham named him Isaac, circumcising him when he was 8 days old, as God had commanded.

Sarah said, "God has brought me laughter and everyone who hears about this will rejoice with me. Who would have said to Abraham that Sarah would nurse a baby? Yet I've given him a son in his old age."

Abraham Sends Hagar and Ishmael Away
GN 21:8-21|1 CHR 1:28

Isaac grew, and Abraham gave a huge feast the day he was weaned from his mother's milk. But Sarah noticed that Hagar and Abraham's son, Ishmael, were making fun of Isaac.

"Get rid of that slave woman and her son," Sarah told Abraham. "Her son must not share Isaac's inheritance."

This upset Abraham very much because he loved both Isaac and Ishmael.

"Don't worry about Ishmael and Hagar," God said. "Listen to Sarah, because it's through Isaac that your descendants will be traced. But I'll make Ishmael into a nation also, because he's your son."

Early the next morning, Abraham strapped food and a container of water to Hagar's shoulders and sent her and Ishmael off. She wandered in the Desert of Beersheba and when the water was gone, she put Ishmael under one of the bushes. Then she went and sat down about 100 yards away, thinking, *I can't watch him die.* And she began to cry.

God heard Hagar crying and the angel of God called to her from heaven and said, "What's the matter, Hagar? Don't be afraid; God heard the boy crying too. Go help him up; I'm going to make his descendants into a great nation."

Then God opened her eyes and she saw a well, so she filled the container with water and gave Ishmael a drink.

God was with Ishmael as he grew up. He lived in the desert and became a skilled archer. Hagar got a wife for him from Egypt while he was living in the Paran Desert.

Abimelech and Abraham Meet at Beersheba
GN 21:22-34

One day Abimelech and the commander of his army, Phicol, went to visit Abraham.

"God is with you in everything you do," Abimelech said. "You've been living in this country as a foreigner, so swear to me before God that you won't betray me or my descendants. Show to me and this country the same loyalty I've shown to you."

"I promise," Abraham said. Then Abraham complained to Abimelech about a well that Abimelech's servants had seized.

"You didn't mention this before, so I'm just now hearing about it," Abimelech said. "I don't know who's responsible."

Then Abraham gave Abimelech sheep and cattle, and they made an agreement.

When Abraham also set apart seven female lambs from the flock, Abimelech asked, "What are they for?"

"Please accept these lambs as a witness that I dug this well," Abraham replied.

So that place was called Beersheba because they made an agreement there. Then Abimelech and Phicol returned to the land of the Philistines.

Abraham planted a tamarisk tree in Beersheba and worshiped the Lord, the Eternal God. He stayed in the land of the Philistines for a long time.

God Tests Abraham
GN 22:1-19

Some time later, God tested Abraham.

"Abraham!" he called.

"Here I am," Abraham replied.

"Take your only son Isaac, whom you love, to the region of Moriah. Sacrifice him there as a burnt offering on a mountain I will show you."

Abraham got up early the next morning and saddled his donkey. He chopped enough wood for the burnt offering and set out for the place God had told him about, taking with him Isaac and two of his servants.

He saw the place in the distance on the third day and said to his servants, "Stay here with the donkey. Isaac and I will go and worship, and then we will return."

Abraham placed the wood for the burnt offering on Isaac's shoulders, and he carried the knife and the material for starting the fire.

As they walked, Isaac said, "Father?"

"Yes, my son?"

"We have fire and wood, but where is the lamb for the burnt offering?"

"God himself will provide the lamb, my son."

And they continued on their way.

When they arrived, Abraham built an altar and arranged the wood on it. After he tied Isaac up and laid him on top of the wood, he raised the knife to kill his son.

But the angel of the Lord called from heaven, "Abraham! Abraham!"

"Here I am," he replied.

"Don't lay a hand on the boy. Don't do anything to him. Now I know that you fear God, because you didn't withhold from me your only son."

Then Abraham looked up and saw a ram caught in a bush by its horns. So he sacrificed it as a burnt offering instead of his son. Abraham called that place *The Lord Will Provide.* And to this day it is said, "On the mountain of the Lord, it will be provided."

The angel of the Lord said to Abraham, "This is what the Lord says, 'I swear by my own name that because you obeyed me and didn't withhold your only son, I will surely bless you. I'll make your descendants as numerous as the stars in the sky and the sand on the seashore. They will conquer the cities of their enemies, and all nations on earth will be blessed through your descendants."

Then Abraham and Isaac returned with the servants to Beersheba, where they settled.

Nahor's Sons
GN 22:20-24

Some time later, Abraham received the news that his brother Nahor and his wife Milcah had eight sons: Uz was the firstborn, next were Buz, Kemuel (the ancestor of the Arameans), Chesed, Hazo, Pildash, Jidlaph, and Bethuel (who later fathered Rebekah).

Nahor's concubine Reumah also had sons: Tebah, Gaham, Tah, and Maakah.

The Death of Sarah
GN 23:1-20

Sarah was 127 years old when she died at Kiriath-Arba (now called Hebron) in Canaan. After Abraham mourned and wept over her, he left her body lying there and visited the local Hittites.

"I'm living here as a foreigner," he said. "Please sell me some property for a burial site so I can bury my wife."

"Sir, we honor you as a mighty leader. Choose the best of our tombs and bury her there. No one will refuse you."

Abraham bowed down before them and said, "Since you are willing, please ask Ephron son of Zohar to sell me the cave of Machpelah at the end of his field as a burial site. I'll pay the full price."

Ephron the Hittite was sitting with the other Hittites by the city gate. He said to Abraham, "No, my lord. In the presence of my people, I'm giving you the field and the cave so you can bury your wife."

Abraham bowed down again and replied, "Please allow me to purchase the field at full price."

"My lord," Ephron replied, "the land is worth 400 pieces of silver, but what is that between us? Bury your wife."

Abraham agreed to Ephron's terms and paid 400 pieces of silver, weighed according to the current commercial rate.

So all the Hittites witnessed as Abraham purchased Ephron's field at Machpelah, near Mamre. This included the cave and all the trees within the borders of the field. So Abraham buried Sarah in the cave there, in the land of Canaan.

Abraham Finds Isaac a Wife
GN 24:1-67|GN 35:8a

Abraham was now very old and the Lord had blessed him in every way. His oldest servant was in charge of everything he owned, so Abraham said, "Put your hand under my thigh and swear in the name of the Lord, the God of heaven and earth, that you won't allow my son to marry one of these Canaanite women. Go back to my homeland and get a wife for Isaac from among my relatives."

"What if the woman won't leave home to travel with me?" the servant asked. "Should I take Isaac back there?"

"No!" Abraham said. "The Lord, the God of heaven, brought me from my father's household, away from my native land, and promised to give this land to my descendants. Therefore, he will send his angel ahead of you to ensure you can get a wife for my son. If the woman won't return with you, then you'll be released from this vow. Just don't take my son back there."

The servant put his hand under Abraham's thigh and vowed to follow his instructions. He loaded ten of Abraham's camels with all kinds of goods and traveled to Mesopotamia, a region with two rivers. When he arrived, he made the camels kneel by the well outside Nahor's city. It was nearly evening, the time the women went out to draw water.

He prayed, "O Lord, God of my master Abraham, grant me success today and be kind to my master. The young women of the city are coming to this spring to draw water. Let this be the sign to confirm the one you've chosen: I'll ask her to give me a drink, and not only will she give me a drink, but my camels too. Then I'll know she's the one you chose for your servant Isaac and that you've been kind to my master."

Before he finished praying, Bethuel's daughter Rebekah came out carrying her water jug on her shoulder. Bethuel's parents were Nahor (Abraham's brother) and Milcah. Rebekah was very beautiful and was still a virgin. She went down to the spring, filled her jug, and headed back.

The servant ran to meet her and said, "Please give me a little water from your jug."

"Drink, my lord," she said, quickly lowering the jug to give him a drink. Afterward she said, "I'll also draw water for your camels until they've had enough to drink."

She quickly emptied her jar into the watering trough, ran back to the well, and drew enough water for all his camels. He silently watched her to confirm whether the Lord had given him success.

When the camels finished drinking, he gave her a gold nose ring weighing a quarter of an ounce and two gold bracelets weighing 5 ounces. Then he asked, "Who's your father? Please tell me if there's room in his house for us to spend the night."

"I'm Bethuel's daughter, and my grandparents are Milcah and Nahor. We have plenty of straw and feed for your camels, and there's room for you to spend the night."

Then the servant bowed down and worshiped the Lord, saying, "Praise the Lord, the God of my master Abraham. He has been kind and faithful by leading me to my master's relatives!"

Rebekah ran home and told her family everything that had happened. Her brother Laban noticed the nose ring and the bracelets she was wearing. As soon as Rebekah finished speaking, Laban ran to meet the man. He found him standing by the camels near the spring.

"You are blessed by the Lord," Laban said. "Why are you standing out here? Come with me; I have a room ready for you and a place for the camels."

So the servant went home with Laban. The camels were unloaded, and straw and feed were provided for them. Water was provided for him and his men to wash their feet. When the food was served, the servant said, "I won't eat until you hear what I have to say."

"Tell us," Laban said.

"I'm Abraham's servant. The Lord blessed my master abundantly and he became wealthy. He gave him sheep and cattle, silver and gold, male and female servants, and camels and donkeys. My master's wife Sarah gave birth to a son, Isaac, in her old age, and my master gave him everything he owns. He made me vow not to get a Canaanite wife for Isaac from where we live, but to come to his father's family instead.

"Then I asked my master, 'What if the woman won't come back with me?'

"He replied, 'The Lord before whom I've walked faithfully will send his angel with you and make your journey a success. You'll be released from this promise if they refuse to let her go with you.'

"When I arrived at the spring today, I silently prayed, 'Lord, God of my master Abraham, please grant me success on this journey. If a young woman comes out to draw water from this spring, I'll ask her for a drink. If she gives me a drink and offers to draw water for my camels too, let her be the one the Lord has chosen for Isaac.'

"Before I finished praying, Rebekah came out carrying her water jug on her shoulder. After she drew water from the spring, I asked her for a drink and she gave it to me. Then she offered to water my camels too.

"I asked her about her family and she told me about you.

"Then I put the ring in her nose and the bracelets on her arms. I bowed down and worshiped the Lord, praising the God of my master, who led me straight to the granddaughter of Abraham's brother. Now tell me whether you'll show kindness and faithfulness to my master, so I can decide what to do next."

Laban and Bethuel answered, "What can we say? The Lord has obviously already made the decision. Let Rebekah become Isaac's wife, as the Lord has directed."

Abraham's servant bowed to the ground and worshiped the Lord. Then he gave Rebekah clothing and gold and silver jewelry; he also gave expensive gifts to her brother and mother. Then he and the men with him ate and drank and spent the night there.

When they got up the next morning, the servant said, "Let me return to my master."

But her brother and mother replied, "Let her stay with us about ten days or so, and then she can go."

"Don't detain me now that the Lord has granted me success," the servant said. "Let me go."

"Let's ask Rebekah," they said. So they called her and asked, "Do you want to go with this man?"

"Yes," she said.

So they blessed Rebekah and said, "May you become the mother of millions; may your descendants conquer the cities of their enemies."

Rebekah got ready and mounted the camels. Then she, her childhood nurse Deborah, and her servants went with Abraham's servant.

Now Isaac had returned from Beer-lahai-roi and was living in the Negev. He was walking and meditating in the field one evening when he looked up and saw camels approaching.

When Rebekah saw Isaac, she got down from her camel and asked the servant, "Who's that man in the field walking toward us?"

"He's my master," he replied.

So she covered her face with her veil.

Then the servant told Isaac everything that had happened. Isaac married Rebekah and brought her into his mother Sarah's tent. He loved her and was comforted after his mother's death.

The Death of Abraham
GN 25:1-11|1 CHR 1:32-33

Abraham had married another woman, whose name was Keturah. Their sons were Zimran, **Jokshan**, Medan, **Midian**, Ishbak, and Shuah.

Jokshan fathered Sheba and **Dedan**.

> **Dedan's** descendants were the Asshurites, the Letushites, and the Leummites.

Midian fathered Ephah, Epher, Hanoch, Abida, and Eldaah.

These were all Abraham's descendants through Keturah.

Abraham died at age 175, joining his ancestors in death. He had lived a long and content life. He left everything he owned to Isaac, but he had given gifts to the sons of his concubines and sent them to live in the land of the east, away from Isaac.

Isaac and Ishmael buried Abraham with Sarah in the Machpelah Cave, in the field east of Mamre that Abraham had purchased from Ephron the Hittite.

After Abraham's death, Isaac settled near Beer-lahai-roi, and God blessed him.

This is the account of Abraham's descendants through Ishmael, the son he had with Hagar, Sarah's Egyptian slave.

These are the names of Ishmael's sons, listed in the order of their birth: Nebaioth, Kedar, Adbeel, Mibsam, Mishma, Dumah, Massa, Hadad, Tema, Jetur, Naphish, and Kedemah. These were also the names of the 12 tribes named after them, based on where they settled and camped.

Ishmael was 137 when he joined his ancestors in death. His descendants settled in the area from Havilah to Shur, near the eastern border of Egypt, going toward Asshur. And they lived in hostility toward their relatives.

**Rebekah Gives Birth to Esau and Jacob
GN 25:19-34|1 CHR 1:34**

Abraham and Sarah were Isaac's parents, and this is the account of Isaac's family line. He was 40 years old when he married Rebekah, who was Bethuel's daughter and Laban's sister. They were Arameans from Paddan-Aram.

Isaac prayed to the Lord for Rebekah because she was unable to have children. And the Lord answered his prayer and she became pregnant with twins. When the babies struggled against each other within her, she asked the Lord, "Why is this happening to me?"

"Two nations are in your womb and they will be rivals," he replied. "One will be stronger than the other, and the older will serve the younger."

When the time came, Rebekah gave birth to twin boys. The firstborn had a reddish color and his whole body was like a hairy robe, so they named him Esau. His brother came out next, holding tightly to Esau's heel, so he was named Jacob. Isaac was 60 years old when he became a father.

The boys grew up and Esau became an outdoorsman — a skillful hunter. But Jacob was content to stay home. Isaac had a taste for wild game and preferred Esau, but Rebekah preferred Jacob.

One day Jacob was cooking some stew when Esau came in from the field, exhausted and hungry.

"I'm famished!" he said to Jacob. "Quick, give me some of that red stew!" (That's why he was also called *Edom*, which means *red*.)

"First sell me your birthright," Jacob replied.

"Look, I'm about to die! What good is my birthright to me?"

"Swear you'll give it to me," Jacob said.

So Esau swore and sold Jacob his birthright. Then Jacob gave him some bread and lentil stew. Esau ate and drank, and then he left, caring nothing for his rights as the firstborn.

God Appears to Isaac in Gerar
GN 26:1-7

Now there was a famine in the land — much like the famine in Abraham's time — and Isaac moved to Gerar, where Abimelech of the Philistines lived.

The Lord had appeared to Isaac and said, "Don't go down to Egypt; stay here for a while and I'll bless you and be with you. I'll give these lands to you and your descendants and confirm the promise I made to your father Abraham. I'll make your descendants as numerous as the stars in the sky. Through them all the nations on earth will be blessed because Abraham obeyed me and did everything I required of him — keeping my laws and commands."

So Isaac stayed in Gerar.

Isaac Encounters Abimelech at Gerar
GN 26:8-33

When the men of Gerar asked Isaac about his wife, he said, "She's my sister." He was afraid to admit she was his wife because he thought, *They might kill me because Rebekah is so beautiful.*

Isaac had been there a while when Abimelech looked down from a window and saw Isaac caressing Rebekah. He summoned Isaac and said, "She's your wife! Why did you say she's your sister?"

"I thought someone might kill me because of her," Isaac said.

"What have you done to us? One of the men might have slept with your wife and you would have been responsible for our guilt."

So Abimelech warned all the people, "Anyone who harms this man or his wife will certainly die."

Isaac planted crops in that land and the same year reaped a hundred times more than he had planted, because the Lord blessed him. His wealth continued to grow until he became very rich. He had so many sheep, goats, cattle, and servants that the Philistines envied him. So they used dirt to fill in all the wells that Abraham's servants had previously dug.

Then Abimelech said to Isaac, "Leave our country; you've become too powerful."

So Isaac moved away and camped for a while in the Valley of Gerar. He reopened the wells that the Philistines had filled in and restored the names his father had given them.

Isaac's servants dug in the valley and discovered a well of fresh water. But the shepherds of Gerar argued with them and said, "That water is ours!" So Isaac named the well *Esek* (which means *argument*). They dug another well, but they argued over that one too, so he named it *Sitnah* (which means *hostility*). He abandoned that one and dug another well. No one fought over it so he named it *Rehoboth*, saying, "Now the Lord has given us space, and we will flourish in the land."

Later he moved up to Beersheba. That night the Lord appeared to him and said, "I am the God of your father, Abraham. Don't be afraid for I am with you. I will bless you and increase your descendants because of my servant Abraham."

Isaac camped there, built an altar, and worshiped the Lord.

One day Abimelech traveled from Gerar to visit Isaac, with Ahuzzath his personal adviser and Phicol the commander of his army.

Isaac said, "Why are you here? You were so unfriendly before and sent me away."

"We can plainly see that the Lord is with you," Abimelech said. "We thought there should be an agreement between us that you'll do us no harm, just as we didn't harm you but always treated you well and sent you away peacefully. And now look how the Lord has blessed you!"

Isaac prepared a feast for them, and they ate and drank. Early the next morning, the men made their vows of peace to each other. Then Isaac sent them on their way and they left without animosity.

The same day, Isaac's servants dug another well. "We've found water!" they told Isaac. He called it *Sheba* (which means *vow*), the same name his father had given it. It's been called *Beersheba* (which means *well of the vow*) ever since.

CHAPTER 5
Jacob, Leah, and Rachel

Jacob Steals Esau's Blessing
GN 27:1-40

When Isaac was old and blind, he called for Esau. "My son," he said. "Yes, Father," Esau replied.

"I'm an old man and will probably die soon. Go out to the field with your bow and arrow and hunt some wild game for me. Prepare my favorite meal. I'll eat and then bless you in the presence of the Lord before I die."

Now Rebekah overheard them. When Esau left she said to Jacob, "Your father told Esau to make his favorite meal so he can bless him before he dies. Now, my son, listen carefully and do what I tell you. Bring me two fat young goats so I can prepare the meal for your father. Then take it to him so he can bless you before he dies."

Jacob said, "But Esau is hairy and I have smooth skin. What if my father touches me and realizes that I tricked him? I'd bring down a curse on myself rather than a blessing!"

"My son, let the curse fall upon me. Just do what I tell you; go and get the goats for me."

So Jacob did and Rebekah prepared the food just the way his father liked it. She then got some of Esau's best clothes from the house and gave them to Jacob to wear. She also covered his hands and the smooth part of his neck with the goatskins. Then she gave him the food and bread she had made.

"My father," Jacob said when he brought the food to Isaac.

"Yes, my son," Isaac answered. "Who is it?"

"Esau, your firstborn," Jacob said. "I've done as you asked. Please sit up and eat so you can bless me."

"How did you find it so quickly, my son?"

"The Lord your God gave me success."

"Come here so I can touch you and determine whether you're really Esau."

Isaac touched him and said, "Your voice sounds like Jacob, but your hands are hairy like Esau's." Isaac prepared to bless him but then he asked, "Are you really Esau?"

"Yes, I am," Jacob replied.

"Bring the food. After I eat I'll give you my blessing."

Jacob brought him the food and some wine. After he finished, Isaac said, "Come kiss me, my son."

When Jacob kissed him, Isaac smelled his clothes. Since he didn't know it was Jacob, Isaac blessed him, saying, "Ah, the smell of my son is like the smell of a field that the Lord has blessed. May God give you heaven's dew and fertile fields — an abundant harvest of grain and new wine. May nations serve you and bow down to you. You and your descendants will rule over your relatives and their descendants, and they will bow down to you. Those who curse you will be cursed and those who bless you will be blessed."

Esau came in from hunting right after Jacob left, bringing the tasty food he had prepared.

"My father," he said, "please sit up so you can give me your blessing."

"Who are you?" Isaac asked.

"Your firstborn, Esau."

Isaac trembled uncontrollably. "Then who hunted and prepared the food I just ate? I blessed him right before you arrived — and indeed he will be blessed!"

Esau cried out loud in anguish and begged, "Bless me too, my father!"

"Your brother tricked me and took your blessing."

"This is the second time he's cheated me," Esau said. "He took my birthright and now he's taken my blessing! No wonder his name is Jacob! "Don't you have just one blessing left for me?"

"I made him master over you and made all his relatives his servants, and I guaranteed him an abundance of grain and new wine. So what can I possibly give you, my son?"

"Do you have only one blessing? Bless me too, my father!" Then Esau wept loudly.

So Isaac said, "You'll live away from the richness of the earth, away from the dew of heaven above. You'll live by your sword and serve your brother. But when you rebel, you'll break free from his control."

Rebekah Sends Jacob Away
GN 26:34-35|GN 27:41-46|GN 28:1-9

Now Esau held a grudge against Jacob because he had stolen his blessing. He thought, *My father will die soon and then I'll kill Jacob.*

When Rebekah heard about Esau's plans, she sent for Jacob. "Esau is consoling himself by planning to kill you. Do what I say, my son. Go immediately to my brother Laban in Haran and stay with him for a while. When your brother calms down and forgets what you did to him, I'll send for you. Why should I lose you both in one day?"

When Esau was 40 years old, he had married Hittite women: (1) Judith, the daughter of Beeri and (2) Basemath, the daughter of Elon. And they made life miserable for Isaac and Rebekah.

So Rebekah said to Isaac, "I'm disgusted with these Hittite women. If Jacob marries one of them, my life won't be worth living!"

So Isaac sent for Jacob and commanded him, "Don't marry any of these Canaanite women. Go immediately to your grandfather Bethuel's house in Paddan-Aram and marry one of your uncle Laban's daughters. May God Almighty bless you and give you many children so that you become many nations. May he give you and your descendants the blessing promised to Abraham so you can take possession of this land God gave him, where you now reside as a foreigner."

So Jacob left to visit his mother's relatives.

Esau found out that Isaac had commanded Jacob not to marry a Canaanite woman and had sent him to Paddan-Aram to find a wife. He realized that Isaac disapproved of Canaanite women. So in addition to his current wives, he married his uncle Ishmael's daughter Mahalath — who was Nebaioth's sister.

God Appears to Jacob at Bethel
GN 28:10-22|GN 35:6

Jacob left Beersheba and set out for Haran. At sundown he arrived in Luz, in Canaan, so he stopped for the night. He lay down to sleep, using one of the stones as a pillow, and dreamed of a stairway reaching from the earth to the sky, with angels of God ascending and descending on it. Suddenly the Lord stood beside him and said, "I am the Lord, the God of your grandfather Abraham and your father Isaac. I'm giving you and your descendants the land on which you are lying. Your descendants will be like the dust of the earth, and you'll spread out to the west and to the east, to the north and to the south. All the nations on earth will be blessed through you and your descendants. I am with you and will watch over you wherever you go, and I'll bring you back to this land. I won't leave you until I've fulfilled my promise."

Jacob woke up afraid and thought, *Surely the Lord is in this place, and I didn't realize it!* How awesome this place is! It must be the house of God, the gateway to heaven."

Early the next morning, Jacob took the stone he had used as a pillow, set it upright as a memorial, and poured oil on it. And he gave the city of Luz a new name, *El-Bethel*, which means *house of God*.

Then he vowed, "Lord, if you'll be with me, watch over me on this journey, give me food and clothing, and allow me to return safely to my father's household, then you'll be my God and this stone I've set up as a memorial will be your house. And I'll give you a tenth of everything you give me."

Jacob Arrives in Paddan-Aram
GN 29:1-14

Jacob continued on his journey and arrived in the land of the east. He saw a well in a field covered with a large stone. The shepherds would wait until all the flocks arrived to roll the stone away and water the sheep. When they finished, they would cover the well again. Jacob approached the well and saw three flocks of sheep and goats lying near the well, waiting for water.

"My brothers, where are you from?" Jacob asked the shepherds.

"We're from Haran," they replied.

"Do you know Laban, Nahor's grandson?"

"Yes, we know him."

"Is he well?"

"Yes, and here comes his daughter Rachel with his sheep."

"Look," Jacob said, "it's still broad daylight and it's too early to round all the animals up for the night. Why not water the sheep and take them out to graze?"

"We can't water the sheep until all the shepherds bring their flocks. Once they're all here, we can roll the stone away."

While they were still talking, Rachel arrived with the sheep, for she was a shepherdess. Jacob rolled the stone away from the well and gave water to his uncle's sheep. Then he kissed Rachel and wept loudly. He told her that he was Rebekah's son, the son of Laban's sister. So she ran and told her father.

As soon as Laban heard that his nephew had arrived, he hurried to meet him. He hugged and kissed him and brought him home, and Jacob told him everything.

"You really are my own flesh and blood!" Laban said.

After Jacob had stayed with him for a month, Laban said, "You shouldn't work for free just because we're family. Tell me what your wages should be."

Now Laban had two daughters: Leah — the oldest — and her sister, Rachel. There was no sparkle in Leah's eyes, but Rachel was shapely and beautiful, and Jacob was in love with her.

"I'll work for you 7 years if you allow me to marry Rachel," Jacob said.

"I'd rather give her to you than to some other man," Laban replied. "Stay with me."

So Jacob served 7 years for Rachel, but they seemed like only a few days to him because of his love for her. Then he said to Laban, "I've completed my time. Give me my wife so I can make love to her."

So Laban prepared a wedding feast and invited everyone. But that night instead of bringing Rachel to Jacob, he brought Leah, and Jacob made love to her.

When morning came, Jacob saw that it was Leah!

"What have you done to me?" Jacob asked Laban. "I served you for Rachel — why did you deceive me?"

Laban replied, "It's not our custom to give the younger daughter in marriage before the firstborn. Finish Leah's week of celebration and then you can marry Rachel in return for another seven years of work."

So Jacob finished the celebration week with Leah, and then he married Rachel. Laban gave Rachel his servant Bilhah and gave Leah his servant Zilpah, to serve them.

Jacob made love to Rachel also, and he loved her more than he loved Leah.

And he worked for Laban another 7 years.

The Lord saw that Leah was unloved, so he enabled her to conceive. But Rachel remained childless. Leah gave birth to a son who she named **Reuben**, saying, "The Lord has seen my misery; surely my husband will love me now."

She gave birth to another son and said, "The Lord heard that I am unloved, and he gave me this son too." So she named him **Simeon**.

She named her next son **Levi**, saying, "Surely now my husband will become attached to me because I've given him three sons."

She had another son and said, "This time I will praise the Lord." So she named him *Judah*. Then she stopped having children.

Bilhah Bears Two Children for Rachel
GN 30:1-8

Rachel wasn't bearing any children, so she was jealous of her sister. "Give me children or I'll die!" she said to Jacob.

Jacob became angry and said, "Am I God? He's the one who's kept you from having children."

Rachel said, "Sleep with my servant Bilhah so she can bear children for me; I can have a family through her."

So Jacob slept with Bilhah and she gave birth to a son.

"God has vindicated me," Rachel said. "He listened to my plea and gave me a son." So she named him **Dan**.

Bilhah gave birth to a second son and Rachel said, "I've battled with my sister and won." So she named him **Naphtali**.

Zilpah Bears Two Children for Leah
GN 30:9-13

When Leah stopped having children, she gave her servant Zilpah to Jacob as a wife. Zilpah gave birth to a son and Leah said, "What good fortune!" So she named him **Gad**.

Zilpah had a second son and Leah said, "I'm so happy! And that's what women will call me." So she named him **Asher**.

Leah Bears Three More Children
GN 30:14-21

During the wheat harvest, Reuben found some mandrake plants in the field and brought them to his mother.

"Please give me some of your son's mandrakes?" Rachel asked Leah.

"Wasn't it enough that you took away my husband? Now you want my son's mandrakes too?"

"Jacob can sleep with you tonight in return," Rachel said.

When Jacob came in from the field that evening, Leah went out to meet him. "I've paid for you with my son's mandrakes; you must sleep with me."

So he slept with her that night.

God answered Leah's prayer and she gave birth to a fifth son. "God has rewarded me for giving my servant to my husband," she said. So she named him **Issachar**.

Leah gave birth to a sixth son and said, "God has given me a precious gift. This time my husband will treat me with honor because I've given him six sons." So she named him **Zebulun**.

Some time later she gave birth to a daughter and named her **Dinah**.

Rachel Gives Birth to Joseph
GN 30:22-24

Then God remembered Rachel; he answered her prayer and enabled her to conceive. She gave birth to a son and said, "God has taken away my disgrace." She named him **Joseph**, saying, "May the Lord give me another son."

CHAPTER 6
Jacob's Return Home

Jacob's Flocks Increase
GN 30:25-43

After Rachel gave birth to Joseph, Jacob said to Laban, "You know how much work I've done for you. Give me my wives and children that I've earned serving you. I want to return to my own land."

"If I've found favor in your eyes, please stay," Laban said. "I learned by divination that the Lord has blessed me because of you. Name your wages and I'll pay them."

Jacob replied, "I've worked hard for you, and your livestock has grown under my care. The little you had before I came has greatly increased, and the Lord blessed you through everything I've done. Now it's time to provide for my own family."

"What should I pay you?" Laban asked.

"Nothing. But do one thing for me. I'll continue tending your flock but allow me today to remove all the goats that are speckled or spotted, along with all the black sheep. They will be my wages. In the future, you can check and determine whether I've been honest. Any goat in my possession that isn't speckled or spotted and any sheep that aren't black will be considered stolen."

"Agreed," Laban said.

That day Laban removed all the streaked and spotted male goats, the female goats that were speckled and spotted or had white patches, and all the black sheep. He put his sons in charge of them. Then he put a three-day journey between himself and Jacob, while Jacob tended the rest of Laban's flock.

Jacob took fresh-cut branches from poplar, almond, and evergreen trees and made white stripes on them by peeling the bark and exposing

45

the white inner wood. Then he put the peeled branches in all the watering troughs. When the flocks were in heat and came to drink, they mated in front of the branches. And they gave birth to young that were striped, speckled, and spotted. Jacob set apart the young of the flock by themselves, but he made the rest face the striped and dark-colored animals that belonged to Laban. Thus he made separate flocks for himself and didn't put them with Laban's animals. Whenever the stronger females were in heat, Jacob placed the branches in the troughs in front of the animals so they would mate near the branches, but he didn't do that if the animals were weak. So the weak animals went to Laban and the strong ones to Jacob. In this way he grew very prosperous and accumulated numerous flocks, servants, camels, and donkeys.

Jacob Flees From Laban
GN 31:1-21

Jacob heard that Laban's sons were saying, "Jacob built his wealth from everything our father owned." He also noticed that Laban's attitude toward him had changed.

Then the Lord said to Jacob, "Return to the land of your father, your grandfather, and your relatives, and I will be with you."

So Jacob sent for Rachel and Leah to meet him in the fields where he was watching his flocks. "Your father's attitude toward me has changed," he said, "but the God of my father has been with me. You know I've worked very hard for him, but he cheated me and changed my wages ten times. However, God hasn't allowed him to harm me. If he said, 'The spotted animals will be your wages,' they were born spotted. If he said, 'The striped ones will be your wages,' they were born striped. So God took your father's cattle and gave them to me.

"In mating season I once had a dream. The angel of God called me and I answered.

"'Look up!' He said. 'All the male goats mating with your flock are striped, spotted, or speckled. I've seen everything Laban has done to you. I am the God of Bethel, where you anointed the pillar and made a vow to me. Now return immediately to your native land.'"

Rachel and Leah replied, "There's nothing left for us to inherit from our father. He treats us like foreigners. Not only did he sell us, he spent all the money you paid him for us. All the wealth God took from our father belongs to us and our children. So do whatever God told you."

When Laban went to shear his sheep, Rachel stole his household gods.

Then Jacob put his children and wives on camels and drove his livestock ahead of him, along with everything he had acquired in Paddan-Aram, without telling Laban he was leaving. So he set out to return to his father Isaac in Canaan, crossing the Euphrates River and heading for the hill country of Gilead.

Laban Pursues Jacob
GN 31:22-55

Three days later, Laban was told that Jacob had run away, so he gathered his relatives and pursued Jacob. Seven days later he caught up with Jacob in the hill country of Gilead, where Jacob had camped. So Laban and his relatives camped nearby. That night God appeared to him in a dream and said, "Make sure you don't harm Jacob in any way."

The next day Laban asked Jacob, "What have you done? You deceived me and secretly carried off my daughters like prisoners of war. If you had told me, I would have sent you away joyfully, singing to the music of tambourines and harps. You didn't even let me kiss my daughters and grandchildren goodbye. You've acted foolishly. I have the power to harm you, but the God of your father warned me last night in a dream to leave you alone. I know you left because you were eager to return home, but why did you steal my gods?"

"I was afraid; I thought you would take your daughters away from me and force them to stay here," Jacob said. "But if anyone has your gods, that person will be put to death. With our relatives as witnesses, see whether we have anything of yours here; if so, take it back."

Jacob didn't know Rachel had stolen the gods.

So Laban searched Jacob's tent, the tent of the two female servants, and Leah's tent, but he found nothing. Then he entered Rachel's tent. Rachel had hidden the household gods inside her camel's saddle and was sitting on it.

"My lord, don't be angry that I can't stand up in your presence," Rachel said. "I'm on my period."

So Laban searched through everything in the tent and didn't find the household gods.

Jacob was very angry and said, "What's my crime? What did I do wrong that you had to hunt me down? You searched through everything I own; what did you find that belongs to you? Put it here in front of our relatives and let them decide which of us is right.

"I've been with you for 20 years now. Your sheep and goats never miscarried, and I never ate any rams from your flock. I didn't bring you animals torn by wild beasts; I took the loss myself. You demanded payment from me for whatever was stolen. The heat consumed me in the daytime and the cold at night, and it was hard to sleep. It was like this the entire 20 years! I worked 14 years for your two daughters and 6 years for your flocks, and you changed my wages ten times. If the God of Abraham, the fearsome God of Isaac, hadn't been with me, you would certainly have sent me away empty-handed. But God saw my suffering and hard work, and last night he rebuked you."

"These are my daughters," Laban said. "Their children are mine and these flocks are mine. Everything you see is mine. Yet what can I do now about my daughters and grandchildren? Come, let's make a covenant to serve as a witness between us."

So Jacob set up a stone as a marker. Then he told his relatives, "Gather some more stones."

So they piled the stones in a heap and ate near it. Laban named it *Jegar-Sahadutha* (which means *witness pile* in Aramaic), and Jacob named it *Galeed* (which means *witness pile* in Hebrew).

Laban said, "This pile of stones is a witness between you and me today." The place was also called *Mizpah* (which means *watchtower*) because Laban said, "May the Lord keep watch between us to ensure we keep this covenant when we're apart. If you mistreat my daughters or marry other women, remember that God is a witness between us and he'll see even if no one else does. This memorial of stones is a witness of our agreement. I won't cross them to harm you and you won't cross them to harm me. May the God of Abraham and the God of Nahor judge between us."

So Jacob took an oath in the name of the fearsome God of his father Isaac to respect the boundary line. He offered a sacrifice there on the mountain and invited his relatives to eat the meal. So they ate and spent the night there.

Early the next morning, Laban kissed his daughters and grandchildren and blessed them. Then he returned home.

Jacob Prepares to Meet Esau
GN 32:1-21

Jacob continued his journey home. At one place God's angels visited him and he said, "This is the camp of God!" So he named that place Mahanaim.

Jacob's brother Esau was living in the region of Seir, in the country of Edom. So Jacob sent messengers to him with this message: "I've been staying with Laban for the past several years. I have cattle and donkeys, sheep and goats, and male and female servants. Now I'm sending this message hoping you'll accept me."

The messengers returned and said, "We gave Esau your message and now he's coming to meet you with 400 men!"

Jacob was frightened and worried, so he divided his people into two groups, along with the sheep, goats, cattle, and camels. He thought, *If Esau attacks one group, the other group might escape.*

Then Jacob prayed, "O God of my grandfather Abraham and my father Isaac — Lord, you told me to return to my country and relatives and that you would make me prosper. I'm unworthy of all the kindness and faithfulness you showed your servant. I crossed this Jordan River with only my staff, but now my household fills two camps. Please protect me from my brother Esau and prevent him from attacking me and my family. You promised to make my descendants as limitless as the sand of the sea."

Then he selected a gift for Esau: 200 female goats, 20 male goats, 200 ewes, 20 rams, 30 female camels with their young, 40 cows, 10 bulls, 20 female donkeys, and 10 male donkeys. He divided them into two groups and put a servant in charge of each. "Go ahead of me and keep some distance between the cattle," he told them.

He instructed the one in the front, "Esau will ask who you belong to, where you're going, and who owns all these animals. Tell him, 'They belong to your servant Jacob and are a gift sent to my lord Esau, and he's coming behind us.'"

He also instructed the second, the third, and all the others who followed the cattle to say the same thing. "And be sure to say, 'Your servant Jacob is coming behind us.'"

He thought, *I'll pacify him with these gifts and perhaps he'll forgive me.*

So Jacob's gifts went on ahead of him, but he spent the night in the camp.

Jacob Wrestles With God
GN 32:22-32

That night Jacob got up and sent his 2 wives, 2 female servants, 11 sons, and all his possessions across the Jabbok River. When he was alone, a man wrestled with him until just before dawn. He couldn't overpower Jacob, so he struck the socket of his hip and dislocated it. Then the man said, "It's almost morning; let me go."

"Not until you bless me," Jacob replied.

"What's your name?"

"Jacob."

"Your name is no longer Jacob, but Israel, because you struggled with God and men, and you won."

"Please tell me your name," Jacob said.

"Why do you want to know my name?" he asked, and then he blessed Jacob.

So Jacob called the place Peniel, saying, "I saw God face to face, yet he spared my life."

The sun rose as he passed Peniel, limping because of his hip. Therefore to this day, the Israelites don't eat the tendon attached to the hip socket, because Jacob had been struck there.

Jacob Reunites With Esau
GN 33:1-17

Then Jacob looked up and saw Esau coming with his 400 men, so he divided the children between Leah, Rachel, and the two female servants. He put the servants and their children in front, Leah and her children next, and Rachel and Joseph last. Then he went ahead of them and bowed down to the ground seven times as he approached his brother.

But Esau ran to Jacob, threw his arms around him, and kissed him. And they were both crying.

Esau looked up, saw the women and children, and asked, "Who are they?"

"They're the children God graciously gave your servant," Jacob replied.

Then the servants and their children approached Esau and bowed down, next came Leah and her children, and then Rachel and Joseph did the same.

Esau asked, "Why did you send all those flocks and cattle?"

"To gain your favor, my lord."

"I already have plenty, my brother. Keep them for yourself."

"No, please accept these gifts from me if I've gained your favor. Now that you've accepted me, seeing your face is like seeing the face of God. Please accept my gifts. God has been kind to me and I have everything I need."

So because Jacob insisted, Esau accepted them.

Then Esau said, "Let's go; I'll lead the way."

But Jacob said, "The children are weak and the ewes and cows are nursing their young. They'll die if they are driven hard even one day. Please, my lord, go ahead while I move slowly at the pace of the animals and the children. I'll meet you in Seir."

"Then let me leave some of my men with you," Esau said.

"Why do that?" Jacob asked. "It's enough that you've accepted me."

So Esau traveled back to Seir, and Jacob went to Sukkoth, where he built a house for himself and shelters for his livestock. That's why the place is called *Sukkoth* (which means *shelters*).

Some time later Jacob arrived safely at Shechem in Canaan and camped in a field near the city. He purchased that part of the field for 100 pieces of silver from Hamor's sons and set up an altar there. He called it *El-Elohe-Israel* (which means *the God of Israel*)

One day Leah and Jacob's daughter Dinah visited the women of Canaan. Hamor the Hivite ruled that area and his son Shechem was the most respected member of his family. When Shechem saw Dinah, he grabbed her and raped her. But then he fell in love with her and spoke to her tenderly to win her affection.

Shechem said to his father, "Get her for me as my wife."

So Hamor and Shechem left to go speak with Jacob.

Meanwhile, Jacob had found out that Shechem violated his daughter. But his sons were in the field with his livestock so he didn't say anything.

While they were talking, Jacob's sons returned. When they found out what had happened, they were shocked and furious because Shechem had done such an intolerable thing to their sister, disgracing their family.

Hamor pleaded with Jacob and his sons, "Shechem is in love with Dinah. Please let him marry her. Let's make an agreement for our sons and daughters to marry each other. Live here with us any place you choose and feel free to trade and purchase land here."

Then Shechem said, "Please grant me this favor and I'll pay whatever you ask for the bride and give you whatever gifts you want. Just let me marry her."

Then Jacob's sons, plotting their revenge, lied and said, "We can't give our sister to a man who isn't circumcised; that would be a disgrace to us. We'll agree only if all your men are circumcised as we are. Then we'll intermarry with you, settle among you, and live together as one nation. But if you won't agree, we'll come get our sister and bring her back home."

So Hamor and Shechem agreed to their proposal. Shechem wasted no time, because he wanted Dinah badly, so he and his father went to their city gate to convince the men.

"Listen," they said. "Let's allow these men to live and trade in our land; there's plenty of room for them and they are peaceful. We can marry their daughters and they can marry ours. But they will only agree if our men are circumcised like they are. Their livestock and property will become ours, so let's agree to their terms."

The men agreed and all the men in the city were circumcised.

Three days later while all of them were still in pain, Dinah's brothers,

Simeon and Levi, attacked the unsuspecting city, killing all the men with their swords. They killed Hamor and Shechem, took Dinah from Shechem's house, and left. Then the rest of Jacob's sons looted the city as revenge for their sister's violation. They seized the flocks, cattle, donkeys, fields, and houses, and everything else in the city. They also took all the women and children as prisoners.

Then Jacob said to Simeon and Levi, "You've brought trouble on me and now the local Canaanites and Perizzites will hate me. There aren't many of us and if they join forces and attack us, our entire family will be destroyed!"

"He shouldn't have treated our sister like a prostitute," they replied.

Jacob Returns to Bethel
GN 35:1-5|GN 35:7-15

Then God said to Jacob, "I am the God who appeared to you at Bethel when you fled from your brother Esau. Now return to settle there, and build me an altar."

So Jacob said to everyone in his household, "Get rid of your idols, purify yourselves, and change your clothes. Let's go up to Bethel. I'll build an altar there to God, who answered me when I was in distress and has never left me."

So they gave Jacob all their idols and earrings, and Jacob buried them under the oak tree near Shechem. When they left, the terror of God fell upon all the cities in the area, and no one pursued them.

Eventually they arrived at Bethel, which Jacob had previously named when he was fleeing from his brother Esau. And he built an altar there.

Later Deborah, who had been Rebekah's nurse, died and was buried under the oak tree south of Bethel. So the tree was named *Allon-Bacuth* (which means *oak of weeping*).

Now that Jacob had returned from Paddan-Aram, God appeared to him again at Bethel and blessed him. "Your name is Jacob, but from now on it will be Israel.

"I am El-Shaddai — God Almighty; be fruitful and increase in number. Nations and kings will descend from you. The land I gave to Abraham and Isaac I also give to you and your descendants."

After God left, Jacob set up a stone there as a memorial and poured on it a drink offering of wine and anointed it with oil.

Rachel Dies Giving Birth to Benjamin
GN 35:16-20

They left Bethel. On the way to Ephrath, Rachel went into labor. She was in terrible pain and had great difficulty giving birth.

"Don't be afraid," the midwife said. "Now you have another son."

But Rachel was dying. With her last breath, she named her son *Ben-Oni* (which means *son of my sorrow*), but Jacob named him *Benjamin* (which means *son of my right hand*).

Rachel was buried on the road to Ephrath, now known as Bethlehem. Jacob set up a stone to mark her tomb, and it's still there to this day.

Esau and Jacob Bury Isaac
GN 35:21-29|1 CHR 2:1-2

Jacob continued traveling and camped on the other side of the tower of Eder. While they lived there, Reuben slept with Bilhah, one of his father's concubines. And Jacob found out about it.

These were Jacob's 12 sons who were born in Paddan-Aram:

With Leah: Reuben (Jacob's firstborn), Simeon, Levi, Judah, Issachar, and Zebulun

With Rachel: Joseph and Benjamin

With Bilhah (Rachel's servant): Dan and Naphtali

With Zilpah (Leah's servant): Gad and Asher

Finally Jacob arrived in Mamre, near Hebron (formerly Kiriath-Arba), where both Abraham and Isaac had lived. Isaac died at the ripe old age of 180, and Esau and Jacob buried him.

Esau's Descendants
GN 36:1-19|1 CHR 1:35-37

This is the family line of Esau (also known as Edom). Esau married Canaanite women:

Adah — Daughter of Elon the Hittite.

Oholibamah — Daughter of Anah and granddaughter of Zibeon the Hivite.

Basemath — His cousin, who was Ishmael's daughter and Nebaioth's sister.

Adah gave birth to **Eliphaz**, Basemath gave birth to **Reuel**, and Oholibamah gave birth to **Jeush, Jalam, and Korah**. They were all born in Canaan.

Esau moved his entire household, cattle, livestock, and all the possessions he had acquired to the hill country of Seir, some distance away from Jacob. The land wasn't big enough to support both of their livestock and possessions.

This is the account of Esau's descendants — the Edomites — who lived in Seir. All these clans descended from Esau:

Eliphaz's sons: Teman, Omar, Zepho, Gatam, and Kenaz. Eliphaz's concubine Timna also gave birth to Amalek. These were grandsons of

53

Esau's wife Adah. They were also the heads of the clans bearing their name.

Reuel's sons: Nahath, Zerah, Shammah, and Mizzah. These were grandsons of Esau's wife Basemath. They were also the heads of the clans bearing their name.

Jeush, Jalam, and Korah were the heads of the clans bearing their names. Their sons were Oholibamah's grandsons.

The Original Inhabitants of Seir
GN 36:20-30|1 CHR 1:38-42

The Horite people lived in Seir before Esau. They were the descendants of a man named Seir. His sons and their tribes were Lotan, Shobal, Zibeon, Anah, Dishon, Ezer, and Dishan. Lotan had a sister named Timna.

Lotan's descendants: Hori and Hemam.

Shobal's descendants: Alvan, Manahath, Ebal, Shepho, and Onam.

Zibeon's descendants: Aiah and Anah. Anah discovered the hot springs in the desert while he was grazing his father's donkeys.

Anah's descendants: Dishon and his sister Oholibamah.

Dishon's descendants: Hemdan, Eshban, Ithran, and Cheran.

Ezer's descendants: Bilhan, Zaavan, and Akan.

Dishan's descendants: Uz and Aran.

These were the leaders of the Horite clans in Seir.

The Kings of Edom
GN 36:31-43|1 CHR 1:43-54

Before any king reigned in Israel, these kings reigned in Edom, in the following order:

(1) Bela son of Beor from Dinhabah

(2) Jobab son of Zerah from Bozrah

(3) Husham from the land of Teman

(4) Hadad son of Bedad from Avith (he defeated the Midianites in the country of Moab)

(5) Samlah from Masrekah

(6) Shaul from Rehoboth-on-the-River

(7) Baal-Hanan son of Achbor

(8) Hadad from Pau (His wife was Mehetabel, the daughter of Matred and granddaughter of Mezahab.)

These were the leaders of clans descended from Esau, and they lived in the places named after them: Timna, Alvah, Jetheth, Oholibamah, Elah, Pinon, Kenaz, Teman, Mibzar, Magdiel, and Iram.

They all descended from Esau, the ancestor of the Edomites.

54

CHAPTER 7
Joseph Sold to Egypt

Joseph Shares His Prophetic Dreams
GN 37:1-11

After Isaac died, Jacob lived in Canaan, where his father had lived as a foreigner, and this is the account of his family.

Joseph was 17 years old and tending the flocks with his brothers, the sons of Bilhah and Zilpah. But Joseph brought bad reports to their father about them.

Now Jacob loved Joseph the most because he'd been born when Jacob was old. So he made him a long, lavish, multi-colored robe with long sleeves. Because their father favored Joseph, his brothers hated him and couldn't say anything nice to him.

One day Joseph said to his brothers, "Listen to this dream I had. We were in the field tying bundles of grain. Suddenly my bundle stood up and your bundles gathered around mine and bowed down to it."

"Do you think you'll become a king and reign over us?" his brothers asked.

And they hated him more because of his dream.

Later Joseph said to his father and brothers, "Listen, I had another dream. This time the sun, moon, and 11 stars bowed down to me."

His father chastised him and said, "What kind of dream is that? Do you think I, your mother, and your brothers will actually bow down to you?"

His brothers were jealous of him, but his father wondered what the dream meant.

One day Jacob told Joseph, "Your brothers are grazing the flocks near Shechem. Go check on them and the flocks, and come back and let me know how they're doing."

"Ok," Joseph replied.

So Joseph left the Valley of Hebron and arrived in Shechem. A man found him wandering in the field and asked, "What are you looking for?"

"I'm looking for my brothers. Do you know where they're grazing the flocks?"

"They left," the man answered. "I heard them say they were going to Dothan."

So Joseph set off for Dothan.

His brothers saw him from a distance and said, "Here comes that dreamer. Let's kill him here in the desert, throw him into one of these wells, and say a wild animal killed him. That will put an end to his dreams!"

"Don't kill him," Reuben said. "Throw him into this well, but don't hurt him." He intended to rescue Joseph and take him back to his father.

When Joseph arrived, they stripped him of his robe and threw him into the well; there was no water in it.

As they sat down to eat their meal, they looked up and saw a caravan of Ishmaelites coming from Gilead. They were Midianite traders and their camels were loaded with spices, balm, and myrrh they were taking down to Egypt.

Judah said to his brothers, "What will we gain if we kill Joseph and cover it up? After all, he's our brother, our own flesh and blood. Let's sell him to the Ishmaelites instead."

His brothers agreed.

When the merchants came by, Joseph's brothers pulled him up out of the well and sold him for 20 pieces of silver. And the Ishmaelites took Joseph to Egypt.

Reuben returned to the well, saw that Joseph wasn't there, and tore his clothes in sorrow. He went to his brothers and said, "The boy is gone! What am I going to do now?"

So they killed a goat and dipped Joseph's robe in the blood, then they took the robe to their father. "We found this," they said. "Doesn't it belong to Joseph?"

Jacob recognized it and said, "Yes, it's my son's robe! A wild animal must have killed and eaten him. Oh, my son Joseph, he has certainly been torn to pieces!"

Then Jacob tore his clothes, put on sackcloth, and mourned for Joseph a long time. His family tried to console him, but he refused to be comforted.

"No," he said, "I'll continue to mourn until I join my son in the grave."

So he continued weeping for Joseph.

Tamar Insists on Her Rights
GN 38:1-26|1 CHR 2:3

Later Judah left home and moved to Adullam, where he stayed with a man named Hirah. There he married Shua, the daughter of a Canaanite man, and they had two sons, **Er** and **Onan**. Later at Chezib, they had another son, **Shelah**.

Years later, Judah arranged for his firstborn Er to marry a woman named Tamar. But Er was wicked, so the Lord took his life.

Then Judah said to Onan, "Sleep with Tamar and fulfill your duty as her brother-in-law to produce descendants for your brother."

But Onan knew the children wouldn't be his, so whenever he slept with Tamar he spilled his semen on the ground. In this way he avoided providing descendants for his brother. But the Lord considered this evil and took his life too.

Judah then said to Tamar, "Live with your father as a widow until my son Shelah grows up." So Tamar stayed with her father.

But Judah was thinking, *What if he dies just like his brother?*

Many years later, Judah's wife died. After his period of mourning, he went up to Timnah to supervise the men who were shearing his sheep. His friend Hirah the Adullamite went with him.

Now someone told Tamar that Judah was on his way to Timnah.

Shelah was now grown and Judah hadn't arranged for Tamar to marry him. So she took off her widow's clothes, disguised herself with a veil, and sat at the entrance to Enaim, which is on the road to Timnah.

Judah noticed her and thought she was a prostitute because she had covered her face. He went over to her and said, "How much do you charge?"

What will you give me?" she asked.

"I'll send you a young goat from my flock."

"Will you leave something as a guarantee until you send it?" she asked.

"What do you want?"

"Your necklace with the seal hanging on it, engraved with your name, and your staff.

So he gave them to her. They slept together and she became pregnant. After she left, she took off her veil and put on her widow's clothes.

Meanwhile, Judah sent his friend Hirah to give the woman the young goat and to get his items back. When he couldn't find her, he asked the men who lived there, "Where is the temple prostitute who was sitting beside the road at Enaim?"

"There's been no temple prostitute here," they said.

So he returned to Judah and said, "I couldn't find her and the men who lived there said no temple prostitute had ever been there."

Then let her keep my things," Judah said. "I tried to pay her but you couldn't find her. If we keep looking for her, people will think we're fools."

About three months later someone told Judah, "Your daughter-in-law Tamar has behaved like a prostitute, and now she's pregnant!"

"Bring her out and let her be burned to death!" Judah said.

As they brought her out, she sent a message to her father-in-law, "I'm pregnant by the man who owns these. Do you recognize them?"

Judah recognized his things and said, "She did the right thing. I was wrong and should have let her marry my son Shelah."

And he didn't sleep with her again.

Tamar Gives Birth to Twins
GN 38:27-30|1 CHR 2:4

Tamar was having twin boys. When she gave birth, one of the babies put his hand out. So the midwife grabbed it, tied a scarlet thread around it, and said, "This one was born first." But he pulled his hand back and his brother was born first instead, so she said, "Well, you've certainly broken your way out!" And he was named **Perez**. Then his brother was born with the scarlet thread on his wrist and he was named **Zerah**.

So all together Judah had fathered five sons.

Potiphar Puts Joseph in Charge
GN 37:36|GN 39:1-6a

Meanwhile, the Ishmaelite merchants had arrived in Egypt and sold Joseph to Potiphar, who was captain of Pharaoh's guard.

The Lord was with Joseph and he prospered while living in Potiphar's house. Potiphar was pleased with Joseph. He realized that the Lord gave Joseph success in everything he did, so he made him his personal attendant, putting him in charge of his house and everything he owned. Then the Lord blessed everything Potiphar had, both in the house and in the field. And he didn't worry about anything except his food.

Potiphar's Wife Tries to Seduce Joseph
GN 39:6b-23

Now Joseph was handsome and well built, and Potiphar's wife soon noticed him. "Come sleep with me," she said.

Joseph replied, "My master trusts me with everything he owns and doesn't worry about anything. No one has more authority than I do. The only thing forbidden to me is you. How could I do such a wicked thing? It would be a sin against God."

Even though she persisted day after day, Joseph refused to sleep with her or even be around her.

One day he went into the house to do his work and the servants weren't there. Potiphar's wife grabbed his robe and said, "Sleep with me!" But he left his clothing in her hand and ran out of the house.

So she called her servants and said, "My husband brought this Hebrew here to make fools of us! He tried to sleep with me but I screamed as loud as I could. Then he left his clothing behind and ran out of the house."

She kept his clothing beside her until Potiphar came home, telling him the same story.

Potiphar was furious with Joseph, so he locked him up in his house where he kept Pharaoh's prisoners.

But the Lord was with Joseph, and he blessed him. The prison warden was pleased with Joseph and put him in charge of all the other prisoners, making him responsible for everything. The warden didn't worry about anything under Joseph's care, because the Lord was with Joseph and gave him success in everything he did.

Joseph Interprets the Dreams of the Cupbearer and Baker
GN 40:1-23

Some time later, the chief cupbearer and chief baker offended their master, Pharaoh — the king of Egypt. He was angry so he put them in the prison in Potiphar's house, where Joseph was being kept. Potiphar assigned Joseph to look after them, and they were there a long time.

One night each of them had a dream, and each dream had its own meaning.

The next morning, Joseph noticed that Pharaoh's officials looked upset. "Why do you look so worried today?" he asked.

"We each had a dream, but there's no one to interpret them."

"Interpretations belong to God," Joseph said. "Tell me your dreams."

The chief cupbearer said, "I dreamed of a grapevine with three branches. It grew leaves and its flowers blossomed and produced clusters of ripe grapes. I squeezed some of the juice from the grapes into Pharaoh's cup and gave it to him."

"This is what the dream means," Joseph said. "The three branches represent three days. Pharaoh will release you in three days and restore you to your position, and you'll give him his cup as usual. But when things are going well for you, please mention me to Pharaoh and help get me out of here. I was kidnapped from the land of the Hebrews, and here in Egypt I've done nothing to deserve being put in prison."

Since Joseph had given the cupbearer a positive interpretation, the chief baker said, "I had a dream too. I was carrying three bread baskets on my head. The top basket had all kinds of bread and pastries for Pharaoh, but the birds ate them."

"The three baskets represent three days," Joseph said. "Pharaoh will release you in three days, cut off your head, and hang your body on a pole. And vultures will eat your flesh."

Three days later, Pharaoh prepared a feast for his birthday and invited all his officials. He released the chief cupbearer and the chief baker in front of everyone. He restored the chief cupbearer to his position but beheaded and hanged the chief baker, just as Joseph had predicted.

But the chief cupbearer forgot all about Joseph.

Joseph Interprets Pharaoh's Dreams
GN 41:1-37

Two years passed. One night Pharaoh dreamed he was standing by the Nile River. Seven healthy, well-fed cows came out of the river and grazed in the grass. Seven ugly and bony cows also came out and stood beside those on the riverbank, and the bony cows ate up the seven healthy cows. Then Pharaoh woke up.

He fell asleep again and had another dream. This time seven heads of plump, ripe grain grew on a single stalk. Then seven heads of thin grain appeared, scorched by the east wind, and they swallowed up the seven healthy heads. Pharaoh woke up and realized he had been dreaming.

In the morning he was worried, so he summoned all the magicians and wise men of Egypt and told them his dreams, but no one could interpret them.

Then the chief cupbearer said to Pharaoh, "I just remembered my mistake! A couple of years ago you were angry with me and the chief baker, and you imprisoned us in Potiphar's house. Each of us had a dream on the same night, with different meanings. A young Hebrew was there too, Potiphar's servant. We told him our dreams and he interpreted them. And things turned out exactly as he said! I was restored to my position and the chief baker was executed."

So Pharaoh sent for Joseph, who shaved and changed his clothes, and then they quickly brought him from the prison to meet with Pharaoh.

"No one can interpret my dream," Pharaoh said to Joseph, "but I heard that you can."

"That's beyond my power," Joseph replied, "but God will give you a good answer."

"In my dream, I was standing on the bank of the Nile River," Pharaoh began. "Seven healthy cows came out of the river and grazed in the grass. And then seven very ugly, skinny cows came out. I'd never seen such ugly cows in the entire land of Egypt! Then the skinny, ugly cows ate up the seven healthy cows. But you couldn't tell that they had eaten them because they looked just as skinny as before.

"In the other dream, I saw seven plump, ripe heads of grain growing on a single stalk. Then seven other heads appeared — withered, thin, and scorched by the east wind. The thin heads swallowed up the seven plump heads. My magicians couldn't explain any of these dreams."

"Both dreams mean the same thing," Joseph said. "God is telling you what he plans to do. The seven healthy cows and the seven plump heads of grain represent seven years of abundance, and the seven skinny cows and withered heads of grain represent seven years of famine. The next seven years will be a period of great abundance for Egypt, but seven years of famine will follow, destroying the land so severely that the period of abundance will be forgotten. The repetition of your dreams means that God has determined these events, and they will take place soon.

"And now you should appoint overseers and give them the authority to collect a fifth of the harvest during the seven years of abundance. They should store the grain in the cities for the future so the country won't be wiped out by the seven years of famine."

Pharaoh and his officials approved of Joseph's plan.

Pharaoh Makes Joseph Governor of Egypt
GN 41:38-57

Pharaoh said to his officials, "Obviously Joseph is filled with God's spirit; we won't find anyone else like him."

Then Pharaoh said to Joseph, "God revealed all this to you, so no one else is as intelligent and wise. I'm appointing you as governor. Even though I'm the king, no one will lift hand or foot in Egypt without your permission. You'll be in charge of my palace and all my people will obey your orders. Your authority will be second only to mine."

Then Pharaoh took off his ring, engraved with the royal seal, and put it on Joseph's finger. He dressed him in a fine linen robe and hung a gold chain around his neck. Then Joseph rode in the chariot reserved for Pharaoh's second-in-command. Everywhere he went people shouted, "Kneel down!"

Pharaoh gave Joseph the Egyptian name Zaphenath-Paneah. He also gave him a wife, whose name was Asenath. She was the daughter of Potiphera, priest of On.

Joseph was 30 years old when he began serving in Pharaoh's court, and he traveled throughout Egypt. During the seven years of plenty, the land produced abundant crops. Joseph collected all the food and stored the grain from the surrounding fields in the cities. There was so much that Joseph stopped measuring it — the grain was like the sand on the seashore. Before the famine came, Joseph and Asenath had two sons. Joseph named his firstborn **Manasseh**, saying, "God made me forget all my suffering and my father's family." He named his second son **Ephraim**, saying, "God has given me children in this land of my suffering."

The seven years of abundance in Egypt ended and the seven years of famine began, just as Joseph had predicted. There was famine in all the surrounding countries but plenty of food in Egypt.

Eventually the famine spread throughout Egypt and the people cried out to Pharaoh for food. "Go to Joseph and do whatever he tells you," he told them.

Joseph opened all the storehouses and sold grain to the Egyptians. The famine was severe throughout the whole world and people from all over traveled to Egypt to buy grain.

CHAPTER 8
Joseph and His Family in Egypt

Joseph's Brothers Go to Egypt
GN 42:1-38

Jacob and his family felt the effects of the famine in Canaan too. So Jacob said to his sons, "Why are you just standing around doing nothing? I heard there's grain in Egypt. Go and buy some; otherwise we'll die."

So ten of Joseph's brothers went down to Egypt to buy grain. Jacob wouldn't allow Joseph's brother Benjamin to go with them, because he was afraid something would happen to him.

Joseph's brothers arrived while he was selling grain, but they didn't recognize him. They bowed down to him with their faces to the ground. Joseph recognized them immediately and remembered the dreams he'd had about them, but he pretended not know them.

"Where are you from?" he asked them harshly.

"We came from Canaan to buy food," they replied.

"You're spies!" he said. "You came to see whether our land is weak."

"No, my lord," they answered. "We're honest men, not spies. Your servants came to buy food."

"No! You came to see how weak we are."

"Your servants are the sons of one man, who lives in Canaan. There were 12 of us, but the youngest is with our father and the other is dead."

"I believe you're spies, but I'm going to test your story. I swear by Pharaoh that you won't leave this place unless I see your youngest brother. One of you must go get him; I'm keeping the rest of you here in prison until I determine if you're telling the truth. If not, then as sure as Pharaoh lives, you are spies!"

Then he put them all in prison for three days.

On the third day, Joseph said, "I'm a God-fearing man, so this is what I'll do. One of you must stay in prison while the rest of you take grain back for your starving families. But you must bring your youngest brother back to prove you've been telling the truth. If I find that you are honest men, I'll let you live."

His brothers agreed.

Then they said to each other, "We're obviously being punished because of what we did to Joseph. He was so distressed when he pleaded for his life, but we wouldn't listen; that's why we're in this trouble."

"I told you not to harm him but you ignored me!" Reuben said. "Now we must answer for his death."

Joseph was using an interpreter, so they didn't realize he could understand them. He turned away and began to cry. When he was able to speak again, he came back, chose Simeon, and had him tied up in front of his brothers.

Joseph ordered his servants to fill his brothers' sacks with grain and to return their money in the sacks. He also gave them supplies for their journey.

Then his brothers loaded the grain on their donkeys and left. When they stopped for the night, one of them opened his sack to get grain for his donkey. In shock, he said, "My money has been returned. It's right here in my sack!"

Their hearts sank and they asked in fear, "What has God done to us?"

When they arrived in Canaan, they told Jacob, "The governor spoke harshly to us and accused us of spying on the land. But we told him we're not spies but brothers, honest men. We also told him about Benjamin and Joseph.

"But he wanted us to prove we're honest, so we had to leave Simeon behind. The man gave us food but ordered us to bring Benjamin back to him. If we do, he'll release Simeon and allow us to buy more food."

Then they emptied their sacks and each man found his money in his bag! They were all frightened, including Jacob.

"Do you want me to lose all my children?" Jacob asked angrily. "Joseph and Simeon are gone, and now you want to take Benjamin too. Everything is going against me!"

Reuben said, "I'll take responsibility for him. You can kill both my sons if I don't bring Benjamin back to you."

"I can't let him go; his brother is dead and he's the only one left. If anything happens to him, you'll send this old man to the grave in sorrow."

The famine was still severe and eventually Jacob's family ate all the food they had brought back from Egypt.

"Go back and buy us a little more food," Jacob said.

"We can't," Judah said. "The governor warned us that we'd never see him again if Benjamin wasn't with us. And he was serious. Let Benjamin come or we won't go."

"Why did you cause me so much trouble by telling him you had another brother?"

"He asked about our family," Judah said. "He asked if you were still alive and if we had another brother. We simply answered his questions. How could we know he'd want to see our brother? Send Benjamin with me and we'll go immediately; otherwise we'll all starve to death. I personally guarantee his safety. You can hold me responsible if I don't bring him back, and I'll bear the blame forever. If we hadn't wasted so much time, we could have been there and back twice by now!"

"Go if you must," Jacob said. "Pack some of our best products and take them to the governor as a gift — balm, honey, spices, myrrh, pistachios, and almonds. Take double the amount of money so you can return what was put into your sacks. Maybe it was a mistake. Take Benjamin and return to Egypt immediately. And may God Almighty grant you mercy so the governor will let Simeon and Benjamin return. And if I must lose my children, so be it."

So they took Benjamin, the gifts, and the extra money and hurried down to Egypt to see Joseph.

When Joseph saw Benjamin with them, he said to his steward, "Take these men to my house, slaughter an animal, and prepare a meal; they'll eat with me at noon."

Joseph's brothers were frightened as the steward took them to Joseph's house. They thought, *He brought us here because of the money that was returned in our sacks. They're going to attack us, take our donkeys, and make us slaves.*

So they approached the steward at the entrance to the house and said, "Sir, we came here the first time to buy food. But when we stopped for the night, we found the exact amount we had paid in our sacks. We don't know who put it there, so we brought it back, along with additional money to buy food."

"It's all right," the steward said. "Don't be afraid. Your God, the God of your father, must have given you that treasure. I received your payment."

Then he released Simeon and brought him out to them.

He took them into Joseph's house, gave them water to wash their feet, and provided food for their donkeys. They'd been told that they would eat there, so they prepared their gifts for Joseph's arrival at noon.

When Joseph came home, they gave him the gifts they had brought and then they bowed to the ground.

He asked them how they were and then asked, "How is your elderly father? Is he still alive?"

"Yes. Our father, your servant, is still alive and well," they said, bowing again.

He looked at his brother Benjamin — his mother's son — and asked, "Is this your youngest brother?" Then he said to Benjamin, "God bless you, my son."

He was overcome with emotion at the sight of his brother, so he hurried out to his private room and wept. After washing his face and gaining control of himself, he returned.

"Serve the food," he said.

The servants served Joseph by himself, his brothers by themselves, and the Egyptians by themselves, because Egyptians find it detestable to eat with Hebrews. Joseph had seated his brothers facing him, and to their amazement they were seated in the order of their ages, from the first-born to the youngest. They were served from Joseph's table and Benjamin received five times more than anyone else. So they ate and drank with Joseph until they were all drunk.

Benjamin Is Found With Joseph's Silver Cup
GN 44:1-34

When his brothers were ready to leave, Joseph instructed his steward, "Fill their sacks with as much food as they can carry, and put their money back in too. Then put my silver cup in the top of the youngest brother's sack."

The steward did as Joseph said.

Early the next morning, his brothers headed out with their donkeys. They were barely out of the city when Joseph said to his steward, "Go after them immediately." And he told him what to say.

The steward caught up with them and said, "Why did you repay kindness with evil? You took my master's cup that he uses to predict the future. You've committed a serious crime!"

"What do you mean, sir?" they asked. "Your servants would never do anything like that! We brought back the money we found in our sacks, so why would we steal silver or gold from your master's house? If you find the cup on any one of us, he must die and the rest of us will become your slaves."

"Ok, but only the person found with it will become my slave; the rest of you will be free to go."

They quickly lowered their sacks to the ground and opened them. Then the steward searched them, beginning with the oldest and ending with the youngest. He found the cup in Benjamin's sack.

They tore their clothes in despair, loaded their donkeys, and returned to the city.

Joseph was still in his house when Judah and his brothers arrived, and they fell to the ground before him.

"What have you done?" Joseph asked. "Don't you know a man like me can predict the future?"

"What can we say, my lord?" Judah replied. "How can we prove our innocence? God has exposed your servants' guilt and now all of us are your slaves."

"I'd never do such a thing!" Joseph said. "Only the guilty man will become my slave. The rest of you can return to your father in peace."

Judah approached him and said, "Pardon your servant, my lord. Let me speak and don't be angry, though you're as powerful as Pharaoh himself. You asked about our family and we told you we have an elderly father. He had two sons born in his old age, and they had the same mother. But the boy's brother is dead; he's the only one left and his father loves him very much.

"Then you told your servants to bring him here so you could see him for yourself. We told you our father would die if the boy left him, but you said we couldn't see you again unless we brought him. So we returned and told our Father what you said.

"Then our father told us to come back and buy more food, but we told him we couldn't unless Benjamin came with us. My father said, 'My wife gave me two sons. A wild animal has certainly torn one of them to pieces, because I haven't seen him since. If you take Benjamin and something happens to him, I'll die in misery.'

"My father's life is wrapped up with the boy's life. And if he isn't with us when we return, he will die and your servants will be responsible for his death. I promised my father that I'd bring him back safely or bear the blame all my life!

"So please let me stay here as my lord's slave and let Benjamin return with his brothers. How can I return if he isn't with me? I couldn't stand to see the misery that would overtake my father."

Joseph Reveals Himself to His Brothers
GN 45:1-28

Joseph could no longer control himself. "Everyone leave!" he ordered his attendants.

When he was alone with his brothers, he wept so loudly that the Egyptians could hear him, and they told Pharaoh's household about it.

"I'm Joseph," he said to his brothers. "Is our father really still alive?"

But they were so terrified that they couldn't respond.

"Come here," Joseph said.

When they did, he said, "I'm your brother Joseph, who you sold into Egypt! Don't be upset and don't be angry with yourselves. God sent me ahead of you to save lives. There's been famine in the land for two years now, and for the next five years, there will be no plowing or harvesting. But God sent me here to make sure you and your descendants survive.

"God sent me here, not you. He made me Pharaoh's adviser, manager of his entire household, and governor of Egypt. Now hurry back and tell my father to come quickly — with his children and grandchildren, flocks and cattle, and everything he has. All of you will live near me in the region of Goshen. I'll provide for all of you during the five years of famine ahead. Otherwise our whole family and all the livestock will starve. You and my brother Benjamin can see that it's really me. Tell my father about the honor shown to me in Egypt and about everything you've seen. Bring him here quickly."

Then Joseph threw his arms around Benjamin and they hugged each other and wept. He also kissed his other brothers and wept, and then he talked with them.

Pharaoh and his officials were pleased when they heard that Joseph's brothers had arrived. Pharaoh told Joseph, "Tell your brothers to load their animals and bring your father and the rest of your family back from Canaan. I'll give them the best land in Egypt and they can enjoy the rich produce of the land. They can take some wagons for their children and wives, and they don't have to worry about their belongings. The best of Egypt will be theirs."

So Joseph gave them wagons, supplies for their journey, and new clothes as Pharaoh had commanded. But he gave Benjamin 300 pieces of silver and 5 sets of clothes. He sent his father 10 donkeys loaded with the finest products of Egypt and 10 female donkeys loaded with grain, bread, and other supplies for the journey. Then he sent his brothers off, saying, "Don't argue on the way!"

When they arrived in Canaan they told Jacob, "Joseph is still alive and he's the governor of Egypt!"

Jacob was stunned and couldn't believe it. But when they told him everything Joseph had said and he saw the carts Joseph had sent, his spirit revived.

"I'm convinced that Joseph is still alive," Jacob said. "I must see him before I die!"

Jacob Goes to Egypt
GN 46:1-7|GN 46:28-34|GN 47:1-12|GN 47:27

So Jacob packed up everything. When it was time to leave, Jacob's sons placed him, their children, and their wives in the wagons Pharaoh had sent. They brought with them all the livestock and the possessions they had acquired in Canaan.

When they arrived in Beersheba, Jacob offered sacrifices to the God of his father Isaac.

That night God spoke in a vision, "Jacob! Jacob!"

"Here I am," he replied.

"I am the God of your father. Don't be afraid to go to Egypt, for I'll make your descendants a great nation there. I'll go with you and will surely bring you back again. And Joseph himself will close your eyes when you die."

They left Beersheba and continued their travels. Jacob sent Judah ahead to ask Joseph to meet them in Goshen, so Joseph prepared his chariot and went to meet his father. As soon as Joseph saw him, he hugged him and wept for a long time.

Finally Jacob said to Joseph, "I'm ready to die now that I've seen for myself that you're still alive."

Joseph instructed his brothers and the rest of his family to say they were shepherds. "Pharaoh will allow you to settle in Goshen because all shepherds are detestable to Egyptians," he told them.

Joseph went to speak to Pharaoh and said, "My father, my brothers, and their families came from Canaan with their flocks, cattle, and everything they own, and now they're in Goshen."

Then he presented five of his brothers to Pharaoh.

"What's your occupation?" Pharaoh asked them.

"Your servants are shepherds," they replied. "We've tended livestock all our lives, just as our ancestors did. We came to live here for a while because the famine is severe in Canaan and our flocks have nowhere to graze. So please allow us to settle in Goshen."

Pharaoh said to Joseph, "Now that your family has joined you, Egypt is theirs. Settle them in the best part of Goshen, and put the most skillful men in charge of my livestock."

Then Joseph brought Jacob to meet Pharaoh, and Jacob greeted him respectfully.

"How old are you?" Pharaoh asked.

"I've wandered from country to country for 130 difficult years," Jacob said. "But my life is short compared to that of my ancestors, who also wandered from place to place."

Then Jacob paid his respects to Pharaoh and left.

So Joseph settled his family in Egypt. He gave them property in the best part of Goshen, in the district of Rameses, as Pharaoh had directed. Joseph also provided them with food, determining the amount based on the size of each family, including the small children. So Jacob and his descendants — the Israelites — made their home there in Goshen. They acquired property and were fruitful, and their population grew rapidly.

The Egyptians Sell Themselves to Pharaoh
GN 47:13-26

The famine was so severe that soon there was no food left in Egypt or Canaan, and the people were starving. Joseph sold grain and put all the money he collected into Pharaoh's treasury. Eventually the Egyptians had spent all their money on grain, so they said to Joseph, "All our money is gone. Give us food or we'll die right before your eyes!"

"I'll sell you food in exchange for your livestock," Joseph said.

So they brought him their horses, sheep, goats, cattle, and donkeys, and Joseph provided them with food for another year.

But the following year they said to Joseph, "We have no money and now you own our livestock. Soon we'll be dead and the land will be deserted. The only thing we have left to offer is ourselves and our land. Give us food to keep us alive and seed to plant in our fields, and we'll be Pharaoh's slaves."

So Joseph purchased all their fields for Pharaoh. All the land in Egypt belonged to him, and the Egyptians were reduced to slaves from one end of Egypt to the other. But Joseph didn't buy the priests' land, because Pharaoh already gave them a food allowance to live on.

Then Joseph said, "Here is some seed for you to plant. But at harvest time, give a fifth of the crop to Pharaoh and keep the other four-fifths as seed for your fields and food for your family."

"You saved our lives," they said. "You've been very kind to us and we will be Pharaoh's slaves."

So Joseph established the law that a fifth of the produce belongs to Pharaoh, and this law is still in effect in Egypt.

Jacob Blesses Ephraim and Manasseh
GN 47:29-31|GN 48:1-22

Some time later, when it was almost time for Jacob to die, he called for Joseph. Joseph was told his father was ill, so he took his two sons, Manasseh and Ephraim, with him to visit Jacob.

When Jacob heard that Joseph had arrived, he gathered his strength and sat up on the bed. He could barely see because of his age, so when he saw Joseph's sons he asked, "Who are they?"

"They're the sons God has given me," Joseph replied.

Jacob said, "Now I'm counting them as mine; Ephraim and Manasseh will be mine just as Reuben and Simeon are mine. Any children after them will be yours, and they will receive their part of the inheritance in Ephraim and Manasseh's territory. I'm doing this because your mother Rachel was unable to have more children. She died in Canaan, not far from Ephrath, as we were returning from Paddan-Aram, and I buried her there beside the road in sorrow. Bring your sons here so I can bless them."

Then Jacob hugged and kissed them. He said to Joseph, "I never expected to see you again, and now God has allowed me to see your children too!"

Then Joseph moved the boys, who were at their grandfather's knees, and bowed with his face to the ground. Afterward he brought them close to Jacob again, with Ephraim on Jacob's left and Manasseh on Jacob's right. But Jacob crossed his arms and put his right hand on Ephraim's head, even though he was the youngest, and put his left hand on Manasseh's head, even though Manasseh was the firstborn.

This upset Joseph and he said, "No, my father, Manasseh is the firstborn; put your right hand on his head." And he lifted his father's right hand to move it.

But Jacob refused and said, "I know, my son, I know. Manasseh's descendants will become a nation, but Ephraim will be greater; his descendants will become a multitude of nations."

Then he blessed Joseph's sons, saying, "Dear God, my grandfather Abraham and my father Isaac walked with you faithfully. You've been my shepherd all my life and you are the Angel who rescued me from all harm. So please bless these boys. May they preserve my name and the names of Abraham and Isaac, and may their descendants be numerous upon the earth."

He said to the boys, "The people of Israel will use your names to pronounce blessings. They will say, 'May God make you as prosperous as Ephraim and Manasseh.'"

In saying this, he put Ephraim ahead of Manasseh.

Then he said to Joseph, "God Almighty appeared to me at Bethel in Canaan. He blessed me and said, 'I'm going to give you many children. Your descendants will become many nations and I'll give them this land as an eternal possession.'

"I'm about to die, but God will be with you and he will take you back to the land of your ancestors. And I'm giving you more land than your brothers. The land of Shechem, which I took from the Amorites with my sword and bow, will belong to you."

Then he said, "If you really love me, please honor my last request. Put your hand under my thigh and swear you won't bury me in Egypt. Take me away from here and bury me with my ancestors."

"I will," Joseph said.

"Swear to me."

So Joseph swore, and Jacob bowed his head in thanks as he lay on the bed.

Jacob's Last Words to His Sons
GN 49:1-28

Then Jacob summoned the rest of his sons and said, "Gather around so I can tell you what will happen to you in the future. Listen closely, my sons, to your father Israel.

Reuben, you are my firstborn, my strength, the first sign of my manhood. Your excellence and power surpass all others. But you're as unstable as a raging flood. You'll no longer excel, because you slept with my concubine and dishonored my bed.

Simeon and Levi are two of a kind — your weapons are instruments of violence. I won't participate in your secret plans or meetings. You killed men in anger and crippled oxen for fun. Cursed is your anger, so fierce, and your fury, so cruel! Your descendants will be scattered among Jacob's descendants and dispersed throughout Israel.

Judah, your brothers will praise you; you'll grab your enemies by the neck and your brothers will bow down to you. You're like a lion who has eaten your prey and returned to the den. As you stretch out and lie down, no one dares to disturb you. You'll hold the royal scepter and your descendants will always rule. Nations will bring you tribute and bow in obedience before you. Your grapevines are numerous; you can tie your donkey and colt to the very best vines and wash your clothing in the blood-red wine. The wine will be so plentiful that your eyes will be bloodshot from drinking it, and your teeth will be as white as the plentiful milk you'll drink.

Zebulun will live by the seashore and become a harbor for ships; your border will extend toward Sidon.

Issachar is a strong donkey lying down between two saddlebags. When you see how good your resting place is and how delightful is your land, you will bend your back to bear the load and be forced to work as a slave.

Dan, you will rule your people as one of the tribes of Israel. You will be like a viper along the roadside that bites the horse's heels, causing its rider to fall backward.

I trust you for deliverance, Lord.

Gad, you will be raided by a band of robbers, but you will turn and attack them.

Asher will dine on rich food and provide food fit for a king.

Naphtali is a doe set free that bears beautiful fawns.

Joseph, you are like a wild donkey near a spring, a wild colt on a hillside. Archers savagely attack him and pursue him with their bows and arrows, but his bow remains steady; his strong arms are strengthened by the power of the Mighty God of Jacob, by the Shepherd and Protector of Israel. It is your father's God who helps you, the Almighty God who blesses you with sunshine and rain from above and water from the deep springs below. He blesses you with many cattle and children. Your father's blessings surpass the blessings of the ancient mountains and the bounty of the eternal hills. May these blessings rest upon he who is set apart from his brothers.

Benjamin, you a ravenous wolf; in the morning you devour your enemies and in the evening you divide the spoil."

These are the 12 tribes of Israel, and their father gave each of them a suitable message.

Joseph Buries Jacob in Canaan
GN 47:28|GN 49:29-33|GN 50:1-14

After blessing his sons, Jacob said, "I'm about to die. Take me back to Canaan and bury me with my father and grandfather in the field and cave at Machpelah, near Mamre. Abraham purchased it as a burial site from Ephron the Hittite, and Abraham, Sarah, Isaac, Rebekah, and Leah are all buried there."

Then he lay down on his bed and breathed his last. He had lived in Egypt 17 years and was 147 when he died.

Joseph hugged and kissed Jacob, weeping over him. Then he directed his physicians to embalm him, and they took the full 40 days required for embalming. The Egyptians mourned for Jacob 70 days.

After the mourning period, Joseph said to Pharaoh's court, "Please ask Pharaoh to allow me to bury my father in Canaan as he made me swear. Then I'll return."

Pharaoh replied, "Yes. Tell him to go keep his promise."

So Joseph went up to bury his father, and all Pharaoh's officials — the elders of his household and the senior officers of Egypt — went with him. Joseph and his brothers took their families with them, leaving their children, flocks, and cattle in Goshen. Soldiers riding in chariots and on horses went with them as well. It was a huge group!

When they reached Atad's threshing floor near the Jordan River, they wept loudly. Joseph performed the mourning ceremonies for his father for seven days. When the local Canaanites saw them, they said, "The Egyptians are in deep mourning!" That's why that place is called Abel-Mizraim.

So Jacob's sons did as he had requested and buried him in Canaan, in the cave and field at Machpelah. Afterward they returned to Egypt.

Joseph Reassures His Brothers
GN 50:15-21

Now that their father was dead, Joseph's brothers said, "What if Joseph holds a grudge against us and plans to pay us back for all the suffering we caused him?" So they sent a message to Joseph, saying, "Our father left instructions before he died that you should forgive us for the terrible way we treated you. So we, the servants of the God of our father, beg you to forgive our sin."

Joseph wept when he received their message.

His brothers then came and bowed down before him. "We are your slaves," they said.

"It's not my place to play God," Joseph said. "You plotted evil against me, but God turned it into good to save many lives. So don't be afraid. I'll take care of you and your children." So Joseph reassured them with his kind words.

Joseph Dies and Is Buried in Egypt
GN 50:22-26

Joseph and his father's family continued living in Egypt. Joseph lived to see Ephraim's children and grandchildren, as well as the birth of the children of Manasseh's son Machir, whom Joseph claimed as his own.

Then Joseph said to his brothers, "Soon I will die, but God will surely come to your aid and lead you out of Egypt to the land he vowed to give Abraham, Isaac, and Jacob."

Then he said to Jacob's descendants, "When God delivers you, promise you'll take my body with you."

So Joseph died at age 110. They embalmed him and buried him in a coffin in Egypt.

CHAPTER 9
Moses' Call to Deliver the Israelites From Egypt

Jacob's Descendants, the Israelites
GN 46:8-27|EX 1:1-5

These are Jacob's descendants who went with him to Egypt (Joseph was already in Egypt):

**Jacob and Leah's sons born in Paddan-Aram,
plus their daughter Dinah
Total descendants – 33**

Reuben's sons: Hanoch, Pallu, Hezron, and Carmi (Reuben was Jacob's firstborn.)
Simeon's sons: Jemuel, Jamin, Ohad, Jachin, Zohar, and Shaul — the son of a Canaanite woman
Levi's sons: Gershon, Kohath, and Merari
Judah's sons: Er, Onan, Shelah, **Perez**, and Zerah (Er and Onan had died in Canaan.)
    Perez's sons: Hezron and Hamul
Issachar's sons: Tola, Puah, Jashub, and Shimron
Zebulun's sons: Sered, Elon, and Jahleel

**Children born to Jacob through Zilpah, the
servant Laban had given to his daughter Leah
Total descendants = 16**

Gad's sons: Zephon, Haggi, Shuni, Ezbon, Eri, Arodi, and Areli
Asher's sons: Imnah, Ishvah, Ishvi, **Beriah**, and their sister Serah
    Beriah's sons: Heber and Malchiel

Rachel and Jacob's sons — Total descendants = 14

Joseph's sons: Manasseh and Ephraim, both born in Egypt. Their mother was Asenath, daughter of Potiphera, priest of On.
Benjamin's sons: Bela, Becher, Ashbel, Gera, Naaman, Ehi, Rosh, Muppim, Huppim, and Ard

**Sons born to Jacob through Bilhah,
the servant Laban had given to his daughter Rachel
Total descendants = 7**

Dan's son: Hushim
Naphtali's sons: Jahziel, Guni, Jezer, and Shillem

Jacob's direct descendants in Egypt — not counting his sons' wives — numbered 70. And his descendants were called the Israelites.

The Egyptians Enslave the Israelites
EX 1:6-22

Joseph, his brothers, and their entire generation died. And their descendants, the Israelites, had many children and became so numerous that they dominated the land and became a threat to the Egyptians.

Eventually a new king ruled Egypt who knew nothing about Joseph. "Listen," he said to the Egyptians, "the Israelites are more numerous and powerful than us. We must find a way to keep them from growing. If there is a war, they might join our enemies and fight against us, and then they'll escape the country!"

So the Egyptians forced the Israelites into hard labor and made them slaves, assigning slave drivers over them to break them down. But the more the Egyptians oppressed the Israelites, the more they multiplied and spread throughout the land. The Egyptians grew very afraid of them so they worked them ruthlessly, making their lives miserable. They forced them to work in the fields and to build with brick and mortar, showing them no mercy. The Israelites built the cities of Pithom and Rameses as supply cities for Pharaoh.

Pharaoh said to the Hebrew midwives, whose names were Shiphrah and Puah, "When you help the Hebrew women deliver their babies, let the girls live but kill all the boys."

But the midwives feared God, so they didn't kill them.

Then Pharaoh summoned them and asked, "Why did you let the boys live?"

The midwives said, "Hebrew women aren't like Egyptian women; they give birth easily and the babies are born before we arrive."

So God was kind to the midwives because they feared him, and he gave them families of their own. Meanwhile, the Israelites continued to grow even more numerous and powerful.

Then Pharaoh ordered his people, "Go throw every newborn Hebrew boy into the Nile River, but let the girls live."

Moses Is Born
EX 2:1-10

Now a man of the tribe of Levi married a Levite woman. She gave birth to a handsome, healthy son and hid him for three months. Soon she couldn't hide him anymore, so she coated a papyrus basket with tar, so it wouldn't sink, and put the baby in it. Then she put the basket among the reeds along the edge of the Nile River. The baby's sister watched from a distance to see what would happen to him.

Pharaoh's daughter went down to the Nile to bathe, and her attendants walked along the riverbank. When she saw the basket in the reeds, she sent her female slave to get it. Pharaoh's daughter opened it and saw the baby crying, and she felt sorry for him.

"This is one of the Hebrew babies," she said.

Then the baby's sister asked her, "Do you want me to get one of the Hebrew women to nurse the baby for you?"

"Yes, go," she replied.

So the girl went and got her mother.

Pharaoh's daughter said, "Nurse this baby for me and I'll pay you."

So his own mother nursed him. When the child grew older, she took him to Pharaoh's daughter, and he became her son. She named him Moses, saying, "I drew him out of the water."

Moses Visits His People
EX 2:11-15

One day after Moses had grown up, he went to visit his own people, the Hebrews, and he watched as they endured hard labor as slaves. Then he saw an Egyptian beating a Hebrew. He looked around and didn't see anyone, so he killed the Egyptian and hid him in the sand. The next day he returned and saw two Hebrews fighting!

"Why are you hitting your fellow Hebrew?" Moses asked the man who had started the fight.

"Who made you our ruler?" the man asked. "You have no right to judge us! Are you going to kill me like you killed that Egyptian?"

So Moses was afraid and thought, *Somehow people found out what I did.*

Soon Pharaoh found out too and he tried to kill Moses, but Moses ran away to Midian.

Moses Makes His Home in Midian
EX 2:16-22

Now Jethro (also called Reuel), the priest of Midian, had seven daughters. One day Moses sat near a well and Jethro's daughters arrived to draw water and fill the troughs for their father's flocks. Some shepherds came and chased them away, but Moses got up and rescued them, and then he watered their flocks.

The girls returned home and Jethro asked, "Why are you home so early today?"

"An Egyptian rescued us from the shepherds. He even drew water for us and watered the flocks!"

"So where is he? Why did you leave him out there? Invite him to dinner."

Moses accepted the invitation and was content to stay and live there with them. Jethro gave his daughter Zipporah to Moses as his wife, and she gave birth to a son who Moses named Gershom, saying, "I've been allowed to live in this foreign land."

God Hears the Israelites' Cry for Help
EX 2:23-25

Many years passed and Pharaoh, the king of Egypt, died. The Israelites continued to moan as they suffered under slavery, and they cried out for help. God heard them and recalled the covenant he had made with Abraham, Isaac, and Jacob. He saw how they suffered and decided it was time to deliver them.

Moses Sees a Burning Bush
EX 3:1-21

One day Moses was tending Jethro's flock. He led them across the desert until he arrived at Sinai, the mountain of God (also called Mount Horeb), and the angel of the Lord appeared to him as a flame of fire from within a bush. *That's strange! Moses thought. I'm going to see why the bush is on fire but isn't burning up.*

As he approached, the Lord called to him from within the bush, "Moses! Moses!"

"Here I am," Moses said.

"Don't come any closer. Take off your sandals because you're standing on holy ground. I am the God of your fathers — the God of Abraham, the God of Isaac, and the God of Jacob."

Moses hid his face because he was afraid to look at God.

"I've certainly heard my people crying out for deliverance from their slave drivers. I've seen their misery and I know all about their suffering and oppression. I'm going to rescue them from the Egyptians and you will bring them up out of Egypt. Now go. I'm sending you to Pharaoh.

"Who am I that I should be assigned this task?" Moses asked.

"I'll be with you," God said. "After you bring the people out of Egypt, you'll worship me on this mountain. That will be the sign that I am the one who sent you."

"If I tell the Israelites that the God of their fathers sent me, they might ask me your name. What should I tell them?"

"I AM WHO I AM. Tell them 'I AM has sent me to you — the Lord, the God of your ancestors Abraham, Isaac, and Jacob.' This is my name forever, the name you'll call me from generation to generation.

"Assemble the elders of Israel and tell them I appeared to you and that I have watched over them and seen everything the Egyptians have done to them. Tell them I have promised to bring them out of their misery, into the land of the Canaanites, Hittites, Amorites, Perizzites, Hivites, and Jebusites — a fertile and spacious land flowing with milk and honey.

"The elders will listen to you; take them with you when you visit Pharaoh. Tell him the Lord, the God of the Hebrews, met with you. Ask him to allow the Israelites to take a three-day journey into the desert to offer sacrifices to the Lord your God. But I know Pharaoh won't let you go unless a mighty hand forces him. So I'll punish the Egyptians with terrifying miracles, and then he'll let you go. I'll make the Egyptians respect you, so you won't leave empty-handed."

God Performs Miracles for Moses
EX 4:1-17|EX 4:19

"But what if they don't believe that you appeared to me and they refuse to listen to me?" Moses asked.

"What's that in your hand?" the Lord asked.

"A staff."

"Throw it on the ground."

Moses did and it became a snake, and he ran from it.

Pick it up by the tail," the Lord said.

When Moses picked up the snake, it turned back into a staff.

"Perform this miracle so they'll believe that the Lord, the God of their ancestors — the God of Abraham, Isaac, and Jacob — appeared to you."

Then he said, "Now put your hand inside your robe."

Moses did so; when he took his hand out, the skin was diseased — white as snow.

"Now put your hand back into your robe," God said.

Moses did and his hand was healthy again.

81

Then the Lord said, "If they don't believe you or pay attention to the first sign, they might believe the second. But if not, take some water from the Nile River, pour it on the ground, and the water will become blood."

Moses said, "Please forgive me, Lord. I've never been a great speaker and I haven't become one since you've been speaking to me. I get tongue-tied and can never think of what to say."

"Who gave humans their mouths? Who makes them deaf or mute? Who gives them sight or makes them blind? Is it not I, the Lord? Now go; I'll help you speak, and teach you what to say."

"Forgive me, Lord, but please send someone else."

And the Lord became very angry with Moses. "Your brother Aaron, the Levite, can speak well. He's already on his way to meet you and he'll be glad to see you. I'll help both of you speak and tell you what to do. You'll be like God, telling Aaron what to say, and he'll speak to the people for you. Everyone who wanted to kill you is dead, so it's safe to return to Egypt. Take your staff so you can perform miracles with it."

Moses Returns to Egypt
EX 4:18|EX 4:20-21|EX 4:24-31

Now the Lord had told Aaron to meet Moses in the desert. So Aaron met Moses at the mountain of God and kissed him. Then Moses told Aaron everything the Lord had told him and also about all the miracles he had commanded him to perform.

Moses returned home and said to his father-in-law Jethro, "Let me return to my people in Egypt to see if any of them are still alive."

"Go," Jethro said. "I wish you well."

So Moses put his wife and sons on a donkey and started back to Egypt, taking the staff of God with him.

The Lord said to Moses, "When you arrive, make sure you perform for Pharaoh all the miracles I've given you the power to do. But I'll harden his heart and he won't let the people go."

Now at a camping place on the way to Egypt, the Lord confronted Moses and was about to kill him. But Zipporah cut off her son's foreskin with a flint knife and touched Moses' feet with it. Because she'd had to circumcise her son, she said to Moses, "Now you're a husband of blood to me!"

So the Lord let Moses live.

Then Moses and Aaron arrived in Egypt and gathered together all the Israelite elders, and Aaron told them everything the Lord had said to Moses. When they heard that the Lord was concerned about them and had seen their misery, they bowed down and worshiped. Moses also performed the miracles for them, and they believed.

Pharaoh Orders Bricks Made Without Straw
EX 5:1-21

Moses and Aaron went to see Pharaoh and said, "The Lord, the God of Israel, says: 'Let my people go so they can honor me in the desert with a festival.'"

"Who is the Lord?" Pharaoh asked. "Why should I obey him and let Israel go? I don't know him and I won't let the people go."

"The God of the Hebrews has met with us. Now let us take a three-day journey into the desert to offer sacrifices to the Lord our God, or he might kill us by disease or war."

"Moses and Aaron, why are you distracting the people from their jobs? Get them back to work! There are too many people for me to allow them to take time off."

That same day Pharaoh ordered the slave drivers and overseers, "Don't supply the people with straw for making bricks anymore; let them gather their own. But don't reduce the quota; require them to make the same number of bricks as before. They're begging to go sacrifice to their God because they're lazy. Make the work harder to keep them occupied, and then they'll have no time to listen to lies."

So the slave drivers and the overseers told the people, "Pharaoh has commanded us not to give you any more straw. Go and get it yourselves wherever you can find it, but you must still make as many bricks as before."

So the people searched all over Egypt to gather stubble to use for straw.

The slave drivers kept urging them, "Finish your assigned work each day, just as you did when straw was provided." And they beat the Israelite overseers who were in charge of the work, asking, "Why aren't you forcing your workers to make as many bricks as they did before?"

So the Israelite overseers appealed to Pharaoh, "Why are you treating your servants this way? We're given no straw but are commanded to make bricks. We're being beaten, but your own people are to blame."

"You're lazy," Pharaoh said, "just lazy! That's why you keep asking to go sacrifice to your Lord. Now get to work. You won't be given any straw, but you must make the same number of bricks."

Then the Israelite overseers realized they were in trouble. As they were leaving, they found Moses and Aaron waiting outside and said, "May the Lord punish you! You've made Pharaoh and his officials hate us; it's as if you've given them a sword to kill us."

God Reassures Moses
EX 5:22-23|EX 6:1-13|EX 6:28-30|EX 7:1-5

Then Moses said, "Lord, speaking to Pharaoh for you has caused nothing but trouble for your people. Why did you send me? He's treating them more cruelly and you haven't rescued your people at all!"

Then the Lord said to Moses, "Soon you'll see what I have planned for Pharaoh. I'm going to use my mighty power to force him to let them go, and he will demand that they leave his country. I am Yahweh. When I revealed myself to Abraham, Isaac, and Jacob as God Almighty, I didn't use the name Yahweh. I made my covenant with them, promising to give them the land of Canaan, where they lived as foreigners. I have certainly heard the Israelites groaning because of their slavery by the Egyptians, and I'm going to honor my covenant.

"Tell them that I'll bring them out from under the bondage of the Egyptians. I'll rescue them from slavery, using my power to inflict terrible punishment on the Egyptians. I'll claim you as my own people and I will be your God. Then you'll know that I am the Lord your God who rescued you from slavery in Egypt. I'll bring you to the land I vowed to give Abraham, Isaac, and Jacob and give it to you as your own possession. I am the Lord."

Moses told the Israelites everything God had said, but they were discouraged and overworked so they refused to listen to him.

Then the Lord said to Moses, "I am the Lord. Tell Pharaoh, king of Egypt, everything I tell you. Tell him to let the Israelites go."

Moses replied, "If the Israelites won't listen to me, why would Pharaoh? I'm such a poor speaker."

"Like I told you, I've made you like God to Pharaoh and Aaron will be your prophet. He will tell Pharaoh to let the Israelites leave his country. But I'll harden Pharaoh's heart and he won't listen to you, even after I perform terrifying miracles. I will punish Egypt severely and bring my people out, tribe by tribe. And the Egyptians will know that I am the Lord."

So the Lord stood firm in his command for Moses and Aaron to lead the Israelites out of Egypt.

Moses and Aaron's Family Record
EX 6:14-27|EX 7:6-7

These were Moses and Aaron's ancestors:

Reuben was the firstborn of Israel (Jacob). Reuben's sons were Hanoch, Pallu, Hezron, and Carmi. They were the ancestors of the clans that bear their names.

Simeon's sons were Jemuel, Jamin, Ohad, Jachin, Zohar, and Shaul

— the son of a Canaanite woman. They were the ancestors of the clans that bear their names

Levi (Jacob's third son) lived 137 years. His sons, as listed in their family records, were **Gershon, Merari, and Kohath**. They were the heads of the Levite clans.

Gershon's sons were Libni and Shimei. Each of them became the ancestor of a clan.

Merari's sons were Mahli and Mushi.

Kohath lived 133 years. His sons were **Amram, Izhar**, Hebron, and **Uzziel**.

Izhar's sons: **Korah**, Nepheg, and Zikri.

Korah's sons: Assir, Elkanah, and Abiasaph. These were the Korahite clans.

Uzziel's sons: Mishael, Elzaphan, and Sithri.

Amram married his father's sister Jochebed. Their sons were **Aaron** and Moses.

Aaron married Elisheba — Amminadab's daughter and Nahshon's sister. Their sons were Nadab, Abihu, **Eleazar**, and Ithamar.

Eleazar married one of Putiel's daughters, and they had a son named Phinehas.

It was this same Moses and Aaron who spoke to Pharaoh, because the Lord had commanded them to bring the Israelites out of Egypt, tribe by tribe. At that time, Moses was 80 years old and Aaron was 83.

Aaron's Staff Becomes a Snake
EX 7:8-13

The Lord said to Moses, "When Pharaoh demands that you perform a miracle, tell Aaron to throw his staff down, and it will become a snake."

So they did just as the Lord commanded. Aaron threw his staff down in front of Pharaoh and his officials, and it became a snake. But Pharaoh summoned his magicians and sorcerers. They used their magic and threw their staffs down, and their staffs became snakes too. But Aaron's staff swallowed up their staffs! However, Pharaoh's heart remained hard and he was unpersuaded, just as the Lord had said.

CHAPTER 10
The Israelites' Freedom From Egypt

God Unleashes Ten Plagues
EX 7:14 – EX 11:10
The Plague of Blood
EX 7:14-24

"Pharaoh is very stubborn and refuses to let the people go," the Lord told Moses. "In the morning when Pharaoh goes to the Nile River, confront him there with the staff that changed into a snake." And he told Moses what to say.

So Moses and Aaron went to the river and said to Pharaoh, "The Lord, the God of the Hebrews, sent me to tell you to let his people go worship him in the desert. So far you haven't listened, but now you will know that he is the Lord."

Then Moses told Aaron, "Strike the Nile River with your staff and then stretch the staff out over the waters of Egypt — over the rivers, canals, ponds, and other water sources. All of them will turn to blood. Blood will be everywhere in Egypt, even in wooden and stone containers, and the Egyptians will have no water to drink at all."

So Aaron raised his staff in the presence of Pharaoh and his officials, and he struck the Nile River. All of Egypt's water turned into blood. The fish died and the river smelled so bad that the Egyptians couldn't drink its water.

But the Egyptian magicians found some water and did the same thing, so Pharaoh's heart remained hard. He refused to listen to Moses and Aaron; instead, he turned and went into his palace and put the whole thing out of his mind. Then the Egyptians dug along the Nile to get drinking water since they couldn't drink from the river.

The Plague of Frogs
EX 7:25|EX 8:1-15

Seven days later the Lord gave Moses further instructions. So Moses and Aaron went to Pharaoh and said, "Let the Lord's people go so they can worship him. If you refuse he will punish your entire country by covering it with frogs, and the Nile will be filled with them. They'll come into your palace, your bedroom, and even onto your bed. They'll enter everyone's houses and get into your ovens and mixing bowls. They'll jump all over your people and your officials."

Then Moses said to Aaron, "Stretch your staff over the rivers, canals, and ponds and make frogs come up and cover Egypt."

So Aaron did, but Pharaoh's magicians also summoned frogs.

Then Pharaoh summoned Moses and Aaron and said, "Pray to the Lord to take the frogs away from us and I'll let your people go offer sacrifices to the Lord."

Moses said, "I'll let you determine the time for me to pray to get rid of all the frogs, except for those in the Nile."

"Tomorrow," Pharaoh said.

Moses replied, "It will stop tomorrow then, so you'll know there's no one like the Lord our God."

Moses and Aaron left Pharaoh, and Moses prayed to the Lord about the frogs. The Lord did what Moses asked and all the frogs in the houses, courtyards, and fields died. The Egyptians gathered them into heaps and the land stank of them. But as soon as there was relief, Pharaoh hardened his heart again and wouldn't let the people go.

The Plague of Gnats
EX 8:16-19

Then the Lord said to Moses, "Tell Aaron to strike the ground with his staff and turn the dust throughout Egypt into gnats."

So gnats infested the entire land, covering the Egyptians and their animals. But when the magicians tried to produce gnats, they couldn't.

Gnats were everywhere and the magicians said to Pharaoh, "This is God's doing!"

But just as the Lord had predicted, Pharaoh remained stubborn.

The Plague of Flies
EX 8:20-32

The Lord gave Moses another message for Pharaoh. So Moses got up early the next morning to confront him as he went to the river. "Let the Lord's people go worship him or he will send swarms of flies upon you and your officials, on your people, and into all your houses; even the ground will be covered with them. But this time he will spare his people in Goshen, and there will be no flies there. Then you will know that the Lord is in this land. He will make a distinction between his people and your people. This miraculous sign will take place tomorrow."

The next day thick swarms of flies infested Pharaoh's palace and the houses of his officials; they were ruining Egypt!

Pharaoh summoned Moses and Aaron and said, "Go sacrifice to your God here in Egypt."

"That wouldn't be right," Moses said. "The sacrifices we offer the Lord our God would be detestable to the Egyptians and they might stone us. We must take a three-day journey into the desert to offer sacrifices, as he commands."

"Ok," Pharaoh said. "You can go into the desert but don't go very far. Now pray for me."

"I'll pray to the Lord as soon as I leave," Moses said. "Tomorrow the flies will go away, but make sure you don't deceive us again. Keep your promise and let the people go offer sacrifices to the Lord."

Then Moses prayed to the Lord, and the flies left; not one fly remained. But again Pharaoh hardened his heart and wouldn't let the people go.

The Plague on Livestock
EX 9:1-7

Moses went to Pharaoh and said, "The Lord, the God of the Hebrews, says that if you refuse to let Israel go and continue to hold them back, tomorrow he will bring a terrible plague on your livestock — your horses, donkeys, camels, cattle, sheep, and goats. But the Lord will make a distinction between Israel and Egypt's livestock. None of the Israelites' animals will die."

The next day all the Egyptians' livestock died. So Pharaoh investigated and found that not even one of the Israelites' animals had died. But his heart was unyielding and he wouldn't let the people go.

The Plague of Boils
EX 9:8-12

Following the Lord's instructions, Moses and Aaron visited Pharaoh again. This time Moses took handfuls of soot from a furnace and tossed it into the air. It became fine dust throughout Egypt, and festering boils broke out on all the people and animals. Even the magicians couldn't appear before Moses because they were covered with boils like all the other Egyptians. But the Lord hardened Pharaoh's heart and he wouldn't listen to Moses and Aaron, just as the Lord had told Moses.

The Plague of Hail
EX 9:13-35

Early the next morning, Moses said to Pharaoh, "Let the Lord's people go worship him or this time he will send the full force of his plagues against all of you, and you will know that there is no one like him in the world. By now he could have struck you all with a plague that would wipe you off the earth, but he spared your life to demonstrate his power and make his name known throughout the world. Yet you're still arrogant and won't let his people go. So at this time tomorrow, he will send the worst hailstorm Egypt has ever seen in all its history. Order your livestock and servants to be brought inside; otherwise they will die."

Some of Pharaoh's officials were afraid because of the Lord's message, so they hurried to bring their servants and livestock inside. But others ignored it and left their servants and livestock in the field.

Then the Lord said to Moses, "Stretch your staff toward the sky."

When Moses did, the Lord sent thunder and rained hail on Egypt, and lightning flashed back and forth. It was the worst storm Egypt had ever seen! The hail struck all the people and animals outside; it beat down everything growing in the fields and stripped every tree. The flax and barley crops were destroyed because the barley was ripe and the flax was budding. But the regular wheat and spelt wheat weren't destroyed, because they ripen later. The only place it didn't hail was in Goshen, where the Israelites lived.

Then Pharaoh summoned Moses and Aaron. "This time I've really sinned," he said. "The Lord is right and we're wrong. We've had enough thunder and hail, so pray to the Lord and I'll let you go; you don't have to stay any longer."

Moses replied, "When I leave the city, I'll spread out my hands to the Lord in prayer. The thunder and hail will stop, and you will know that the earth is the Lord's. But I know that, even now, you and your officials don't fear the Lord God."

So Moses left the city and spread out his hands, and the thunder, hail, and rain stopped. As soon as it was over, Pharaoh sinned again. He and his officials hardened their hearts and wouldn't let the Israelites go.

The Plague of Locusts
EX 10:1-20

Then the Lord said to Moses, "Go visit Pharaoh. I've made him and his officials stubborn in order to perform my signs. I did this so you can tell your children and grandchildren how I punished the Egyptians, and so you will know that I am the Lord."

So Moses and Aaron said to Pharaoh, "The Lord, the God of the Hebrews, has a message for you: How long will you refuse to humble yourself before him? Let his people go so they can worship him. If you refuse he will bring locusts into Egypt tomorrow. They'll be so numerous that you won't be able to see the ground. They'll devour all the trees in your fields and what little you had left after the hail. They'll fill all the Egyptians' houses. No one has ever seen anything like it in the history of Egypt!"

Then Moses left.

Pharaoh's officials said, "How long will you allow this man to cause us so much trouble? Let the people go worship the Lord their God. Don't you realize yet that Egypt is being ruined?"

So Pharaoh called Moses and Aaron back and said, "You can go worship the Lord your God, but who will be going?"

"Our young and old, our sons and daughters, our flocks and cattle. We must all hold a festival to honor the Lord."

"The Lord really *would* be with you if I let you take your women and children!" Pharaoh said. "Clearly you're up to no good. You've been asking to go worship the Lord, so go, but take only the men."

Then he ordered Moses and Aaron to leave.

And the Lord said to Moses, "Stretch your staff out over Egypt."

When Moses did, the Lord made an east wind blow across the land all day and all night, and by morning it had brought swarms of locusts. Never before had there been such a plague of locusts, and there never would be again. They invaded every area of Egypt and covered the ground until it was black. They devoured all that was left after the hail — everything growing in the fields and all the fruit on the trees. Nothing green remained on any tree or plant in Egypt.

Pharaoh quickly summoned Moses and Aaron and said, "I've sinned against the Lord your God and against you. Forgive me once more and pray to the Lord to take this deadly plague away."

So Moses left Pharaoh and prayed. Then the Lord reversed the wind's direction, and a very strong west wind carried the locusts into the Red Sea until none was left anywhere in Egypt. But the Lord hardened Pharaoh's heart and he wouldn't let the Israelites go.

The Plague of Darkness
EX 4:22-23|EX 10:21-27

Then the Lord said to Moses, "Stretch your hand toward the sky and darkness will spread over Egypt — a darkness that can be felt."

So Moses stretched out his hand and total darkness covered Egypt for three days. No one could see anyone else or even move, but all the Israelites had light where they lived.

Pharaoh summoned Moses and said, "Take your women and children and go worship the Lord; just leave your flocks and cattle behind."

"Not even a hoof can be left behind," Moses said. "Our livestock must go with us so we can present sacrifices and burnt offerings to the Lord our God. We won't know until we get there which animals we should use."

But the Lord hardened Pharaoh's heart and he wasn't willing to let them go.

The Plague on the Firstborn
EX 10:28-29|EX 11:1|EX 11:4-10

"Get out of my sight!" Pharaoh said to Moses. "Make sure I never see you again! If I do, you will die."

"Ok," Moses replied, "you'll never see me again. But this is what the Lord says: 'Israel is my firstborn son and I told you to let my son go worship me. But you refused, so I'm going to kill your firstborn son.'

"About midnight the Lord will go throughout Egypt and every firstborn son will die — from Pharaoh's firstborn, to the firstborn of the female slave at her hand mill, to the firstborn of the cattle. There will be loud crying throughout Egypt — worse than has ever been or ever will be again. But it will be so peaceful among the Israelites that not even a dog will bark. Then you will know that the Lord makes a distinction between the Egyptians and the Israelites. All your officials will bow down before me and beg me to take my people and leave. And indeed I will go!"

Burning with anger, Moses left Pharaoh.

Even though Moses and Aaron performed all these miracles, the Lord hardened Pharaoh's heart and he wouldn't let the Israelites leave his country. The Lord had told Moses that Pharaoh's refusal would allow him to perform mighty miracles in Egypt and that Pharaoh would drive them out completely after the final plague.

The Passover and the Festival of Unleavened Bread
EX 12:1-30

The Lord told Moses and Aaron, "This month will be the first month of the year for you. Tell the whole community of Israel that on the 10th day of this month, each man must take a lamb or a young goat for his family. Any household too small to eat a whole lamb must share one with their nearest neighbor, based on the number of people and how much they can eat. The animals must be one-year-old males without defect.

"Take care of them until the 14th day of the month and then slaughter them at twilight and let the blood drain into a basin. Put some of the blood on the sides and tops of the doorframes of the houses where they will eat the animals that night. Don't eat the meat raw or boiled in water — roast it over fire with the head, legs, and internal organs. Eat it with bitter herbs and bread made without yeast. Don't leave any meat until morning; burn whatever is left over. Eat the meal quickly, fully dressed, wearing your sandals, and carrying your staff; this is the Lord's Passover.

"That night I will go throughout Egypt and kill every firstborn male of both humans and animals, executing judgment on all the gods of Egypt. I am the Lord. When I see the blood marking your houses, it will be a sign and the plague of death won't touch you when I strike Egypt. I will pass over you.

"For the generations to come, commemorate this day and celebrate the Festival of Unleavened Bread to the Lord, because on this day I brought your tribes out of Egypt. In the first month of each year — for seven days — from the evening of the 14th until the evening of the 21st, eat unleavened bread — bread made without yeast. Anyone who eats anything made with yeast during this time, whether foreigner or native-born, must be cut off from Israel. On the first day, remove the yeast from your houses and keep it out for seven days. Wherever you live, you must eat unleavened bread. Hold a sacred assembly on the first day and another on the seventh day. Don't do any work during this time, except to prepare food."

So Moses summoned all the elders of Israel and said, "Go immediately and select the animals for your families and slaughter them for the Passover. Dip a bunch of hyssop into the blood and put some on the top and on both sides of the doorframe. No one should leave the house until morning. When the Lord strikes down the Egyptians, he will pass over the houses with blood on the doorframe, and he won't permit the destroyer to enter and kill you.

"After you enter the land the Lord has promised, you and your descendants must obey these rules and celebrate the Passover Festival each year from now on. When your children ask what the ceremony means, tell them it's a Passover sacrifice to the Lord, who passed over your houses in Egypt and spared you when he struck down the Egyptians."

The Israelites bowed down and worshiped, and they did everything the Lord had commanded.

At midnight the Lord struck down all the firstborn in Egypt, from the firstborn of Pharaoh — who sat on the throne — to the firstborn of the prisoner in the dungeon, as well as the firstborn of all the livestock. When everyone woke up, there was loud crying throughout the land, because there was someone dead in every Egyptian household.

The Israelites Leave Egypt
EX 11:2-3|EX 12:31-42

That night Pharaoh summoned Moses and Aaron and said, "Take the Israelites, your flocks, and your cattle and go worship the Lord as you requested. And please bless me."

And the Egyptians urged the Israelites, "Hurry up and leave or we'll all die!"

Then the Lord said, "The Israelites must ask the Egyptian women living near them for clothing and silver and gold jewelry, which you'll put on your sons and daughters."

So the Israelites did as Moses instructed. The Lord had made the Egyptians cooperative, and Moses himself was highly regarded by Pharaoh's officials and by the people. So they gave the Israelites what they asked for. In this way the Egyptians were stripped of their wealth.

When the Israelites left Egypt, they traveled from Rameses to Sukkoth with about 600,000 men on foot, besides women and children. Many other people went with them, along with large droves of flocks and cattle. They carried unleavened dough on their shoulders, in kneading troughs wrapped in clothing, and used it to bake loaves of unleavened bread. The dough had no yeast because they didn't have time to prepare food before being driven out of Egypt.

The Lord's people had lived in Egypt 430 years but, on that last day, all the Israelite tribes left. This night is dedicated to the Lord because he kept his promise to bring them out of Egypt, and the Israelites were to commemorate it each year for the generations to come.

God Gives Passover Restrictions at Sukkoth
EX 12:43-50

The Lord said to Moses and Aaron, "These are the rules for the Passover meal: The whole community of Israel must participate. Don't break any of the animals' bones. Eat the meal inside; don't take any of it outside the house.

"Any slave you purchased may eat the meal after you circumcise him, but no temporary resident or hired worker may eat it. A foreigner may not celebrate the Lord's Passover unless he decides to live among you and circumcises all the males in his household, and then he may take part like one born in the land. No uncircumcised male may eat the meal, whether he is native-born or a foreign resident."

The Israelites agreed to do everything the Lord had commanded.

God Claims Israel's Firstborn
EX 12:51|EX 13:1-16

On the same day the Lord brought the Israelites out of Egypt, tribe by tribe, he said to Moses, "Dedicate every firstborn male to me; every firstborn human and every firstborn animal belongs to me."

Then Moses said to the people, "Remember this day in the month of Abib, because the Lord brought you with a mighty hand out of Egypt, out of the land of slavery. When he brings you into the land of the Canaanites, Hittites, Amorites, Hivites, and Jebusites — the land flowing with milk and honey that he promised through your ancestors — observe this ceremony every year at the appointed time in the month of Abib. For seven days, eat unleavened bread and hold a festival to the Lord on the seventh day. There must be no yeast anywhere in your land.

"At that time, tell your children you're celebrating because the Lord brought you out of Egypt. This celebration will remind you, like a symbol on your hand or on your forehead, that the Lord brought you out of Egypt with his mighty hand and that you must keep his law on your lips.

"After the Lord gives you the land of the Canaanites, give him the firstborn males of your sons and your livestock; they belong to the Lord. But you must buy back all your firstborn sons. You can buy back every firstborn donkey with a lamb, or break its neck if you don't want to buy it back.

"In days to come when your children ask you what it means, tell them, 'The Lord brought us out of Egypt with his mighty hand. Pharaoh stubbornly refused to let us go, so the Lord killed the firstborn of their families and their animals. That's why we sacrifice every firstborn male animal to the Lord but buy back our firstborn sons.'"

God Leads the Way
EX 13:17-22|EX 14:1-4

When Pharaoh let the Israelites go, they left armed for battle. But God didn't lead them by the shortest route, through the Philistine country. He knew that if they were attacked, they might regret leaving Egypt and return there. So he led them in a roundabout way through the desert toward the Red Sea.

Moses took the bones of Joseph with him because Joseph had told the Israelites, "God will surely come to your aid and you must take my bones with you when you leave." So they had promised.

After leaving Sukkoth, they camped at Etham on the edge of the desert. During the day the Lord went ahead of them in a pillar of cloud to guide them and at night in a pillar of fire to give them light. In this way they could travel by day or night.

Then the Lord said to Moses, "Tell the Israelites to turn back and camp near Pi-Hahiroth, between Migdol and the sea, across from Baal-Zephon. Pharaoh will think you are wandering around in confusion, trapped in the desert. I'll harden his heart and he will come after you. But I'll display my glory by defeating Pharaoh and his army, and the Egyptians will know that I am the Lord."

So the Israelites camped near Pi-Hahiroth.

Pharaoh Pursues the Israelites
EX 14:5-31|EX 15:19

When the Egyptians told Pharaoh that the Israelites had actually escaped, Pharaoh and his officials had second thoughts. "We let our slaves go! What have we done?" they asked. So Pharaoh had his chariot and army prepared — his horses, horsemen, and troops, including 600 of his best chariots, all led by commanders. The Lord had hardened Pharaoh's heart and he pursued the Israelites, who had boldly left Egypt, catching up to them as they camped by the sea near Pi-Hahiroth, across from Baal-Zephon.

The Israelites looked up and saw the Egyptians marching after them. They were terrified and cried out to the Lord.

Then the Israelites said to Moses, "Did you bring us to the desert to die because there were no graves in Egypt? What have you done to us? Didn't we tell you to leave us alone and let us serve the Egyptians? That would have been better than dying in the desert!"

The Lord said to Moses, "Why are they crying out to me? Tell them to move on. Stretch your staff out over the sea to divide the water so they can cross on dry ground. I'll harden the Egyptians' hearts and they will go in after them. In this way I'll gain glory through Pharaoh, his army, his chariots, and his horsemen — and the Egyptians will know that I am the Lord."

"Don't be afraid," Moses said. "Stand firm and watch the Lord deliver you today. The Egyptians you see today you will never see again. Be at peace; the Lord will fight for you."

The angel of God and the pillar of cloud had been traveling in front of Israel's army; now they both moved from the front and got behind them, between the armies of Egypt and Israel. The cloud lit up the darkness and the Egyptians and Israelites didn't approach each other all night.

Then Moses stretched his hand over the sea, and the Lord sent a strong east wind that blew all night and divided the waters. So the Israelites went through the sea on dry ground, with a wall of water on their right and a wall of water on their left.

The Egyptians and all Pharaoh's horses, chariots, and horsemen pursued them into the sea. Just before dawn, the Lord looked down on the Egyptian army from the fiery cloud and threw it into confusion. He jammed their chariot wheels so that they had difficulty driving.

"Let's get away from the Israelites!" the Egyptians said. "The Lord is fighting for them against us."

Then the Lord said to Moses, "Stretch your hand over the sea so that the waters flow back over them all."

At daybreak Moses stretched his hand over the sea. The Egyptians tried to escape, but the water covered Pharaoh's entire army. The Lord swept them into the sea and not one of them survived.

But the Israelites crossed the sea on dry ground, with a wall of water on their right and a wall of water on their left. On that day when the Lord rescued them, the Israelites saw his mighty hand. They saw the Egyptians lying dead on the shore, so they feared the Lord and put their trust in him and in his servant Moses.

Moses and Miriam Sing Praises
EX 15:1-18|EX 15:20-21

Then Moses and the Israelites sang this song to the Lord:

> "I'll sing to the Lord because he is highly exalted. He has hurled both horse and driver into the Red Sea. The Lord is my strength and my defense; he has become my salvation. He's my God and I'll praise him; he's my father's God and I'll exalt him. The Lord is a warrior and Yahweh is his name. He has hurled Pharaoh's chariots and his army into the sea. Pharaoh's best officers are drowned. The deep waters covered them and they sank to the depths like a stone. With the tremendous force of your right arm, Lord, you crushed the enemy. In majestic triumph you overthrew those who opposed you. You unleashed your burning anger and it consumed them like straw. With one blast of your breath, the surging waters piled up and stood up like a wall; the deep waters became solid in the heart of the sea.
>
> The enemy boasted, 'I'll pursue them and overtake them. I'll divide the spoils and consume them. I'll draw my sword

and destroy them.' But you blew with your breath and the sea covered them, and they sank like lead in the raging waters. Who among the gods is like you, Lord? Who is like you — majestic in holiness, awesome in glory, performing great wonders? You stretched out your right hand and the earth swallowed your enemies.

In your unfailing love, you'll lead the people you redeemed. In your strength you'll guide them to your holy land. The nations will hear about this and tremble; the Philistines are gripped with fear. The chiefs of Edom will be terrified, and the leaders of Moab will tremble. Struck by terror and fear, the people of Canaan will panic. Your powerful arm will keep them still as a stone, Lord, until your people whom you rescued for your very own pass them by. You'll bring them in and plant them on your own mountain — the place you chose as your dwelling, the sanctuary your hands established. The Lord will reign forever and ever."

Then Miriam the prophetess — Aaron and Moses' sister — played her tambourine. All the women followed her, playing their tambourines and dancing to them. "Sing to the Lord, for he's highly exalted," Miriam sang. "Both horse and driver he has hurled into the sea!"

God Provides Water at Marah
EX 15:22-27

Moses led the Israelites from the Red Sea to the Desert of Shur. They traveled in the desert for three days and found no water. At one place they found water but couldn't drink because it was *bitter*. (That's why the place is called *Marah*.) So the people complained to Moses, "What are we going to drink?"

Moses cried out to the Lord, and the Lord showed him a piece of wood and told him to throw it into the water. When he threw it in, the water became fit to drink.

While they were there, the Lord gave them the following instructions by which he would test their faithfulness to him, "Listen carefully to the Lord your God, do what's right, pay attention to my commands, and I'll spare you all the diseases I brought upon the Egyptians, for I am the Lord who heals you."

Then they arrived at Elim, where there were 12 springs and 70 palm trees, and they camped there near the water.

God Provides Manna and Quail
EX 16:1-36|NM 11:7-9

The Israelites left Elim. On the 15th day of the 2nd month after they had left Egypt, they arrived at the Desert of Sin, which is between Elim and Sinai. They complained to Moses and Aaron, saying, "In Egypt we sat around pots of meat and ate all the food we wanted, but you brought us out into this desert to starve us all to death. It would have been better if the Lord had killed us in Egypt!"

Then the Lord said to Moses, "I've heard the Israelites complaining. Tell them they will eat meat at twilight and be filled with bread in the morning. Then they will know that I am the Lord their God. I'll rain down bread from heaven for you, and each day the people must go out to gather enough for that day. On the sixth day, they must gather twice as much as they gather on other days and prepare what they bring in. In this way I'll test them and see whether they will follow my instructions."

So Moses and Aaron said to the Israelites, "We've done nothing but carry out God's commands, so it is God you're complaining about, not us. He has heard your complaining against him and in the morning you'll see his glory. You'll know that it is the Lord when he gives you meat to eat in the evening and all the bread you want in the morning."

Then Moses told Aaron, "Tell all the Israelites to come before the Lord."

While Aaron was speaking to them, they looked toward the desert and saw the glorious presence of the Lord appear in a cloud.

That evening quail came and covered the camp, and in the morning there was a layer of dew, which had settled on the camp the night before. When the dew evaporated, thin flakes like frost appeared on the ground. It looked like coriander seeds and was white like gum resin.

The Israelites asked each other, "*What is it?*" (That's why they called the bread *manna*.)

Moses said, "This is the bread the Lord has given you to eat. Gather as much as you need, two quarts for each person in your tent. Don't keep any of it until morning."

The Israelites did as they were told. When they measured it by the quart, the one who gathered much didn't have too much and the one who gathered little didn't have too little. They all gathered only as much as they needed. They made flour by grinding it in hand mills or pounding it in mortars. Then they boiled it in a pot and formed it into cakes, which tasted like pastries baked with olive oil and honey. A two-quart container was used for the manna, as a standard of dry measure.

But some of the people paid no attention to Moses and kept some manna until morning, but it was full of maggots and began to smell. And Moses was angry with them.

Each morning they gathered as much as they needed, and when the sun grew hot, the manna melted away. On the sixth day, they gathered twice as much — four quarts for each person — and the leaders of the community reported this to Moses.

Moses responded, "The Lord commanded that tomorrow must be a holy day of rest, a holy Sabbath dedicated to the Lord. So they can cook whatever they want today and save the leftovers until morning."

This time when they saved it for the next day, as Moses commanded, it didn't stink or become infested with maggots.

"Go ahead and eat it," Moses said. "You won't find any on the ground today because it's the Sabbath. You must gather the manna for six days, but on the seventh day — the Sabbath — there won't be any."

But some people still went out to gather manna on the seventh day, and they found none.

Then the Lord said to Moses, "How long will these people refuse to keep my commands? They must realize that the Sabbath is the Lord's gift; that's why on the sixth day he provides enough bread for two days. Everyone must avoid going out on the Sabbath to look for food."

So the people rested on the Sabbath.

Then Moses said, "The Lord has commanded us to preserve some manna for our descendants, and store it in his presence. In this way they can see the bread he gave us to eat in the desert when he brought us out of Egypt." Then he said to Aaron, "Put two quarts of manna in a jar."

Eventually this jar was kept in the Ark of the Covenant with the tablets of the Ten Commandments.

The Israelites would eat manna 40 years until they settled in Canaan.

God Provides Water From a Rock
EX 17:1-7

The Israelites left the Desert of Sin, traveling from place to place as the Lord commanded. They camped at Rephidim, but there was no water.

"We need water to drink!" they complained to Moses.

"Why are you complaining and testing the Lord?" he asked.

But they were very thirsty and said, "Why did you bring us out of Egypt? Now we, our children, and our livestock will die of thirst?"

"What should I do?" Moses cried out to the Lord. "They're almost ready to stone me!"

"Take some of Israel's elders and the staff you used to strike the Nile and go ahead of the people," the Lord said. "I will stand before you on the rock at Mount Sinai. Strike the rock and water will come out for the people to drink."

So Moses did this in the presence of the elders. And he called the place *Massah* (which means *test*) and *Meribah* (which means *complaining*) because the Israelites complained and tested the Lord asking, "Is the Lord among us or not?"

The Israelites Defeat the Amalekites
EX 17:8-16

While the Israelites were at Rephidim, the Amalekites attacked them. Moses said to Joshua, "Choose some of our men and go fight them. Tomorrow I'll stand on top of the hill with the staff of God in my hands."

So Joshua fought the Amalekites, and Moses, Aaron, and Hur went to the top of the hill. As long as Moses held up his hands, the Israelites began winning, but whenever he lowered his hands, the Amalekites began winning. When Moses' hands grew tired, Aaron and Hur sat him on a stone. They stood, one on each side, and held his hands up so that they remained steady until sunset. In this way Joshua defeated the Amalekites.

Then the Lord said to Moses, "Write this victory down so it can be remembered, and read it to Joshua, because I'll completely erase the memory of the Amalekites from under heaven."

Moses built an altar and called it *Yahweh-Nissi*, which means *The Lord is my Banner*. "Hold high the banner of the Lord!" he said. "The Lord will be at war against the Amalekites forever."

Jethro Visits Moses
EX 18:1-27

Now Jethro, the priest of Midian and Moses' father-in-law, heard how God had brought his people out of Egypt and about everything else he had done for Moses and the Israelites.

Moses had sent his wife Zipporah and their two sons to stay with Jethro. He had named his first son **Gershom** because he was at that time a foreigner in the land. He named his second son **Eliezer**, saying, "The God my father worshiped rescued me when Pharaoh tried to kill me."

Jethro had sent a message to Moses that he was coming to see him, along with Moses' wife and sons.

So they traveled to the desert, where Moses was camped near the mountain of God. Moses went to meet his father-in-law, bowing down and kissing him. After they asked about each other's health, they went into the tent. Moses told Jethro about everything the Lord had done to

Pharaoh and the Egyptians, about all the hardships they had experienced along the way, and how the Lord had rescued them.

Jethro was delighted and he said, "All praise is due to the Lord, who rescued you from slavery under Pharaoh and the arrogant Egyptians. Now I know that the Lord is greater than all other gods."

Then Jethro offered a burnt offering and other sacrifices to God, and Aaron and all the elders of Israel came to eat with him in God's presence.

The next day Moses took his seat to settle disputes for the people; many were waiting and they kept him busy from morning until evening.

Jethro asked, "Why are you doing this all by yourself?"

"Because the people come to seek God's will," Moses said. "When two people have a dispute, I decide which one of them is right, and I tell them God's commands."

"This isn't good," Jethro said. "You're going to wear out both yourself and the people this way. It's too much work for you to handle alone. Follow my advice and God will be with you. Continue to bring their disputes to God, teach them his commands, and show them what to do and how to behave. But appoint capable men as leaders over groups of thousands, hundreds, fifties, and tens. They must be God-fearing men who are honest and can't be bribed. Have them handle the simple cases themselves but bring the difficult cases to you. They'll share your load and make it lighter. If you do as God commands, you'll be able to handle the pressure and all these people will go home satisfied."

So Moses followed Jethro's suggestion and appointed the leaders and gave them instructions. Then Moses and Jethro said goodbye and Jethro returned home.

CHAPTER 11
The Ten Commandments
and Other Laws

The Israelites left Rephidim. On the first day of the third month after leaving Egypt, they entered the Sinai Desert and camped in front of the mountain.

Then the Lord called Moses from the mountain, and Moses went up. The Lord said, "Tell Jacob's descendants, the Israelites, 'You saw what I did to Egypt and how I carried you on eagles' wings and brought you here to me. Now if you obey me fully and keep my covenant, I'll choose you out of all nations to be my own special people. Even though the whole earth is mine, you'll be for me a kingdom of priests and a holy nation.'"

So Moses went back and summoned the elders and told them everything the Lord had commanded. "We will do everything the Lord has said," the people responded.

Moses returned to the Lord and told him what the people had said.

Then the Lord said, "Go help the people purify themselves today and tomorrow. Have them wash their clothes and be ready by the third day, when I'll come down on Mount Sinai in a dense cloud. They'll see it and hear me speaking to you, and then they will always trust you. Tell them to be careful not to approach the mountain or touch the foot of it. Kill any person or animal who disobeys, but don't touch them — instead, stone them or shoot them with arrows. The people can approach the mountain only when they hear a long blast from the trumpet."

So Moses descended the mountain and gave the people God's instructions. He also told them to abstain from sex.

On the morning of the third day, thunder roared and lightning flashed, and a thick cloud descended upon the mountain. The people heard a long, loud trumpet blast and everyone trembled with fear. Then Moses led them outside the camp to the foot of Mount Sinai to meet with the Lord, who descended on the mountain in fire and covered it in smoke. The smoke spiraled up like smoke from a furnace, and the whole mountain shook violently as the trumpet grew louder and louder. Each time Moses spoke, God answered him with a voice as loud as thunder.

Then the Lord called Moses to the top of the mountain. Moses went up and the Lord said, "Warn the people not to cross the boundary or they will die. Even the priests who normally approach me must consecrate themselves, or I will punish them."

Moses said, "You warned us to put a boundary around Mount Sinai to set it apart as holy, so the people can't come up the mountain."

"Go back down and bring Aaron up with you," the Lord replied, "but the priests and the people must not come up here, or I will punish them."

So Moses went down and told the people what the Lord had said.

God Gives the Ten Commandments
EX 20:1-21

Then God said, "I am the Lord your God, who brought you out of Egypt, out of the land of slavery.

1. Do not worship any other god but me.
2. Do not carve out idols in the image of anything in heaven above, on the earth beneath, or in the waters below. Do not bow down to them or worship them, because I, the Lord your God, am a jealous God, punishing the children for the sin of the parents to the third and fourth generation of those who hate me, but showing love to a thousand generations of those who love me and keep my commandments.
3. Do not misuse my name. I am the Lord your God and anyone who misuses my name will not go unpunished.
4. Observe the Sabbath day by keeping it holy. You can do all your work in six days, but the seventh day must be dedicated to the Lord your God as a day of rest. Neither you, your children, your servants, your livestock, nor foreign residents may do any work on the Sabbath. I made the heavens, the earth, the sea, and everything in them in six days, but I rested on the seventh day. That's why I blessed the Sabbath day and made it holy.
5. Honor your father and mother so you may have long life in the land I'm giving you.

6. Do not commit murder.
7. Do not commit adultery.
8. Do not steal.
9. Do not give false testimony against your neighbor.
10. Do not covet your neighbor's house, wife, servants, livestock, or anything that belongs to your neighbor."

When the people saw the thunder and lightning, heard the trumpet, and saw the mountain smoking, they trembled with fear and stayed a good distance away from the mountain. They said to Moses, "We'll die if God speaks to us! Speak to us yourself and we will listen."

"Don't be afraid," Moses said. "God has come in this way to test you so that your fear of him will help you obey him and keep you from sinning."

But the people remained at a distance while Moses approached the thick darkness where God was.

Laws About Idols and Altars
EX 20:22-26

Then the Lord gave Moses these instructions for the Israelites: You've heard me speak to you from heaven with your own ears; remember you must worship only me and not make any gods of silver and gold to worship. Build an altar made of earth for me and sacrifice your burnt offerings, peace offerings, sheep, goats, and cattle on it. In every place I choose for you to worship me, I'll come and bless you. If you make the altar out of stones, don't use a tool to shape them; otherwise you'll defile them. And don't build an altar with steps leading up to it; you might expose yourself going up.

Laws About Hebrew Servants
EX 21:1-11

If you buy a Hebrew servant, he may serve you no longer than six years. In the seventh year, you must set him free without owing you anything. He must leave alone if he came alone or with his wife if she came with him. But if his master gives him a wife and they have children, the woman and her children will belong to her master and only the man will go free.

If the servant loves his master, wife, and children and doesn't want to go free, his master must take him to the place of worship, have him stand against the door or doorpost, and pierce his ear with an awl. Then he will be his servant for life.

If a man sells his daughter as a servant, she won't be set free like the male servants. If her master isn't pleased with her, he must let her father buy her back. He has no right to sell her to foreigners, because he broke their contract. If he selects her for his son, he must grant her the rights of a daughter. If he marries another woman, he must not deprive the first one of her food, clothing, and marital rights. If he won't provide her with these three things, he must let her go free, without receiving any payment.

Laws About Personal Injuries
EX 21:12-36

Anyone who assaults and kills someone must put to death. But if it was an accident I permitted, I'll appoint a place of refuge where he can safely flee. If anyone gets angry, deliberately plans a murder, and then runs to my altar for protection, you must drag him away and put him to death.

Anyone who attacks or curses his father or mother must be put to death.

A kidnapper must be put to death, whether the victim has been sold or is still in the kidnapper's possession.

If during a fight one person hits another with his fist or with a stone, but it doesn't result in death, don't punish him. If the victim is confined to bed but later is able to walk outside with a cane, the aggressor must pay for the time the victim lost and take care of him until his injury has healed.

If a slave dies as a direct result of a beating with a stick, the slave owner must be punished, but don't punish him if the slave recovers after a day or two, since the slave is his property.

If people are fighting and they hit a pregnant woman, causing her to give birth prematurely but there is no serious injury, the offender must be fined whatever the woman's husband demands and the court allows. But if there's serious injury, take life for life, eye for eye, tooth for tooth, hand for hand, foot for foot, burn for burn, wound for wound, and bruise for bruise.

An owner who hits his slave in the eye and injures it must set the slave free to compensate for the eye. An owner who knocks out the tooth of his slave must set the slave free to compensate for the tooth.

If a bull gores someone to death, whether an adult or a child, stone the bull to death and don't eat its meat. But don't hold the bull's owner responsible. However, if the owner was warned of the bull's habit of goring people and he still didn't keep it penned up, stone the bull and put its owner to death. But if the dead man's relatives allow him to pay a fine to save his life, he must pay whatever is demanded. If the bull kills a slave, its owner must pay 30 pieces of silver to the slave's master and stone the bull to death.

If an ox or a donkey falls into a pit because the person who dug it didn't cover it up, the one who dug it must pay the owner for the loss and take the dead animal in exchange.

If someone's bull injures another person's bull and it dies, the two parties should sell the live one and divide the money and the dead animal equally. But if the owner knew the bull had a habit of goring and he didn't keep it penned up, he must pay, animal for animal, and take the dead animal in exchange.

Laws About Protection of Property
EX 22:1-15

If a person steals an ox and slaughters or sells it, he must replace it with five oxen; if he steals a sheep and slaughters it or sells it, he must replace it with four sheep. If the thief doesn't own anything and can't pay for what he stole, he must be sold as a slave to make the payment. If the stolen animal — whether a cow, donkey, or sheep — is found alive in his possession, he must pay two for one.

If a thief is caught breaking into a house and is killed, the one who killed him is guilty of murder only if it happens during the day. He's not guilty if it happens at night.

If livestock are out grazing and they stray and graze in someone else's field, the livestock's owner must make restitution from the best of his own field or vineyard.

Anyone who starts a fire that spreads through weeds to another person's field must pay for the damage, whether it burns the grain growing there or the grain that has been cut and stacked.

If anyone agrees to hold his neighbor's money or valuables and they are stolen, the thief must pay back double if he is caught. But if the thief isn't found, the owner of the house must appear before the judges so they can determine whether the owner himself stole the other person's property. In cases of dispute about possession of an ox, donkey, sheep, clothing, or any other property, both parties must bring their case to the judges. The person found guilty must pay double compensation to the other party.

If someone agrees to keep his neighbor's donkey, ox, sheep, or any other animal and it dies, is injured, or gets away while no one is looking, he must swear before the Lord that he didn't steal the animal. The owner must accept this and no restitution is required. But if the animal was stolen, restitution must be made to the owner. If a wild animal killed it, the neighbor must bring the remains as evidence, and he won't be required to pay for the dead animal.

If anyone borrows an animal and it is injured or dies while the owner is away, he must pay for it. But if the owner was present, he owes nothing. If the animal was rented, the money paid for it covers the loss.

Laws About Social Responsibility
EX 22:16-20|EX 22:22-31|EX 23:13b|EX 34:17|EX 34:19-20

If a man seduces a virgin who isn't engaged to be married, he must pay the bride-price to her family and marry her. If her father absolutely refuses, he must still pay the bride-price for virgins.

Don't allow a sorceress to live.

Put to death anyone who has sex with an animal.

Don't take advantage of widows or fatherless children. If you do, I'll hear them when they cry out to me. My anger will burn against you and I'll kill you with the sword. Then your wives will become widows and your children will be fatherless.

If you lend money to any of my people who are poor, don't charge interest like a creditor would. If you take your neighbor's cloak as collateral for a loan, return it to him by sunset. He has nothing else to sleep in and it's the only covering he has to keep warm. I am merciful and when he cries out to me, I'll listen.

Don't make any idols. Destroy anyone who offers sacrifices to any god other than the Lord. Don't pray to other gods or even mention their names. Don't speak evil of God or curse your leaders.

Give me the offerings from the harvest of your crops and wine when they're due.

Give me your firstborn sons. The first offspring of every womb belongs to me, including all the firstborn males of your livestock, whether from cattle or flock. Let the animals stay with their mothers for seven days and give them to me on the eighth day. Redeem the firstborn donkey with a lamb, but if you don't redeem it, break its neck. Redeem all your firstborn sons.

No one is to appear before me empty-handed.

You are my holy people, so don't eat the meat of an animal killed by wild beasts; give it to the dogs.

Laws of Justice and Mercy
EX 22:21|EX 23:1-9

Don't spread false rumors. Don't follow the crowd when they do wrong, and don't be swayed by them to pervert justice in court. Don't help a guilty person by giving false evidence or false testimony. Don't show favoritism in a lawsuit just because a person is poor, and don't deny them justice either.

Don't falsely accuse anyone and don't put an innocent person to death; I'll punish anyone who does such a thing. Don't accept a bribe — it blinds people to what is right and twists justice.

If your enemy's ox or donkey wanders off, return it to its owner. If his donkey falls down under its load, don't just leave it there; help him get the donkey up.

Don't mistreat or oppress a foreigner; remember that you were foreigners in Egypt, so you know how it feels.

Laws About the Sabbath
EX 23:10-12|EX 34:21|EX 31:12-17|EX 35:1-3

Moses assembled the whole Israelite community and gave them the following commands from the Lord:

Do your work in six days, but rest on the seventh day and do no work, even during the plowing and harvest seasons. This allows your ox and donkey to rest, and allows foreign residents and slaves born in your household to be refreshed.

Plant in your fields and gather its produce for six years, but let the land rest and don't gather anything during the seventh year. Allow the poor to gather the food and let the wild animals eat what's left. The same applies to your vineyards and olive trees.

Observe my Sabbaths. This will be a sign between me and you forever, a lasting covenant, so you'll know I am the Lord, who has set you apart. The Sabbath will be a sacred day and anyone who desecrates it must be put to death. Those who do any work on that day must be cut off from their people and put to death. You can work six days of the week, but the seventh day is a day of sabbath rest, holy to the Lord. Don't even light a fire in your house on the Sabbath. It will be a sign between me and the Israelites, because I made the heavens and the earth in six days and on the seventh day rested and was refreshed.

Laws About the Three Annual Festivals
EX 23:13a|EX 23:14-19a|EX 34:18|EX 34:22-26

All the men must travel three times a year to worship the Sovereign Lord, the God of Israel, and celebrate three festivals to honor me:

The Festival of Unleavened Bread – Celebrate the Festival of Unleavened Bread at the appointed time in the month of Abib, because that's the month you came out of Egypt. Eat bread made without yeast for seven days, as I commanded you. Don't come without an offering.

The Festival of Harvest – Celebrate the Festival of Harvest each spring by bringing me the first crops of your wheat harvest.

The Festival of Ingathering – Celebrate the Festival of Ingathering in autumn at the end of the harvest season, when you gather all your crops from the field.

When you sacrifice an animal and offer its blood to me, don't offer it with anything containing yeast and don't let any of the sacrifice from the Passover Feast remain until morning. Bring the best of the first crops of your soil to the house of the Lord your God.

When you travel each year to appear before the Lord your God, I'll drive out nations before you, enlarge your territory, and protect your land from anyone who desires it. Make sure you do everything I've commanded you.

God's Angel Will Prepare the Way
EX 23:20-32|EX 24:3-4

Then the Lord said: I'm sending an angel ahead to protect you on the journey and lead you to the place I've prepared. Pay attention and obey him. Don't rebel against him, because he won't forgive you. Obey him and do everything I command, and I will be an enemy to your enemies and oppose those who oppose you. My angel will lead you into the land of the Amorites, Hittites, Perizzites, Canaanites, Hivites, and Jebusites, and I'll wipe them out. Don't bow down to or worship their gods, and don't follow their religious practices. You must completely destroy them and smash their sacred stone pillars. Worship the Lord your God and I'll bless your food and water and protect you from sickness. No one in your land will miscarry or be infertile, and I'll give you long, full lives.

I'll cause every nation you encounter to be terrified of you, and I will throw them into confusion. I'll make all your enemies turn and run from you. I'll throw them into a panic and drive the Hivites, Canaanites, and Hittites out. But I won't drive them all out in the first year, because the land would become deserted and there would be too many wild animals for you to handle. I'll drive the people out little by little until there are enough of you to take possession of the land.

I'll establish your borders from the Red Sea to the Mediterranean Sea and from the desert to the Euphrates River. I'll give you power over the people who live in the land and you'll drive them out. Don't make a covenant with them or with their gods. Don't let them remain in your land or they will cause you to sin against me. If you worship their gods, it will certainly be a trap for you.

So Moses told the people all the Lord's commands, and they responded, "We will do everything the Lord said."

Moses then wrote down everything the Lord had told him.

The Covenant Is Confirmed
EX 24:1-2|EX 24:5-18

After the Lord finished giving the laws, he said to Moses, "Bring Aaron, his sons Nadab and Abihu, and 70 of the Israelite elders up the mountain. But you must approach me alone. The others must not come near me; they must worship at a distance. And the people must not come up at all."

Moses got up early the next morning and built an altar at the foot of the mountain and set up 12 stone pillars representing the 12 tribes of Israel. Then he summoned young men to offer burnt offerings and sacrifice young bulls as peace offerings to the Lord. Moses put half of the blood in bowls and splashed the other half against the altar. Then he read the Book of the Covenant to the people.

"We will obey everything the Lord said," they responded.

Then Moses splattered the blood on the people and said, "This blood is confirmation of the covenant that the Lord has made with you in giving these commandments."

Then Moses, Aaron, Nadab and Abihu, and the 70 elders ascended the mountain and saw the God of Israel. Under his feet was something that looked like pavement. It was made of sapphire as blue as the sky. But God didn't harm the elders when they went up; they saw God and ate and drank with him.

Then the Lord told Moses, "Come further up the mountain and remain here, and I'll give you the tablets of stone with the commandments I wrote for the people's instruction."

So Moses took his assistant Joshua and prepared to continue ascending Sinai, God's mountain.

The glorious presence of the Lord settled upon the mountain and a cloud covered it for six days. On the seventh day, the Lord called to Moses from the cloud.

"Wait here until we come back," Moses said to the elders. "Aaron and Hur are here to solve any disputes."

Then Moses entered the cloud and went up the mountain. And he stayed there 40 days and 40 nights.

To the Israelites, the glorious presence of the Lord looked like a consuming fire on top of the mountain.

God Gives Instructions for the Tabernacle
EX 25:8-9|EX 31:18

The Lord gave Moses instructions for building a Tabernacle, a holy sanctuary where he could live among the Israelites. He instructed Moses to build it and all its furnishings according to a specific plan.

When the Lord finished speaking to Moses on Mount Sinai, he gave him the two tablets of stone with the Ten Commandments, inscribed by the finger of God.

The Israelites Worship a Golden Calf
EX 32:1-35|EX 33:1-6

Moses took so long coming down from the mountain that the people gathered around Aaron and said, "Make us gods to lead us. We don't know what happened to that man Moses, who brought us out of Egypt."

"Take off the gold earrings that your wives, your sons, and your daughters are wearing and bring them to me," Aaron said.

So they all brought Aaron their earrings and he used a tool to fashion them into a calf-shaped idol.

Then they said, "Israel, this is our god who brought us out of Egypt."

Aaron built an altar in front of the calf and announced, "Tomorrow there will be a feast to the Lord."

The next day the people rose early and sacrificed burnt offerings and presented peace offerings. Afterward they ate and drank and engaged in shameful dancing.

The Lord said to Moses, "Go down! Your people whom you brought out of Egypt have become corrupt. They were so quick to disobey me and made themselves a calf-shaped idol. They bowed down and sacrificed to it, claiming it brought them out of Egypt!

"Now leave me alone. They're stubborn and my anger will burn against them. I'll destroy them, and then I'll make you into a great nation."

But Moses sought the favor of the Lord his God. "Lord," he said, "why should your anger burn against your people, whom you brought out of Egypt with great power and a mighty hand? Why should the Egyptians say, 'He brought them out only to kill them in the mountains and wipe them off the face of the earth'? Turn from your fierce anger; change your mind and don't bring disaster on your people. Remember your servants Abraham, Isaac, and Jacob. You swore by your own name to make their descendants as numerous as the stars in the sky and give them the land you promised them as an inheritance forever."

So the Lord changed his mind and didn't unleash disaster on his people.

Moses descended the mountain with the two tablets of the Ten Commandments, inscribed on both the front and back. God himself had made the tablets, and he had written the commandments himself.

Joshua had heard the people shouting below and he said to Moses, "It sounds like war in the camp."

"It isn't the sound of victory or defeat," Moses replied. "It's the sound of a celebration."

When Moses approached the camp and saw the calf and the people dancing, he was furious and threw the tablets down, breaking them into pieces at the foot of the mountain. Then he threw the calf into the fire, ground it to powder, scattered it in the water, and made the Israelites drink it.

"How did these people convince you to lead them into such great sin?" He asked Aaron.

"Don't be angry, my lord," Aaron replied. "You know how prone they are to evil. They didn't know what had happened to you and asked me to make gods to lead us. I asked for everyone's gold jewelry and they gave it to me. I threw it into the fire and this calf just came out!"

Moses saw that Aaron had let the people get completely out of control, and now they had made fools of themselves in front of their enemies. So he stood at the camp's entrance and said, "Whoever is on the Lord's side, come over here!"

And everyone from the tribe of Levi gathered around him.

Then Moses said, "The Lord, the God of Israel, has given the following instructions: strap a sword to your side; go through the camp, from one end to the other; and kill your brothers, friends, and neighbors."

The Levites did as Moses commanded and about 300 people died that day.

Afterward Moses said to the Levites, "Today the Lord has set you apart to serve him and has blessed you because you didn't spare even your closest relatives."

The next day Moses said to the people, "You've committed a terrible sin, but I'm going up to the Lord to see if he will forgive you."

Then he went back to the Lord and said, "These people have committed such a terrible sin by making themselves gods of gold. But please forgive them; if you won't, then blot me out of the record you've written."

The Lord replied, "I'll erase the name of everyone who has sinned against me. Now go lead the people to the place I told you about. But when the time comes, I will punish them."

Then the Lord struck the people with a plague.

"Take these people you brought out of Egypt, leave this place, and go up to the land flowing with milk and honey, which I swore to give to Abraham, Isaac, and Jacob and their descendants," the Lord said. "I'll send an angel to guide you and I'll drive out the Canaanites, Amorites,

Hittites, Perizzites, Hivites, and Jebusites. But I'm not going with you; these people are hard-headed, and if I'm with them for even a moment, I might destroy them on the way. Tell them to take off their jewelry and I'll decide what to do with them."

When Moses told the Israelites, they mourned and removed their jewelry at Mount Sinai and never wore it again from that point on.

Moses Sets Up the Tent of Meeting
EX 33:7-11

Now Moses used to set up a tent some distance outside the camp, and he called it the tent of meeting. Anyone who wanted to consult the Lord would go there. Whenever Moses went, everyone stood at their tent entrance and watched until he entered the tent. Then the pillar of cloud would come down and hover at the entrance while the Lord spoke with Moses. Whenever the people saw the pillar of cloud there, they bowed and worshiped at their tent entrance. The Lord would speak to Moses face to face, as one speaks to a friend. Then Moses would return to the camp, but his young assistant Joshua, son of Nun, didn't leave the tent.

Moses Sees God's Glory
EX 33:12-23

Moses said to the Lord, "You've been telling me to lead these people, but you haven't told me who you'll send with me. You said you know me by name and that you're pleased with me. If that's true, tell me your plans so I can serve you and continue to please you. Remember that you've chosen this nation to be your people."

The Lord replied, "I'll go with you and set your mind at ease."

"Don't make us leave if you don't go with us," Moses said. "How will anyone know that you're pleased with me and with your people unless you go with us? Your presence sets us apart from everyone else on the earth."

"I'll do what you ask because I'm pleased with you and I know you by name."

"Then please show me your glorious presence," Moses asked.

"I'll make all my goodness pass in front of you, and I'll proclaim my name, Yahweh, in your presence. I'll show mercy to whom I choose to show mercy, and I'll show compassion to whom I choose to show compassion. But you can't see my face, because no one can see me and live. There's a place near me where you can stand on a rock. When my glory passes by, I'll put you in an opening in the rock and cover you with my hand until I pass by. Then I'll remove my hand and you'll see my back, but my face must not be seen."

God Gives Moses New Stone Tablets
EX 34:1-16|EX 34:27-28

Then the Lord said to Moses, "Cut two stone tablets like the first ones, and I'll write the same words on them that were on the ones you smashed. Be ready by morning and then come up to the top of Mount Sinai. Don't let anyone come with you or come anywhere on the mountain; don't even allow the flocks and cattle to graze in front of it."

So Moses did as the Lord commanded and carried the two stone tablets up Mount Sinai. The Lord came down in the cloud and stood there with him and proclaimed his name, Yahweh. He passed in front of Moses and continued proclaiming, "Yahweh, Yahweh, the compassionate and gracious God, slow to anger, abounding in love and faithfulness, maintaining love to thousands, and forgiving wickedness, rebellion, and sin. Yet punishing the guilty and their children and grandchildren for the sin of the parents to the third and fourth generation."

Moses immediately bowed to the ground and worshiped. "Lord," he said, "if you're pleased with us, then please go with us. Although these people are stubborn, forgive our wickedness and sin, and accept us as your own people."

The Lord said, "I'm making a covenant with Israel and will perform miracles that have never before been seen in any nation in the world. You and all the people living around you will see the awesome things that I, the Lord, will do for you. Obey my commandments and I'll drive out the Amorites, Canaanites, Hittites, Perizzites, Hivites, and Jebusites. Be sure not to make a treaty with them, or they will be a trap to you. Break down their altars, smash their sacred pillars, and cut down their Asherah poles. Don't worship any other god; my very name is Jealous because I am a jealous God.

"When they offer sacrifices to their gods, they'll invite you to join them and you might eat their sacrifices. If you marry their daughters, you risk joining them when they prostitute themselves to their gods."

And then God repeated the commands he had given Moses earlier.

Afterward the Lord said to Moses, "Write down all these instructions, for they represent the terms of the covenant I am making with you and with Israel."

Moses remained there on the mountain with the Lord 40 days and 40 nights. In all that time, he ate and drank nothing. And the Lord wrote the terms of the covenant — the Ten Commandments — on the stone tablets.

Moses' Shining Face
EX 34:29-35

When Moses came down from Mount Sinai with the two tablets of the Ten Commandments, he was not aware that his face was shining as a result of being in the Lord's presence. So Aaron and all the Israelites were afraid to come near him. But Moses called them, so they approached him and he spoke to them, and he gave them all the commands the Lord had given him.

When Moses finished speaking to them, he put a veil over his face. But he removed the veil whenever he entered the Lord's presence to speak with him. When he came out and told the Israelites what God had commanded, his face was shining again, so Moses would put the veil back on until he went back to speak with the Lord.

CHAPTER 12
The Building of the Tabernacle

Moses Gathers Materials for the Tabernacle
EX 25:1-7|EX 35:4-29|EX 31:7-11

Moses said, "Everyone who is willing should bring to the Lord an offering of gold, silver, and bronze; blue, purple, and scarlet thread; fine linen; goat hair; fine leather and ram skins dyed red; acacia wood; olive oil for the lamps; spices for the anointing oil and fragrant incense; and onyx stones and other gems to be mounted on the priests' linen apron and chestpiece.

"He's given all the skilled craftsmen the ability to make everything he commanded: the Tabernacle with its tent and covering, clasps, frames, crossbars, posts and bases, and other furnishings; the Ark containing the Ten Commandments, with its poles, its lid, and the curtain that shields it; the table with its poles and equipment, which holds the bread of the Presence; the pure gold lampstand and its accessories, lamps, and oil for the light; the incense altar with its poles, the anointing oil, and the fragrant incense; the curtain for the Tabernacle's entrance; the altar for burning offerings, its bronze grate, poles, and equipment; the washbasin and its stand; the courtyard curtains, their posts and bases, and the curtain for the entrance to the courtyard; the tent pegs and ropes for the Tabernacle and courtyard; the fine woven, sacred clothing for Aaron and his sons when they serve as priests in the sanctuary; and the anointing oil and fragrant incense for the Holy Place. You must make them just as the Lord commanded."

So the Israelites returned to their tents and all who were willing, men and women alike, returned with their offerings to the Lord for the materials for the Tabernacle, everything needed for the sacred clothing and for worship. They brought all kinds of gold jewelry — brooches, earrings, rings, and necklaces — and presented them as a special offering to the Lord. Some people brought blue, purple, or scarlet yarn, fine linen, goat hair, ram skins dyed red, and fine leather. Others brought silver or bronze; some brought acacia wood. Some of the women weaved blue, purple, or scarlet yarn; fine linen; and goat hair and brought it as an offering.

The leaders brought onyx stones and other gems to be mounted on the linen apron and chestpiece. They also brought spices and olive oil for the lamps, the anointing oil, and the fragrant incense. The Israelites freely brought their offerings to the Lord for all the work he had commanded through Moses.

God Appoints Bezalel and Oholiab as Craftsmen
EX 31:1-6|EX 35:30-35|EX 36:1-7|EX 38:22-23

Moses said, "The Lord has chosen Bezalel — who is Uri's son and Hur's grandson — from the tribe of Judah. He has filled him with his Spirit, giving him wisdom, ability, and skills to use gold, silver, and bronze to make artistic designs. He is skilled in cutting and setting jewels, carving wood, and has mastered all kinds of artistic crafts. The Lord also appointed Oholiab son of Ahisamak, from the tribe of Dan, to work together with Bezalel to complete the work that the Lord had commanded. He gave them both the ability to teach others their skills. Both of them are skilled engravers, designers, weavers, and embroiderers, using blue, purple, and scarlet thread, and fine linen. They are excellent craftsmen and designers. They and all the other men to whom the Lord has given the skills must carry out the work of constructing the sanctuary just as the Lord commanded."

Moses summoned Bezalel, Oholiab, and the other craftsmen and gave them all the offerings the Israelites had brought for constructing the sanctuary. The people continued bringing voluntary offerings morning after morning. So all the craftsmen stopped working and said to Moses, "The people are bringing more than enough for the work the Lord commanded."

Then Moses sent the order throughout the camp that no one should bring any more offerings, because they already had an abundance, so they stopped bringing their gifts.

The Workers Build the Tabernacle
EX 26:1-32|EX 26:36-37|EX 36:8-38

Moses gave the craftsmen the instructions for the Tabernacle that the Lord had given him on Mount Sinai.

They made 10 curtains of finely woven linen for the Tabernacle, decorated with blue, purple, and scarlet thread and embroidered with cherubim. All the curtains were 42 feet long and 6 feet wide. They sewed 5 of the curtains together and did the same with the other 5. Then they used blue thread to make 50 loops and put them along the edge of the last curtain in each set, so that the loops matched each other. Then they made 50 gold clasps to join the 2 sets of curtains together into 1 piece.

They made 11 curtains out of goat-hair cloth to serve as a cover for the Tabernacle. Each curtain was 45 feet long and 6 feet wide. They sewed 5 of the curtains together to make one long curtain and did the same with the other 6, allowing 3 feet of material from the second set of curtains to hang over the front the Tabernacle. Then they made 50 loops along the edge of the last curtain in each set. They made 50 bronze clasps to join the covering into one piece. Then they covered the material with a layer of tanned ram skins and covered that with another layer of fine leather. They let the remaining 3 feet of the tent covering hang over the back of the Tabernacle and the extra 18 inches hang over each side so that the Tabernacle would be completely covered.

For the Tabernacle's framework, they used acacia wood to construct upright frames. Each frame was 15 feet high and 27 inches wide, with 2 matching pegs so the frames could be joined together. They made 20 frames for the south side of the Tabernacle and 40 silver bases to go under them — 2 bases for each frame — so that the pegs fit into the bases. They did the same for the north side. For the back, the west end, they made 6 frames. They made 2 additional frames, one for each corner, and they were joined at the bottom and attached at the top with a single ring. So for the rear there were 8 frames and 16 silver bases — 2 under each frame.

They also made crossbars out of acacia wood to link the frames: 5 for the south side of the Tabernacle, 5 for the north, and 5 for the rear. The center crossbar ran through the middle of the frames from one end to the other. They overlaid the frames and crossbars with gold and made gold rings to hold the crossbars.

For the inside of the Tabernacle, they made a curtain of fine linen, woven with blue, purple, and scarlet thread, and embroidered it with cherubim. To hold the curtain, they used acacia wood to make 4 posts, covered them with gold, and fitted them with gold hooks. Then they made 4 silver bases to hold the posts. For the entrance to the tent, they made another curtain of finely woven linen embroidered with blue, purple, and scarlet thread. They made 5 posts for the curtain and fitted them with hooks.

They overlaid the tops of the posts and the hooks with gold and made 5 bronze bases for the posts.

The Workers Build the Ark of the Covenant
EX 25:10-15|EX 25:17-20|EX 37:1-9

They made the Ark of the Covenant out of acacia wood. It was 45 inches long, 27 inches wide, and 27 inches high. They overlaid it inside and out with pure gold and put a gold border around it. They made 4 gold carrying rings and fastened them to the Ark's 4 feet, with 2 rings on one side and 2 rings on the other. They made carrying poles of acacia wood, covered them with gold, and inserted the poles into the rings on each side of the Ark to carry it. These poles had to remain in the rings; they couldn't be removed. They made the cover for the Ark out of pure gold. It was 45 inches long and 27 inches wide. Then they hammered each end of the cover into the shape of a cherub so that they were of one piece with the cover. The cherubim faced each other, looking down toward the cover. Their wings stretched out toward each other, covering the top of the Ark.

The Workers Build the Table for the Sacred Bread
EX 25:23-29|EX 37:10-16

They made the table for the sacred bread out of acacia wood. It was 36 inches long, 18 inches wide, and 27 inches high. They overlaid it with pure gold and made a gold border around it. They also made a 3-inch-wide strip of wood to go around the table and fastened it to the legs. Then they placed a gold border around the strip. They made 4 gold rings and attached one to each of the legs, close to the rim, to hold the poles for carrying the table. The carrying poles were made of acacia wood and overlaid with gold. And the articles for the table were made from pure gold — its plates, dishes, and the bowls and pitchers for pouring out drink offerings.

The Workers Build the Tabernacle Lampstand
EX 25:31-36|EX 25:38-40|EX 37:17-24|NM 8:4

They made the lampstand and accessories according to the pattern shown to Moses on the mountain. The lampstand and all its accessories were hammered from 75 pounds of pure gold, including its base and shaft. All its cups were shaped like almond flowers, with buds and blossoms. 6 branches extended from the sides — 3 on one side and 3 on the other. 3 cups were on each of the 6 branches extending from the lampstand. 4 cups were on the shaft. There was one bud below each of the 3 pairs of branches.

They also made the 7 lamps, the tongs, and the trays out of pure gold. The buds and the branches were all of one piece with the lampstand.

So the lampstand was made of hammered gold from its base to its blossoms.

The Workers Build the Altar of Incense
EX 30:1-5|EX 37:25-29

For burning incense, they made a square altar out of acacia wood. It was 18 inches long, 18 inches wide, and 36 inches high — with horns at the corners carved from the same piece of wood as the altar. They overlaid the top, sides, and the horns with pure gold, and put a gold border around it. They made the poles for carrying the altar out of acacia wood and overlaid them with gold. They made 2 gold rings for the altar below the gold border — one on each side — to hold the poles.

Using his expert incense-mixing skills, Bezalel made the sacred anointing oil and the pure, fragrant incense.

The Workers Build the Altar of Burnt Offering
EX 27:1-8|EX 38:1-7

Next they built an altar for burning offerings, just as God had shown Moses on the mountain. They made it out of acacia wood. It was square, made in the shape of a hollow wooden box, 7½ feet wide, 7½ feet long, and 4½ feet high. They made horns for each of its 4 corners so that the horns and altar were all one piece, and overlaid the altar with bronze. They made all its equipment with bronze — its pans to remove the ashes, shovels, sprinkling bowls, meat forks, and firepans. They made a bronze grating for a strainer and put it under the rim, halfway down the altar. They made 4 bronze rings and put them on the 4 corners of the grating to hold the 2 poles, which they made of acacia wood and overlaid with bronze. Then they inserted the poles through the rings on each side of the altar for carrying it.

The Workers Build the Washing Basin
EX 38:8|EX 30:17-18a

They made the bronze washing basin, along with its bronze stand, using the mirrors of the women who served at the Tabernacle entrance.

The Workers Build the Tabernacle Courtyard
EX 27:9-19|EX 38:9-20

Next they made the enclosure for the Tabernacle courtyard using curtains of fine linen. The courtyard was 150 feet long on the south and north and 75 feet wide on the east and west. They used 20 bronze posts on bronze stands for the south and north and 10 for the west. Then they hung curtains on all the posts using silver hooks and rods. They placed 3 bronze posts on each side of the entrance at the east and hung curtains on them that were 22½ feet long.

The curtain for the entrance of the enclosure was made of fine linen and embroidered with blue, purple, and scarlet thread. It was hung on 4 posts set in 4 bronze bases, using silver hooks and rods. It was 30 feet long and, like the curtains of the courtyard walls, 7½ feet high. All the other articles for everyday use in the service of the Tabernacle were bronze, including all the tent pegs used to support the Tabernacle and the courtyard curtains.

God Gives Instructions for the Tabernacle Tax
EX 30:11-16|EX 38:21|EX 38:24-31

The Lord had said to Moses, "When you take a census to count the Israelites, each man 20 years or older who crosses over and is registered must pay the Lord a price for his life so no plague will strike him. They must give an offering of approximately 6 ounces of silver, measured according to the official standard, using the correct weight. Everyone must give the same amount, whether rich or poor. Use the atonement money for the care of the Tabernacle. It will be a reminder to the Israelites before the Lord that they have paid for protection for their lives."

Moses had assigned Aaron's son Ithamar the responsibility of keeping a record of the metals used for the Tabernacle. The total amount of gold from the special offering was about 2,195 pounds, measured according to the official standard.

The silver collected from all the men who would cross over was about 7,550 pounds — there was a total of 603,550 men. 7,500 pounds of the silver was used to cast the 100 bases for the sanctuary walls and the inner curtain — 75 pounds for each base. Another 50 pounds of silver was used to make the hooks for the posts, overlay the tops of the posts, and make the bands.

The bronze from the special offering totaled 5,310 pounds. They used it to make the bases for the entrance to the Tabernacle, the bronze altar with its bronze grating and equipment, the bases for the surrounding courtyard and entrance, and all the tent pegs for the Tabernacle and surrounding courtyard.

God Gives Instructions for the Anointing Oil
EX 30:22-33

Then the Lord said to Moses, "Mix a gallon of olive oil with the following fine spices: 12½ pounds of liquid myrrh, 6¼ pounds of fragrant cinnamon, 6¼ pounds of fragrant cane, and 12½ pounds of cassia — measured according to the official standard. Mix it like perfume to make sacred anointing oil, and anoint the Tabernacle, the Ark of the Covenant, the table and all its equipment, the lampstand and its accessories, the altar of incense, the altar of burnt offering and all its equipment, and the basin with its stand. Consecrate them so they will be completely holy, and whatever touches them will become holy.

"Use the oil to anoint Aaron and his sons and consecrate them to serve me as priests. Tell the Israelites this is my sacred anointing oil for the generations to come. They shouldn't pour it on anyone other than a priest or use the same blend to make any other oil. Whoever does must be cut off from their people. It is sacred and they must treat it as sacred."

God Gives Instructions for the Incense
EX 30:34-38

Then the Lord said to Moses, "Gather fragrant spices in equal amounts — myrrh resin, aromatic shellfish, and plant resin — and pure frankincense, and make a fragrant blend of incense, with the skill of a perfumer. Add salt so it will be pure and sacred. Grind some of it to powder and place it in front of the Ark of the Covenant in the Tabernacle, where I'll meet with you. It will be most holy to you. Consider it holy to the Lord. Don't make any incense with this formula for yourselves, to enjoy its fragrance. Whoever does must be cut off from their people."

God Gives Instructions for the Priests' Clothing
EX 28:1-5|EX 39:1

"Send for your brother Aaron and his sons —Nadab, Abihu, Eleazar, and Ithamar. Set them apart from the Israelites so they can serve me as priests. Tell the skilled workers whom I've filled with wisdom to make sacred clothing for Aaron to distinguish him as High Priest, set apart for my service to minister in the sanctuary. They must make a chestpiece, a linen apron, a robe, an embroidered ankle-length shirt, a turban, and a sash. They must use gold, and also blue, purple, and scarlet thread to weave fine linen cloth for the sacred priestly clothing."

So the craftsmen made the magnificent clothing just as the Lord had commanded.

The Linen Apron
EX 28:6-14|EX 39:2-7

The apron was made of finely spun linen, woven with blue, purple, and scarlet thread. Thin sheets of gold were hammered out, cut into strands, and skillfully woven into the thread and linen. Shoulder straps were attached to the sides of the apron to hold it up. Its skillfully woven waistband was made of the same material, and embroidered; it was attached to the front and formed one piece with the apron.

They mounted 2 onyx stones in gold settings and attached them to the shoulder straps. A skilled craftsman engraved the stones with the names of the 12 tribes of Israel in the order of their birth — 6 names on one stone and the remaining 6 on the other. Then they fastened the stones on the apron's shoulder pieces so Aaron would always wear their names on his shoulders and the Lord would always remember his people. They made 2 more gold settings and attached 2 chains of pure gold, braided like a rope, as the Lord commanded Moses.

The Chestpiece
EX 28:15-30|EX 39:8-21

Skilled craftsmen fashioned a chestpiece to be used for making decisions. It was made of the same material and design as the linen apron and was folded into a 9-inch-square pouch. 4 rows of precious stones were mounted on it, 12 stones in all. The first row contained a red carnelian, a pale green topaz, and an emerald; the second row contained a turquoise, a sapphire, and a diamond; the third row contained an orange jacinth, an agate, and a purple amethyst; the fourth row contained a blue-green beryl, an onyx, and a green jasper. All of them were mounted in gold filigree settings. Each stone was engraved like a seal with the name of one Jacob's sons to represent the 12 tribes of Israel. In this way Aaron would bear their names over his heart whenever he entered the Holy Place, so the Lord would always remember his people. They also put the Urim and the Thummim in the chestpiece so he would always carry over his heart the objects used for making decisions for the Lord's people.

They made 2 braided chains of pure gold and 2 gold rings. Then they fastened the rings to the front corners of the chestpiece and fastened the 2 gold chains to the rings. The other ends of the chains were fastened to the 2 gold settings on the linen apron's shoulder straps. They made 4 more gold rings and attached 2 of them to the lower inside corners of the chestpiece next to the linen apron. The other 2 rings were attached to the bottom of the shoulder pieces on the front of the linen apron, close to the seam just above the apron's waistband. They tied the chestpiece's rings to the apron's rings with blue cord, connecting it to the waistband so it wouldn't come loose — as the Lord commanded Moses.

Other Priestly Clothing
EX 28:31-43|EX 39:22-31

The linen apron's robe was woven entirely of blue wool, with an opening for the head in the center and a woven collar around it so it wouldn't tear. Woven pomegranates of fine linen and blue, purple, and scarlet thread were attached around the hem of the robe. They made bells of pure gold and attached them around the hem between the pomegranates so that the bells and pomegranates alternated around the hem of the robe. The robe was for Aaron to wear while ministering. The bells would be heard when he entered and exited the Holy Place before the Lord, so that he wouldn't die.

Everything that Aaron and his sons wore was made of fine linen woven with blue, purple, and scarlet thread, including their robes, turbans, decorative head coverings, underwear, and even their embroidered sashes.

Finally, they made the medallion, a sacred sign of holiness. It was made out of pure gold and was engraved like an inscription on a seal with the words: HOLY TO THE LORD. It was attached with a blue cord to the front of the turban. Aaron would continually wear it on his forehead to accept the responsibility for any sins the Israelites committed. In this way when he offered their sacred gifts, they would be acceptable to the Lord.

Aaron's ankle-length shirt and turban were made of fine linen, and the sash was embroidered. They also made ankle-length shirts, sashes, and caps for the priests to give them dignity and honor. These clothes were for Aaron and his sons to wear when they were anointed and ordained to serve the Lord as priests.

Linen underclothing was made for Aaron and his sons to cover the body from waist to thigh. They had to wear them whenever they entered the Tabernacle or approached the altar to minister in the Holy Place, otherwise they would incur guilt and die. This would be a permanent law for Aaron and his descendants.

Moses Inspects the Tabernacle
EX 39:32-43

Finally, the Tabernacle was complete and the Israelites brought it to Moses: the tent and all its furnishings, its clasps, frames, crossbars, posts, and bases; the covering of ram skins dyed red and the covering of durable leather and the shielding curtain; the Ark of the Covenant with its poles and the atonement cover; the table with all its articles and the sacred bread; the pure gold lampstand with its row of lamps and all its accessories, and the olive oil for the light; the gold altar, the anointing oil, the fragrant incense, and the curtain for the Tabernacle entrance; the bronze altar with its bronze grating, poles, and accessories; the basin with its stand; the courtyard curtain with its posts and bases, and the curtain for the entrance to the courtyard; the ropes and tent pegs for the courtyard; all the furnishings for the Tabernacle; and the woven clothing Aaron and his sons would wear for ministering in the sanctuary as priests.

Moses inspected the work and saw that they had completed it just as the Lord had commanded, so he blessed them.

The People Set Up the Tabernacle
EX 25:16|EX 25:21-22|EX 25:30|EX 25:37|EX 26:33-35
EX 27:20-21|EX 30:6-10|EX 30:18b-21|EX 40:1-11
EX 40:17-35|LV 8:10-11|LV 24:1-9|NM 8:1-3

The Lord had told Moses to set up the Tabernacle in the second year, on the first day of the first month and had given him instructions. So they put the bases in place, erected the frames, inserted the crossbars, and set up the posts. Then they spread the tent over the Tabernacle and put the protective covering over it.

They put the tablets of the Ten Commandments that God had given Moses into the Ark, and they put the atonement cover over it. God would meet with Moses above the cover between the two cherubim to give him all his commands for the Israelites.

They hung the curtain from the hooks and placed the Ark of the Covenant behind the curtain to shield it. The room that held the Ark was called the Most Holy Place and the curtain separated it from the Holy Place.

They placed the table on the north side of the Tabernacle outside the curtain and set out the bread so it would be in the Lord's presence at all times. The Lord had given the following instructions: "Use 24 quarts of the finest flour to bake 12 loaves of bread. Arrange them in 2 stacks of 6 and place them before the Lord on the table of pure gold. Put pure incense near each stack to be offered as a food offering to the Lord in place of the bread. Each Sabbath, set the bread out regularly as an offering on the Israelites' behalf; this is an eternal covenant. The bread belongs to Aaron and his descendants. They must eat it in a holy place because it is the most holy part of their permanent share of the food offerings presented to the Lord."

They placed the pure gold lampstand in front of the curtain shielding the Ark of the Covenant. This was on the south side of the Tabernacle opposite the table. Then the Lord said to Moses, "The Israelites must bring pure oil from crushed olives to the Tabernacle. Aaron must use this oil to light the lamps. Tell Aaron to set up the seven lamps so that they all light up the area in front of the lampstand."

So Aaron set up in the Lord's presence the seven lamps so that they faced forward on the lampstand to light the space in front of it. Aaron and his sons were responsible for keeping the lamps burning from evening until morning. This would be a permanent law among the Israelites for the generations to come.

They placed the gold altar of incense in front of the curtain that shields the Ark of the Covenant. Aaron would be responsible for burning fragrant incense on the altar every morning and evening when he tended the lamps, so the incense would burn regularly before the Lord for the generations to come. No unauthorized incense or burnt, grain, or drink offering was to be offered on this altar. Once a year, for the generations to come, Aaron would purify the altar by smearing its horns with the blood of the animal sacrificed for sin. The altar is especially holy, dedicated to the Lord.

They hung the curtain at the Tabernacle entrance and placed the altar of burnt offering in front of it. Then they placed the basin between the Tabernacle and the altar and put water in it for washing. Moses, Aaron, and Aaron's sons would use it to wash their hands and feet whenever they entered the Tabernacle or approached the altar, as the Lord commanded. In this way they wouldn't die. It would be a permanent law for Aaron and his descendants for the generations to come.

Then Moses set up the courtyard around the Tabernacle and altar and put up the curtain at the entrance to the courtyard. And so Moses finished the work.

When they finished setting up the Tabernacle, Moses used the anointing oil to dedicate the Tabernacle and all its furnishings to the Lord, making them holy. He sprinkled some of the oil on the burnt altar seven times, so it would be especially holy, along with all its utensils and the basin with its stand.

Then the cloud of the Lord covered the Tabernacle and his glory filled it, so Moses couldn't enter.

Offerings at the Tabernacle Dedication
NM 7:1-89

Then the leaders of each tribe brought offerings before the Lord at the Tabernacle: 6 covered carts and 12 oxen — an ox from each leader and a cart from every two.

The Lord said to Moses, "Accept these items and give them to the Levites to use for transporting the Tabernacle."

So Moses gave 2 carts and 4 oxen to the Gershon clan, and 4 carts and 8 oxen to the Merari clan. Aaron's son, Ithamar the priest, supervised them. But Moses didn't give carts and oxen to the Kohath clan, because they were required to carry the sacred objects on their shoulders.

Then the Lord said to Moses, "Each day, one leader must bring his offering for the dedication of the altar." So when the altar was anointed, they presented their offerings there in the following order:

Day 1: Nahshon son of Amminadab, the leader of the tribe of Judah
Day 2: Nethanel son of Zuar, the leader of the tribe of Issachar
Day 3: Eliab son of Helon, the leader of the tribe of Zebulun
Day 4: Elizur son of Shedeur, the leader of the tribe of Reuben
Day 5: Shelumiel son of Zurishaddai, the leader of the tribe of Simeon
Day 6: Eliasaph son of Deuel, the leader of the tribe of Gad
Day 7: Elishama son of Ammihud, the leader of the tribe of Ephraim
Day 8: Gamaliel son of Pedahzur, the leader of the tribe of Manasseh
Day 9: Abidan son of Gideoni, the leader of the tribe of Benjamin
Day 10: Ahiezer son of Ammishaddai, the leader of the tribe of Dan
Day 11: Pagiel son of Okran, the leader of the tribe of Asher
Day 12: Ahira son of Enan, the leader of the tribe of Naphtali

And each leader brought the same offerings:
* A **silver platter** that weighed over 3 pounds and a silver sprinkling bowl weighing almost 2 pounds, according to the official standard. Both were filled with a grain offering consisting of the finest flour mixed with olive oil.
* A **gold dish** weighing 4 ounces and filled with incense
* A **burnt offering**: a young bull, a ram, and a one-year-old male lamb
* A **sin offering**: a male goat
* A **peace offering**: 2 bulls, 5 rams, 5 male goats, and 5 one-year-old male lambs

So the Israelite leaders' offerings for the altar dedication equaled: 12 silver platters, 12 silver sprinkling bowls, and 12 gold dishes. Altogether, the silver dishes weighed about 60 pounds, according to the official standard, and the gold dishes weighed about 3 pounds.

The total number of animals for the burnt offering equaled 12 young bulls, 12 rams, and 12 one-year-old male lambs, together with their grain offering. Twelve male goats were used for the sin offering. And for the peace offering 24 bulls, 60 rams, 60 male goats, and 60 one-year-old male lambs were used.

Then Moses entered the Tabernacle and the Lord spoke to him from between the two cherubim, which sat above the atonement cover on the Ark of the Covenant.

The Israelites Celebrate the Passover
NM 9:1-14

In the first month of the second year after they left Egypt, the Lord said to Moses in the Sinai Desert, "The Israelites must celebrate the Passover at the appointed time — at twilight on the 14th day of this month, according to the regulations I gave you."

So they celebrated the Passover in the Sinai Desert at the appointed time, just as the Lord commanded. But some of them couldn't celebrate the Passover on the 14th because they had touched a dead body and become ceremonially unclean. So they said to Moses and Aaron, "We touched a dead body and have become unclean, but why should that keep us from presenting the Lord's offering with everyone else at the appointed time?"

"I will find out what the Lord commands," Moses replied.

Then the Lord gave Moses the following instructions: "When you or your descendants are unclean because of a dead body or are away on a trip, you must celebrate the Lord's Passover a month later — at twilight on the 14th day of the *second* month. Don't break the lambs' bones. Eat the lamb, unleavened bread, and bitter herbs, and don't leave any until morning. Follow all the normal regulations for the Passover. But anyone else who fails to celebrate the Passover at the appointed time will suffer the consequences of their sin and must be cut off from their people. The same rules apply for foreign residents as for native-born Israelites. They also must follow all the regulations for the Lord's Passover if they want to participate."

CHAPTER 13
The Ordination of the Priests

Moses Ordains the Priests
EX 29:1-37|EX 40:12-16|LV 8:1-9|LV 8:12-36
Moses Prepares the Priests for Ordination
EX 29:1-9|EX 40:12-16|LV 8:1-9 |LV 8:12-13

The Lord gave Moses the following instructions for consecrating and ordaining Aaron and his sons to serve him as priests: Choose a young bull and two rams that have no defects. Use the finest wheat flour and no yeast to make loaves of bread, cakes mixed with olive oil, and thin wafers spread with oil, and place them all in a basket. Bring Aaron and his sons, their sacred clothing, the anointing oil, the bull for the sin offering, the two rams, and the basket of unleavened bread to the Tabernacle entrance, and assemble the Israelite community there.

So Moses obeyed God, and when the community assembled, he said, "We're here to do what the Lord commanded."

Then he brought Aaron and his sons forward and had them engage in a ritual washing. He put the ankle-length shirt and robe on Aaron and tied the sash around his waist. Then he put the linen apron on him and fastened it with its decorative sash. He put on the chestpiece and put the Urim and Thummim inside. Then Moses put the turban on Aaron's head and attached the sacred, engraved gold medallion to the front. He consecrated Aaron by pouring anointing oil on his head.

Finally, Moses anointed Aaron's sons just as he had their father. He dressed them in their ankle-length shirts, tied on their sashes, and fastened their caps, as the Lord commanded. This ceremony ordained them and their descendants to forever serve the Lord as priests.

Moses Offers the Sin Offering for the Priests
EX 29:10-14|LV 8:14-17

Following the Lord's instructions, Moses then presented the bull for the sin offering, and Aaron and his sons laid their hands on its head. Moses slaughtered it there in the Lord's presence and used his finger to smear some of the blood on the four horns of the altar. He poured out the rest of the blood at the altar's base. In this way he purified the altar to make it suitable to offer the sacrifices for the forgiveness of sins. Then Moses burned on the altar all the fat around the internal organs, the best part of the liver, and both kidneys with their fat. But he burned the rest of the bull — its skin, meat, the food in its stomach, and the waste in its intestines — outside the camp.

Moses Offers the Burnt Offering for the Priests
EX 29:15-20|EX 29:22-25|LV 8:18-29

Moses then presented the ram for the burnt offering, and Aaron and his sons laid their hands on its head. Moses slaughtered the ram and splashed the blood against all four sides of the altar. He cut the ram into pieces and washed the internal organs and hind legs with water, and burned the head, the fat, and the rest of the ram on the altar. This burnt offering was a pleasing aroma presented to the Lord.

Then Aaron and his sons laid their hands on the head of the other ram — the ordination ram — and Moses slaughtered it and put some of its blood on Aaron's right earlobe, his right thumb, and the big toe of his right foot. He did the same to Aaron's sons. Then he splashed the rest of the blood against the four sides of the altar. Since this was the ordination ram, Moses cut away its fat, including the fat of the tail, the fat around the internal organs, the best part of the liver, both kidneys with their fat, and the right thigh.

And from the basket of the sacred unleavened bread, he took one loaf, one cake mixed with olive oil, and one thin wafer spread with oil and gave them to Aaron and his sons. They lifted them before the Lord to dedicate them as a special offering. Moses then took the items from them and burned them on top of the fat portions and on the right thigh as an ordination offering. This food offering was a pleasing aroma presented to the Lord.

Aaron and His Sons Complete Their Ordination
EX 29:21|EX 29:26|EX 29:31-34|LV 8:30-32

Then Moses mixed some blood from the altar with some anointing oil and sprinkled it on Aaron, his sons, and their clothing. This demonstrated that they and their clothing had been set apart as holy.

Moses also lifted up the breast of the ram to the Lord as a special offering. Then he said to Aaron and his sons, "Boil the meat in a sacred place, at the Tabernacle entrance, and eat it there with the leftover bread from the basket of ordination offerings. Any food left over in the morning must be burned and not eaten, because it is holy. And remember that only the priests can eat this sacred food."

Instructions for the Future Installation of Priests
EX 29:27-30

The Lord gave Moses the following instructions: In the future when the Israelites offer the breast and thigh of a ram, either to ordain a priest or as a peace offering, the meat belongs to the Lord, and it must be set aside for the priests. This law will never change.

Aaron's sacred clothing must be preserved for his descendants to wear when they are anointed and ordained. They must wear these clothes for seven days as they enter the Tabernacle to minister in the Holy Place.

The Seven-Day Ordination Ceremony
EX 29:35-37|LV 8:33-36

Then Moses said to the priests, "Everything that has been done today was commanded by the Lord to make atonement for your sins. To complete your ordination, you must stay at the Tabernacle entrance for seven days and seven nights as the Lord commanded. Each day you must sacrifice a young bull for the forgiveness of your sins and to purify the altar. You must also anoint the altar with the special oil. Then the altar will be completely holy and whatever touches it will become holy. Do not leave before your time is completed. Do what the Lord requires so you won't die."

So Aaron and his sons did everything the Lord commanded through Moses.

The Levites Are Set Apart
NM 8:5-26

The Lord gave Moses the following instructions: Set the Levites apart and purify them. Sprinkle them with the water of purification, and then have them shave their whole bodies and wash their clothes so they will be ceremonially clean. Bring the Levites before the Lord at the Tabernacle entrance and assemble the whole Israelite community. The Israelites must lay their hands on them, and Aaron must present the Levites as a special offering from the Israelites so they can to do the Lord's work.

Then the Levites must offer a young bull with its required grain offering and another young bull for a sin offering to make atonement for themselves. They must lay their hands on the bulls' heads and present the animals as a special offering to the Lord. Then they must stand in front of Aaron and his sons so they can present the Levites as a special gift to me. After their purification and dedication, they will be qualified to work in the Tabernacle.

The Levites have been set apart from the other Israelites. They will belong to me and they must be given to me completely. I have claimed them as a substitute for the firstborn sons of Israel. Every firstborn male in Israel, whether human or animal, is mine. I set them apart for myself when I struck down all of Egypt's firstborn. I have set the Levites apart as gifts to Aaron and his sons to serve at the Tabernacle on behalf of the Israelites and to make atonement for them. In this way no plague will strike them when they approach the sanctuary.

Men age 25 or older can work in the Tabernacle, but they must retire from their regular service at age 50. They may assist their fellow Levites in performing their duties, but they themselves must not be responsible for the work.

So Moses, Aaron, and the whole Israelite community dedicated the Levites just as the Lord commanded, and the Levites purified themselves and washed their clothes. Then Aaron presented them to the Lord as a special offering and made atonement for them. After that, the Levites reported to the Tabernacle under the supervision of Aaron and his sons.

Introduction for Offering Regulations
LV 1:1-2|LV 7:37-38

On the day the Lord commanded the Israelites to bring him their offerings, these are the laws he gave for the ordination offering, the burnt offering, the grain offering, the peace offering, the sin offering, and the guilt offering. He gave these instructions to Moses in the desert at Mount Sinai. The Lord called to Moses from the Tabernacle and said, "Tell the Israelites that when they bring a burnt offering to the Lord, they may bring an animal from either the cattle or the flock."

Regulations for the Burnt Offering
LV 1:1-17|LV 6:8-13

A Burnt Offering From the Cattle
LV 1:3-9

Burnt offerings from the cattle must be a male without defect. Bring the young bull into the Lord's presence at the Tabernacle entrance so I can make sure it's acceptable. Lay your hand on its head and it will be accepted as a sacrifice to take away your sins. Slaughter it there on the altar and have Aaron's descendants, the priests, splash the blood against its sides. Skin the burnt offering and cut it into pieces while the priests arrange wood on the altar and light the fire. Then they will arrange the pieces, the head, and the fat on the wood. Wash the internal organs and the legs and a priest will burn them on the altar. This burnt offering is a pleasing aroma to the Lord.

A Burnt Offering From the Flock
LV 1:10-13

Burnt offerings of sheep or goats must be a male without defect. Slaughter it in my presence at the north side of the altar. The priests will splash its blood against the sides of the altar. Cut it into pieces and the priest will arrange them, with the head and the fat on the burning wood. Wash the internal organs and the legs and a priest will burn them on the altar. This burnt offering is a pleasing aroma to the Lord.

A Burnt Offering From the Birds
LV 1:14-17

Burnt offerings of birds may be a dove or a young pigeon. The priest will bring it to the altar, wring off the head, and burn it on the altar, draining its blood out on the side. He must remove the crop and the feathers and throw them down east of the altar, where the ashes are. He will tear it open by the wings, not dividing it completely, and then burn it on the wood. This burnt offering is a pleasing aroma to the Lord.

Burnt Offering Instructions for the Priests
LV 6:8-13

The Lord gave Moses the following instructions for Aaron and his sons: The burnt offering must remain on the firewood on top of the altar and the fire must not be extinguished. The next day, the priest will put on his priestly clothing — his linen undergarment and robe — remove the ashes of the burnt offering that the fire has consumed, and put them beside the altar. Then he must change into his everyday clothes and dispose of the ashes outside the camp in a ceremonially clean place. Every morning the priest must add fresh firewood, arrange the burnt offering next to the fat of the peace offerings, and burn them. Keep the fire burning on the altar continuously; it must not go out!

Regulations for the Grain Offering
LV 2:1-16|LV 6:14-23

Uncooked Grain Offerings
LV 2:1-2a

Use only the finest flour for raw grain offerings presented to the Lord. Pour olive oil on the flour, sprinkle on incense, and take it to the priests.

Cooked Grain Offerings
LV 2:4-8a|LV 2:11|LV 2:13

Cooked grain offerings must consist of the finest flour and olive oil, and contain no yeast.

For grain offerings **baked in an oven**: Make thick loaves mixed with olive oil or thin loaves brushed with olive oil.

For grain offerings **prepared on a griddle**: Crumble it and pour oil on it.

For grain offerings **cooked in a pan**: Make it of the finest flour and olive oil.

Bring the cooked grain offering to the Lord and present it to the priest. Every grain offering brought to the Lord must be made without yeast or honey because neither yeast nor honey can be burned.

You must season all your grain offerings with salt, which represents the covenant between you and God.

Firstfruits Grain Offerings
LV 2:12|LV 2:14-16

For firstfruits grain offerings to the Lord, roast crushed heads of fresh grain, along with oil and incense. The priest will burn the symbolic portion as a food offering presented to the Lord. You may bring honey or yeast to the Lord as a firstfruits offering, but don't burn them on the altar.

Grain Offering Instructions for the Priests
LV 2:2b-3|LV 2:8b-10|LV 6:14-23

The presiding priest must bring the grain offering before the Lord, in front of the altar. Take a handful of the flour and olive oil, and all the incense, and burn it on the altar as a symbol that the full portion has been offered to the Lord. The aroma of this food offering is pleasing to the Lord.

The rest of the grain offering belongs to Aaron and his sons. It must not be prepared with yeast, and they must eat it in the sacred courtyard of the Tabernacle. I have given it to them as their share of the food offerings presented to me. Like the sin and guilt offerings, it is most holy because it was taken from food offered to the Lord. Any of Aaron's male descendants may eat from these offerings. This is their permanent right for all generations to come. Whoever touches this food offering must be holy; therefore no one but the priests may consume it.

Each descendant of Aaron anointed to succeed him must offer to the Lord a regular grain offering of two quarts of the finest flour, half in the morning and half in the evening. It must be mixed well with oil and cooked on a griddle, and then presented broken in pieces, as an aroma pleasing to the Lord. This share is the Lord's forever. Every grain offering of a priest must be burned completely; it must not be eaten."

Regulations for the Peace Offering
LV 3:1-17|LV 7:11-21

General Regulations for Peace Offerings
LV 19:5-8

When you sacrifice a peace offering to the Lord, do it according to my regulations so it will be accepted. You may eat it on the day you sacrifice it or on the next day, but burn up anything left over until the third day because then it will be impure and won't be accepted. Those who eat it will be punished because they have profaned that which is holy to the Lord; they must be cut off from their people.

Peace Offerings of Cattle
LV 3:1-5

Bulls or cows presented as peace offerings must be presented before the Lord without defect. Lay your hand on the animal's head and slaughter it at the Tabernacle entrance. Then the priests will splatter the blood against all four sides of the altar. Present part of the sacrifice as a food offering to the Lord: all the fat surrounding the internal organs, both kidneys with their fat, and the best part of the liver. Burn them on the altar along with the burnt offering. This offering is a pleasing aroma to the Lord.

Peace Offerings of the Flock
LV 3:6-16a

Goats or sheep offered from the flock as a peace offering to the Lord may be male or female, but must be without defect. Present the animal before the Lord, lay your hand on its head, and slaughter it in front of the Tabernacle. The priests will then splatter its blood against all four sides of the altar. Present part of the sacrifice as a food offering to the Lord: all the fat surrounding the internal organs, both kidneys with their fat, and the best part of the liver. For the sheep, also include the entire fat of the tail, cut off near the backbone. Burn them on the altar. This offering is a pleasing aroma to the Lord.

God Forbids Eating Fat
LV 3:16b|LV 3:17|LV 7:22-25

Don't eat the fat of cattle, sheep, or goats. If you find an animal that has died of natural causes or has been killed by wild animals, you may use its fat for any other purpose, but you must not eat it. Don't eat the fat of an animal offered as a special gift to the Lord. Anyone who does so must be cut off from their people. This is a lasting command for the generations to come, wherever you live. You must not eat any fat, because all of it belongs to the Lord.

The Priests' Portion of the Peace Offering
LV 7:28-36

Those who bring a peace offering as a special sacrifice to the Lord must present with their own hands the animal fat and the breast. The priest will burn the fat on the altar, and then the breast must first be lifted before the Lord as a special offering and then given to priests. You must also give as a contribution the right thigh of your peace offerings to the officiating priest who offers the blood and the fat of the peace offering. From the Israelites' peace offerings, I have given the breast and the thigh to the priests as a permanent portion for the generations to come.

Peace Offerings as an Expression of Thankfulness
LV 7:11-15

For a peace offering presented as an expression of thankfulness, also offer in addition to the animal sacrifice various types of bread: (1) thick loaves made without yeast and mixed with olive oil, (2) thin loaves made without yeast and brushed with olive oil, (3) thick loaves of the finest flour, well-kneaded and mixed with oil, and (4) thick loaves of bread made with yeast.

Offer one of each kind as a special gift to the Lord; they will belong to the priest who splashed the blood against the altar. The meat of the thanksgiving peace offering must be eaten on the same day it's offered; none of it may be saved until morning.

Peace Offerings as the Result of a Vow
LV 7:16-18

But if the offering is the result of a vow or is a voluntary offering, anything left over may be eaten the next day. However, anything left on the third day must be burned up. If any of it is eaten on the third day, the person who offered it won't be accepted by the Lord and will receive no credit for it, because the meat has become contaminated, and the person who eats it will be held responsible for his sin.

Purity During the Peace Offerings
LV 7:19-21

Anyone ceremonially clean may eat the peace offering belonging to the Lord, but those who eat the meat in an unclean state must be cut off from their people.

Don't eat meat that touches anything ceremonially unclean; you must burn it up. And those who become defiled by human uncleanness, an unclean animal, or any unclean, detestable creature must not eat any of the meat; otherwise they must be cut off from their people.

Regulations for the Sin Offering
LV 4:1-35|LV 5:1-13|LV 6:24-30

The Sin Offering for the High Priest
LV 4:1-12

The Lord gave Moses the following laws for those who sin unintentionally, doing what is forbidden by the Lord's commands:

If the High Priest sins, bringing guilt on the people, he must offer to the Lord a young bull without defect. He must bring the bull to the Tabernacle entrance, lay his hand on its head, and slaughter it before the Lord. Then he will carry some of the bull's blood into the Tabernacle, dip his finger into it, and sprinkle it before the Lord seven times — in front of the sanctuary curtain.

He must smear some of the blood on the horns of the incense altar and pour the rest of it at the base of the altar of burnt offering. As with the peace offering, he must remove all the fat around the internal organs, both kidneys with their fat, the fat near the loins, and the best part of the liver, and burn them on the altar. But he must take the rest of the bull — its skin, meat, head, legs, internal organs, and excrement — outside the camp to a ceremonially clean place and burn it there on a wood fire on the ash heap.

The Sin Offering for the Israelite Community
LV 4:13-21|NM 15:22-26

If the whole Israelite community sins without realizing it and violates the Lord's commands, the community must present the following in front of the Tabernacle when they become aware of their sin: A young bull for a burnt offering as an aroma pleasing to the Lord; the prescribed grain and liquid offerings; and a male goat for a sin offering. The elders must lay their hands on the bull's head and slaughter it before the Lord. Then the High Priest must take some of the bull's blood into the Tabernacle, dip his finger into the blood, and sprinkle it before the Lord seven times in front of the curtain. He must put some of the blood on the horns of the incense altar and pour the rest of the blood out at the base of the altar of burnt offering near the Tabernacle entrance. Just as with the bull offered for the sins of the High Priest, he must remove all the fat and burn it on the altar. Then he will take the bull outside the camp and burn it. In this way the priest will make atonement for the whole Israelite community, and they will be forgiven because their sin wasn't intentional and they presented the required offerings to the Lord.

The Sin Offering for a Leader
LV 4:22-26

When a leader sins without realizing it and violates the commands of the Lord his God, he must offer a male goat without defect when he becomes aware of his sin. He must lay his hand on the goat's head and slaughter it at the place where burnt offerings are slaughtered before the Lord, as a sacrifice for his sin. Then the priest will dip his finger in the blood and smear it on the horns of the altar of burnt offering and pour out the rest of the blood at the altar's base. As with the peace offering, he will burn all the fat on the altar. In this way the priest will make atonement for the leader's sin, and he will be forgiven.

The Sin Offering for an Individual
LV 4:27-35|NM 15:27-29

Individuals in the community who sin without realizing it and violate the commands of the Lord must offer a one-year-old female goat without defect when they become aware of their sin. They must lay their hand on its head and slaughter it at the place of the burnt offering. Then the priest must dip his finger in the blood and put it on the horns of the altar of burnt offering and pour out the rest at the altar's base. As with the peace offering, they will remove all the fat, and the priest will burn it on the altar as a pleasing aroma to the Lord. In this way the priest will make atonement for them, and they will be forgiven.

Lambs brought as a sin offering must be a female without defect. They must lay their hand on its head and slaughter it at the place of the burnt offering. Then the priest must dip his finger in the blood and put it on the horns of the altar of burnt offering and pour out the rest at the altar's base. As with the peace offering, they will remove all the fat, and the priest will burn it on the altar on top of the food offerings presented to the Lord. In this way the priest will make atonement for them, and they will be forgiven.

These laws apply to everyone who sins unintentionally, whether a native-born Israelite or a foreign resident.

Offenses That Require a Sin Offering
LV 5:1-6

People will be responsible for their sin in any of the following situations:

1. Refusing an official summons to testify about something one has knowledge about.
2. Touching something unclean. This includes the carcass of any

140

unclean animal or crawling creature, and anything unclean that comes from a human.
3. Carelessly promising to do anything, whether good or evil.

They may unknowingly do these things, but when they become aware that they're guilty, they must confess their sin. They must bring to the Lord a female lamb or goat as a sin offering, and the priest will make atonement for their sin.

Acceptable Sin Offerings for the Poor
LV 5:7-13

Those who can't afford a lamb or goat must bring two doves or two young pigeons to the Lord as restitution — one for a sin offering and the other for a burnt offering. The priest will offer the first bird for the sin offering. He will break its neck, without severing the head from the body, splash some of the blood against the side of the altar, and drain the rest out at the altar's base. Then the priest will offer the other bird as a burnt offering, according to regulations, and make atonement for their sin, and they will be forgiven.

Those who can't afford two doves or two young pigeons must offer two quarts of the finest flour. They must not put olive oil or frankincense on it, because it's a sin offering. The priest will take a handful of it as a symbol that it belongs to the Lord and burn it on the altar on top of the food offerings. In this way the priest will make atonement for any sins they have committed, and they will be forgiven. The rest of the offering will belong to the priest, just as in the case of the grain offering.

Sin Offering Instructions for the Priests
LV 6:24-30

The Lord gave Moses these instructions for Aaron and his sons: The sin offering is most holy and must be slaughtered before the Lord in the same place the burnt offering is slaughtered. The priest who offers it must eat it in a holy place, in the Tabernacle courtyard. Any male in the priest's family may eat this most holy offering. But they must not eat any sin offering whose blood is brought into the Tabernacle to make atonement in the Holy Place; it must be burned up.

Anyone who touches the animal's flesh must be holy, and any blood spattered on clothing must be washed in the sanctuary area. If the meat is cooked in a clay pot, break the pot, but if cooked in a bronze pot, scrub it and rinse with water.

But anyone who sins defiantly blasphemes the Lord and must be cut off from the Israelites, because they despised the Lord's word and disobeyed his commandments. They will be responsible for the consequences of their sin.

Regulations for the Guilt Offering
LV 5:14-19|LV 6:1-7|LV 7:1-10
Restitution for Things Belonging to God
LV 5:14-19|LV 7:1-10|NM 5:9-10

Then the Lord gave Moses the following regulations: Those who unintentionally fail to give the offerings that belong only to the Lord must bring as repayment a ram from the flock without defect. Or one of equal value may be purchased with silver, according to the official standard of the sanctuary. In addition, they must make restitution by paying an additional 20% of its value and giving it all to the priest. The priest will make atonement for them with the ram as a guilt offering, and they will be forgiven.

Those who unintentionally break any of the Lord's commands are still guilty and will be held responsible. They must bring to the priest a ram without defect or buy one of equal value. In this way the priest will make atonement for them, and they will be forgiven. This is a guilt offering, because they are guilty of sinning against the Lord.

The guilt offering must be slaughtered in the place where the burnt offerings are slaughtered, and its blood must be splashed against the sides of the altar. Offer the fat on its tail and the fat covering the internal organs, both kidneys with their fat, near the loins, and the best part of the liver. The priest will burn them on the altar as a food offering presented to the Lord. Any male in a priest's family may eat it, but it must be eaten in a sacred place because it is most holy.

The same law applies to both the sin offering and the guilt offering: They belong to the priest who offers the sacrifice. The priest who offers a burnt offering may keep its skin for himself. Every grain offering baked in an oven, prepared in a pan, or cooked on a griddle belongs to the priest who offers it, and every grain offering, whether dry or mixed with olive oil, belongs equally to all of the priests.

All the sacred offerings the Israelites bring to the Lord belong only to the priests.

Restitution for Things Belonging to Others
NM 5:5-8|LV 6:1-7

Those who wrong another person are unfaithful to the Lord. They are guilty and must confess their sin.

Suppose a person sins against the Lord by doing any of the following:

- ❧ Failing to return property given for safekeeping
- ❧ Robbing or taking advantage of someone by fraud or force
- ❧ Failing to return lost property
- ❧ Falsely swearing innocence before God about any of these sins

When they realize their guilt about these or any similar sins, they must return to the owner in full whatever they received by dishonest means or for the wrong they have done, plus an additional 20%. But if the person wronged has died and has no close relative to whom the restitution may be given, the restitution belongs to the Lord and must be given to the priest.

They must also offer a guilt offering to the Lord as a penalty, and bring to the priest a ram without defect or purchase one of equal value. In this way the priest will make atonement for them before the Lord, and they will be forgiven.

Supplementary Offerings
NM 15:1-21

The Lord gave Moses these instructions for the Israelites to observe after entering the land: Offerings from the cattle or the flock may be presented to the Lord as a burnt offering, a sacrifice in fulfillment of a vow, a voluntary offering, or an offering at your annual festivals; these offerings will produce an aroma pleasing to the Lord. All burnt offerings must be accompanied by a proportional grain offering mixed with oil, as well as a wine offering, as follows:

Animal	Flour	Oil	Wine
Lamb or goat	2 Quarts	1 Quart	1 Quart
Ram	4 Quarts	1/3 Gallon	1/3 Gallon
Bull	6 Quarts	2 Quarts	2 Quarts

When more than one animal is offered, increase the grain and liquid offering proportionately.

All native-born Israelites must follow these instructions. And foreign and temporary residents must follow the same instructions. When you eat food in the land that I am giving you, set aside a portion as an offering to the Lord. When you bake bread, present the first loaf as a special offering to the Lord, just as when you offer the first grain from the threshing floor. These are permanent laws for the generation to come.

The Priests Begin Their Ministry
LV 9:1-24

On the eighth day after the ordination ceremony was completed, Moses summoned Aaron, his sons, and the Israelite leaders. He said to Aaron, "Present before the Lord a young bull calf for your sin offering and a ram for your burnt offering, both without defect. Then tell the Israelites that the Lord will appear to them today; therefore they must present the following offerings:

(1) A male goat for a sin offering
(2) A one-year-old calf and one-year-old lamb with no defects for a burnt offering
(3) A bull and a ram for a peace offering
(4) A grain offering mixed with olive oil

The people brought these things to the Tabernacle entrance and assembled there before the Lord. Then Moses said, "This is what the Lord has commanded so his glorious presence may appear."

Moses said to Aaron, "Come to the altar and sacrifice the offerings to make atonement for yourself and the people."

So Aaron approached the altar and slaughtered the calf as a sacrifice for his sins. His sons brought him the blood, and he dipped his finger in it and smeared some on the altar horns; he poured out the rest of the blood at the altar's base. Then he burned the fat, the kidneys, and the best part of the liver on the altar, and he burned up the meat and skin outside the camp.

He slaughtered the ram for his burnt offering. When his sons handed him the blood, he splashed it against the four sides of the altar. They handed him the head and each piece of the burnt offering, and he burned them on the altar. Then he washed the internal organs and hind legs, placed them on top of the burnt offering, and burned them as well.

Then Aaron slaughtered the goat for the people's sin offering and offered it as he did with his own sin offering. He also offered the burnt offering for the people according to the prescribed regulations. Then he took a handful of the grain offering and burned it on the altar, in addition to the morning's burnt offering.

Finally, he slaughtered the bull and ram as a peace offering for the people. His sons handed him the blood, and he splashed it against the four sides of the altar. But they placed all the fat portions of the animals on the breasts, and Aaron burned the fat on the altar. Then Aaron lifted up the breasts and the right thigh before the Lord as a special offering, as Moses commanded.

After sacrificing all these offerings, Aaron lifted his hands toward the people and blessed them. Then he stepped down from the altar.

Moses and Aaron entered the Tabernacle. When they came back out, they blessed the people, and the Lord appeared to them in all his glory. Suddenly, fire blazed from the presence of the Lord and consumed the burnt offering and the fat portions on the altar. When the Israelites saw this, they shouted with joy and bowed with their faces to the ground.

The Priestly Blessing
NM 6:22-27

The Lord gave Moses the following instructions: Tell Aaron and his sons that when they bless the Israelites, they must say: "May the Lord bless and protect you, be kind and gracious to you, and show you favor and give you peace."

When the priests bless the people in my name, I will bless them.

Nadab and Abihu Sin Against the Lord
LV 10:1-7

Now two of Aaron's sons, Nadab and Abihu, put burning coals in their firepans, added incense, and offered unauthorized fire before the Lord, going against his commands. So fire blazed from the presence of the Lord and consumed them, and they died.

And Moses said to Aaron, "This is what the Lord meant when he said: 'I must be treated as holy by my priests who approach me; I must be honored in the sight of all the people.'"

Aaron remained silent.

Moses summoned Mishael and Elzaphan, the sons of Aaron's uncle Uzziel, and said, "Come carry your cousins outside the camp, away from the front of the sanctuary."

So they came and carried Aaron's sons, who were still in their priestly garments, outside the camp, as Moses had commanded.

Then Moses said to Aaron and his remaining sons, Eleazar and Ithamar, "Don't mourn by leaving your hair uncombed and tearing your clothing. If you do, you will die and the Lord will punish the whole community. But the rest of the Israelites may mourn for those destroyed by the Lord's fire. You have been anointed with the Lord's anointing oil, so don't leave the Tabernacle entrance or you will die."

So they did as Moses said.

Rules for the Priests
LV 10:8-15

Then the Lord said to Aaron, "You and your sons must not drink wine or any other alcoholic drink when you go into the Tabernacle. If you do, you will die. This is a permanent law for the generations to come. You must distinguish between the holy and the common, between the unclean and the clean. You must teach the Israelites all the commands the Lord has given them through Moses."

Then Moses said to Aaron, Eleazar, and Ithamar, "Use the grain offering left over from the offering to the Lord to prepare bread without yeast. Eat it beside the altar, because it is especially holy and must be eaten in a holy place. This is your share of the food offered to the Lord, as he commanded. The breast and thigh that were lifted up as a special offering with the fat portions may be eaten by your entire family, as long as you eat them in a ceremonially clean place. They have been given to you and your descendants as your permanent share of the Israelites' peace offerings."

The Priests Fail to Eat the Sin Offering
LV 10:16-20

Later, Moses asked about the goat for the sin offering and discovered that it had already been burned up. He was angry with Eleazar and Ithamar and asked, "Why didn't you eat it in a sacred place? It is especially holy and was given to you to bear the guilt of the community and make atonement before the Lord. Since its blood was not taken into the inner sanctuary, you should have eaten the goat in a sacred place, as I commanded."

Aaron replied to Moses, "Would the Lord have been pleased if I had eaten the sin offering on a tragic day like this? Today we sacrificed our sin and burnt offerings before the Lord, but still these terrible things have happened to me."

So Moses was satisfied with Aaron's response.

CHAPTER 14
Laws Regarding Purity

Instructions About Clean and Unclean Food
LV 11:1-47
Introduction Regarding Clean and Unclean Food
LV 11:1-2a|LV 11:46-47

The Lord gave Moses and Aaron instructions for the Israelites regarding food:

These are the regulations for animals, birds, water creatures, and crawling creatures. You must distinguish between the clean and the unclean, between animals that may be eaten and those that may not be eaten.

Food Considered Clean
LV 11:2b-12|LV 11:39-40

The following are clean and you may eat them:

1. **Any animal living on land that both has divided hoofs and chews the cud**. Now some animals only have one of these features, but not both, and you must not eat them. For example, do not eat:

   ♥ The camel, rock badger, and rabbit – They chew the cud but do not have divided hoofs.

   ♥ The pig – It has divided hoofs but does not chew the cud. You must not eat their meat or touch their carcasses. Every animal that does not have divided hoofs or does not chew the cud is ceremonially unclean for you.

2. **Any creature living in the waters that has fins and scales**. You must consider all water creatures that don't have fins and scales as unclean. You must not eat their meat and you must regard their carcasses as unclean.

If an animal that you are allowed to eat dies, those who touch, eat, or carry away its carcass must wash their clothes, and they will be unclean until evening.

Food Considered Unclean
LV 11:13-38|LV 11:41-45|LV 17:15-16

The following are **unclean**; they are detestable and you must not eat them:

Certain birds: This includes eagles, vultures, buzzards, falcons, crows, ostriches, owls, hawks, seagulls, pelicans, storks, herons, hoopoes, and bats.

Flying insects that walk on four legs. However, you may eat those that have jointed legs so they can hop, such as locusts, crickets, and grasshoppers. But all other flying insects that have four legs will make you unclean.

Four-legged animals that walk on paws and animals with hoofs, unless their hoofs are divided and they chew the cud. Whoever touches their carcasses must wash their clothes, and they will be unclean until evening.

Animals that scurry along the ground. Moles, rats, mice, and lizards are unclean. Whoever touches their carcasses will be unclean until evening. If these animals fall on something after they die, that article, whatever its use, will be unclean — whether it's made of wood, cloth, leather, or sackcloth. Wash it in water and it will be unclean until evening.

If the animal falls into a clay pot, everything in it will be unclean and you must break the pot. Water from this pot that touches any edible food makes that food unclean, and any liquid drank from that pot is unclean. If an unclean carcass falls on an oven or cooking pot, it must be destroyed.

If a carcass falls into a spring or a cistern for collecting water, the water remains clean, but whoever removes the animal becomes unclean. If a carcass falls on unplanted seeds, the seeds remain clean. But if the seeds are soaking in water, they are unclean.

Small animals that move along the ground. Small animals that move on their belly, walk on all fours, or walk on many feet are unclean and you must not eat them.

Any Israelite or foreigner who eats an animal that has died a natural death or was killed by wild animals must wash their clothes and bathe, and they will be ceremonially unclean until evening. But if they don't follow these instructions, they will be held responsible. I am the Lord your God who delivered you from slavery in Egypt to be your God; therefore do not defile yourselves with these creatures. Consecrate yourselves and be holy, because I am holy.

Regulations for Purification After Childbirth
LV 12:1-8

The Lord gave Moses the following regulations for a woman after childbirth: A woman who gives birth to a son will be ceremonially unclean for 7 days, just as she is unclean during her monthly period. On the eighth day, the boy must be circumcised. Then the woman must wait 33 days to be purified from her bleeding. She must not touch anything sacred or go to the sanctuary until her purification is complete. If she gives birth to a daughter, she will be unclean for 14 days. Then she must wait 66 days to be purified from her bleeding.

When her purification for childbirth is over, she must bring to the Tabernacle entrance a one-year-old lamb for a burnt offering and a young pigeon or dove for a sin offering. But if she can't afford a lamb, she must bring two doves or two young pigeons, one for a burnt offering and the other for a sin offering. The priest will present her offerings before the Lord to purify her, and then she will be ceremonially clean from her flow of blood.

Regulations About Defiling Skin Diseases
LV 13:1-46

The Lord gave Moses and Aaron the following regulations:

For swelling, a rash, or sores on the skin that might develop into a defiling skin disease. Those affected must be brought to Aaron or one of the other priests, who will examine the affected area. If the hair has turned white and the problem appears to be more than skin deep, it's a defiling skin disease and the priest will pronounce them ceremonially unclean. If the affected area is white but does not appear to be more than skin deep and the hair in it has not turned white, the priest will isolate them for seven days and then conduct another examination. If the condition is still the same but has not spread, the priest will isolate them for another seven days and then conduct another examination. If the sore has faded and has not spread, the priest will pronounce them clean, because it was only a rash. They must wash their clothes and they will then be completely clean. But if the rash continues to spread after they have been pronounced clean, the priest must examine them again and pronounce them unclean, because it's obviously a defiling skin disease.

For a defiling skin disease. The priest must examine those affected.

149

If the sore is white and filled with pus and the hair has turned white, it's a chronic skin disease and the priest will pronounce them unclean. He won't isolate them for observation, because it's obvious they're unclean.

Now if after the examination the disease covers the skin from head to foot and has all turned white, the priest will pronounce them clean. But if any open sores appear, the priest will pronounce them unclean, because they have a defiling disease. If the sores change and turn white, the priest will pronounce them completely clean.

For boils that have healed. If white swelling or a reddish-white spot appears in place of the boil, the priest must examine it. If it appears to be more than skin deep and the hair in it has turned white, the priest will pronounce them unclean because the boil has become a defiling skin disease. But if the boil has faded, there's no white hair in it, and it's not more than skin deep, the priest will isolate them for seven days. Now if the boil is spreading, the priest will pronounce them unclean because it's a defiling disease. But if the spot is unchanged and has not spread, it's only a scar from the boil, and the priest will pronounce them clean.

For burns on the skin. If a reddish-white or white spot appears in the raw flesh of the burn, the priest must examine it. If the hair in it has turned white and the spot appears to be more than skin deep, a defiling disease has developed in the burn and the priest will pronounce them unclean. But if the priest finds no white hair in the spot, it's not more than skin deep, and it has faded, the priest will isolate them for seven days and then examine them again. If it's spreading, the priest will pronounce them unclean, because it's a defiling skin disease. But if the spot has faded and has not spread, it's only a scar from the burn, and the priest will pronounce them clean.

For sores on the head or chin. If the sore appears to be more than skin deep and has thin, yellow hair in it, the priest will pronounce them unclean, because it's a defiling skin disease. Now if the sore doesn't seem to be more than skin deep but there's still no healthy hair in it, the priest will isolate them for seven days and then examine them again. If the sore hasn't spread and there's no yellow hair in it and it doesn't appear to be more than skin deep, the person must shave, except for the area around the sore. The priest must keep them isolated another seven days and then examine them. If it has not spread and appears to be no more than skin deep, the priest will pronounce them clean. They must wash their clothes, and they will be completely clean. But if the sore spreads after they're pronounced clean, the priest does not need to look for yellow hair, because it's clear they're unclean. But if the sore seems unchanged to the priest and healthy hair has grown in it, they are healed and the priest will pronounce them clean.

For bald spots. A man who has lost all his hair or only the hair from the front of his scalp is clean. But if the priest finds that he has a reddish-white sore in the bald area, it's a defiling disease and the priest will pronounce him unclean.

For harmless rashes. The priest must examine any man or woman who has white spots on the skin. If the spots are dull white, it's only a harmless rash and those affected are clean.

Those with defiling skin diseases must tear their clothing, leave their hair uncombed, cover the lower part of their face, and call out, 'Unclean! Unclean!' They will remain unclean as long as they have the disease, and they must live alone outside the camp.

Cleansing From Defiling Skin Diseases
LV 14:1-32

The Lord gave Moses the following regulations for the ceremonial cleansing of those afflicted with a skin disease:

The priest must examine them outside the camp. If they have been healed, he will purify them using two clean birds, cedar wood, scarlet yarn, and hyssop. The priest will have someone slaughter one of the birds over a clay pot filled with fresh spring water. He will then dip the live bird, cedar wood, scarlet yarn, and hyssop, into the mixture of blood and water. He will then use the mixture to sprinkle seven times those being purified and then pronounce them clean. After that, he must release the live bird and allow it to fly away freely.

Those being purified must wash their clothes, shave all their hair, and bathe, and then they will be ceremonially clean. Afterward they may return to the camp, but they must stay outside their tent for seven days. On the seventh day, they must shave all their hair again: their head, beard, eyebrows, and all the rest of their hair. They must wash their clothes and bathe themselves with water, and then they will be completely clean.

On the eighth day, they must bring two male lambs and a one-year-old female lamb, each without defect; a pint of olive oil; and for a grain offering, 6 quarts of the finest flour mixed with olive oil. The presiding priest will present those being purified, along with their offerings, before the Lord at the Tabernacle entrance.

The priest will offer one of the male lambs as a guilt offering, along with the pint of oil, and lift them up before the Lord as a special offering. He will slaughter the lamb in the sanctuary area where the sin and burnt offerings are slaughtered. Like the sin offering, the guilt offering belongs to the priest; it is especially holy.

The priest will put some of the blood of the guilt offering on the right ear lobe, right thumb, and big toe of the right foot of those being purified. He will then pour some olive oil in the palm of his left hand, dip his right finger into it, and sprinkle it before the Lord seven times. The priest will put some of the oil on their right ear lobe, right thumb, and big toe of the right foot, just as he did with the blood of the guilt offering. The priest will put the rest of the oil in his palm on their head. Through this process the priest will purify them before the Lord.

Then the priest will make atonement for them by sacrificing the sin offering and slaughtering the burnt offering. He will offer the burnt offering on the altar with the grain offering, and they will be clean.

Those who are too poor to afford these items may bring one male lamb as a guilt offering, two quarts of the finest flour mixed with olive oil for a grain offering, and a pint of oil. Depending on what they can afford, they must also bring two doves or two young pigeons, one for a sin offering and the other for a burnt offering.

They must bring these items for their cleansing to the priest on the eighth day, to be presented before the Lord at the Tabernacle entrance. The priest will make atonement for them using the same procedures as for presenting the regular offerings.

Regulations About Defiling Mildew on Clothing
LV 13:47-59

If a greenish or reddish spot appears on your woolen or linen clothing or fabric, or on anything made of leather, it's contaminated with mildew. Let the priest examine the affected area and isolate the article for seven days. Afterward he must examine it again. If it has spread, it's harmful mildew and the article is unclean; the fabric must be burned.

But if the priest examines the fabric and the mildew hasn't spread, he will order that the article be washed. Then he'll isolate it another seven days. Afterward the priest will examine it again. If the mildew hasn't spread but hasn't changed color, it's unclean and must be burned, no matter where the mildew appears. But if the mildew has faded, the priest will cut off the affected part. Now if the mildew reappears later, it's clearly spreading and must be burned. Any article that has been washed and no longer contains mildew must be washed again, and then it will be clean.

The Lord gave Moses and Aaron the following regulations for houses contaminated with mildew. (These laws would apply when the Israelites entered the land of Canaan, which the Lord was giving them as a possession.):

The owner of the affected house must tell the priest about the contamination. Before the priest goes inside to examine the mildew, the house must be emptied; otherwise everything inside will be pronounced unclean. Then he will inspect the house. If the mildew on the walls has greenish or reddish spots that appear to be eating into the wall, the priest will quarantine the house for seven days. Anyone who goes into the house while it's quarantined will be unclean until evening. Anyone who sleeps or eats in the house must wash their clothes. On the seventh day, he will return to inspect the house again. If the mildew has spread, he will order that the contaminated stones be torn out and replaced with other stones. All the inside walls must be scraped. The contaminated stones and scraped material must be dumped into an unclean place outside the city. Then the house must be plastered with new clay.

If the defiling mildew reappears after all this, the priest must examine it again. If the mildew has spread, it's clearly harmful and the house is unclean. It must be torn down — all the stones, timbers, and plaster — and hauled outside the city to an unclean place.

But if the mildew has not spread after the house has been plastered, the priest will pronounce it clean, because the defiling mildew is gone. He will purify the house using two birds, cedar wood, scarlet yarn, and hyssop. The priest will slaughter one of the birds over a clay pot filled with fresh spring water. He will then dip the live bird, cedar wood, scarlet yarn, and hyssop into the mixture of blood and water and sprinkle the house seven times, thus purifying the house. Afterward, he must release the live bird outside the city and allow it to fly away freely. In this way he will make atonement for the house, and it will be clean.

These are the regulations for defiling skin diseases and defiling mildews found in fabric or in a house, to determine when something is clean or unclean.

Bodily Discharges Causing Uncleanness
LV 15:1-33
Introduction Regarding Bodily Discharges
LV 15:1-2a|LV 15:31-33

The Lord gave Moses and Aaron the following instructions: You must protect the Israelites from things that make them unclean; otherwise they will die for defiling my Tabernacle, which stands in their midst. These are the regulations the Israelites must follow for a man with a discharge; anyone made unclean by a discharge, emission of semen, or flow of blood; and anyone who has sex with someone who is ceremonially unclean.

Male Discharges
LV 15:2b-18

These are the instructions for the Israelites regarding a man with an unclean bodily discharge from his male organ: The discharge will make him unclean, whether it flows from his body or is blocked. Any bed he lies on and any furniture he sits on will be unclean.

Those who have any sort of contact with him must wash their clothes and bathe, and they will be unclean until evening. For example:

* If they touch him, his bed, or his furniture
* If he spits on them
* If they touch or pick up any saddle or seat he sits on
* If he touches them without rinsing his hands

A clay pot that the man touches must be broken, and any wooden container must be rinsed with water.

When the man is cured of his discharge, he must wait seven days and then wash his clothes and bathe in fresh spring water, and he will be ceremonially clean. On the eighth day, he must bring two doves or two young pigeons before the Lord at the Tabernacle entrance. The priest will sacrifice one for a sin offering and the other for a burnt offering. In this way he will purify the man of his discharge.

A man who has a semen emission must bathe his whole body, and he will be unclean until evening. Any clothing or leather that has semen on it must be washed, and it will be unclean until evening. After sexual intercourse, both the man and the woman must bathe, and they will be unclean until evening.

Female Discharges
LV 15:19-30

When a woman has her monthly period, her impurity will last seven days, and anyone who touches her will be unclean until evening.

Anything she lies on or sits on during her period will be unclean.

Anyone who touches her bed or anything she sits on must wash their clothes and bathe, and they will be unclean until evening.

If a man has sex with her and comes in contact with her blood, he will be unclean for seven days, and any bed he lies on will be unclean.

If a woman's flow of blood continues beyond her monthly period or she has several days of bleeding unrelated to her period, she will be unclean as long as she has the discharge, just as she is during her period.

When the woman is cured of her discharge, she must wait seven days and then she will be ceremonially clean. On the eighth day, she must bring two doves or two young pigeons to the Tabernacle entrance. The priest will sacrifice one for a sin offering and the other for a burnt offering. In this way he will purify the woman of her discharge.

The Water for Purifying Uncleanness
NM 19:1-22

The Lord gave Moses and Aaron the following instructions: The Israelites must bring a red young female cow that has no defects and has never been put to work. Give it to Eleazar the priest and take it outside the camp and slaughter it in his presence. Then Eleazar must use his finger to sprinkle the blood seven times toward the front of the Tabernacle. As Eleazar watches, the cow's skin, flesh, blood, and excrement must be burned. Then he will throw cedar wood, hyssop, and scarlet wool onto the burning cow. After that, he must wash his clothes and bathe. He may then enter the camp, but he'll be ceremonially unclean until evening. The man who burned the cow must also wash his clothes and bathe, and he'll also be unclean until evening.

Have someone who is ceremonially clean gather the ashes and put them in a ceremonially clean place outside the camp. They must be kept there for the Israelite community to prepare the water used for purification from sin. The man who gathers the ashes must also wash his clothes, and he'll be unclean until evening. This will be a permanent law for both Israelites and foreign residents.

Those who touch a human corpse will be unclean for seven days. They must cleanse themselves with the purification water on the third and the seventh day, and then they'll be clean. If a person dies in a tent, anyone who enters the tent and anyone who is already in it will be unclean for seven days, and every open container without a lid on it will be unclean.

Anyone outdoors who touches someone who has been killed or has died a natural death, or touches a human bone or a grave, will be unclean for seven days.

To begin the purification process, someone who is ceremonially clean must put some ashes from the burnt purification offering into a jar and stir in fresh water. He will dip some hyssop in the water and on the third and seventh days sprinkle the tent and all the furnishings, as well as the people who were there. He will do the same to those who touched a human bone, a grave, or a corpse. On the seventh day, those who are being purified must wash their clothes and bathe, and they will be clean by evening.

The man who sprinkled the purification water must also wash his clothes, and anyone else who touches this water will be unclean until evening. Anything that an unclean person touches becomes unclean, and anyone who touches that item is unclean until evening.

Those who fail to purify themselves defile the Lord's Tabernacle and must be cut off from Israel. They remain defiled because they weren't sprinkled with the water. This is a permanent law.

CHAPTER 15
Holy Festivals and Other Laws

The Day of Atonement
LV 16:1-34

The High Priest's Preparation
LV 16:1-2|LV 16:4

Because Aaron's sons had offered unholy fire to the Lord and died as a result, the Lord gave Moses the following instructions for his brother, the priest:

Aaron must not enter the Most Holy Place behind the inner curtain whenever he pleases; otherwise he will die. For the Lord will appear in a cloud there over the atonement cover that sits on the Ark of the Covenant.

Before he enters the Most Holy Place on the Day of Atonement, he must first bathe himself and then put on the sacred linen clothing: the undergarments and ankle-length shirt; he must tie the sash around his waist and put on the turban.

The High Priest's Atonement for Himself
LV 16:3|LV 16:6|LV 16:11-14

Before entering the Most Holy Place, Aaron must first bring a young bull for a sin offering and a ram for a burnt offering. He must slaughter the bull as a sin offering to make atonement for himself and his household. He will take a firepan full of burning coals from the altar that stands before the Lord and two handfuls of finely ground incense. He must bring these items behind the veil into the Most Holy Place. There in the Lord's presence, he will put the incense on the fire and its smoke will conceal the atonement cover, so that he won't die. He must use his finger to sprinkle some of the bull's blood on the atonement cover and then sprinkle some in front of it seven times.

The High Priest's Atonement for the People
LV 16:5|LV 16:7-9|LV 16:15-19

From the Israelite community, Aaron must take two male goats for a sin offering and a ram for a burnt offering. Present the two goats to the Lord at the Tabernacle entrance and then cast lots to determine which goat will be offered to the Lord and which will be the scapegoat.

Aaron will slaughter the goat chosen for the Lord as a sin offering for the people. Just as was done with the bull's blood, take the goat's blood behind the veil into the Most Holy Place and sprinkle it on and in front of the atonement cover. In this way he will purify the Most Holy Place from the Israelites' sins and uncleanness. Do the same for the Tabernacle, which stands in the midst of their uncleanness.

No one else is allowed inside the Tabernacle from the time Aaron goes into the Most Holy Place to make atonement for himself, his household, and the whole community of Israel. Everyone must remain outside until he comes out.

When Aaron comes out, he will purify the altar by putting some of the bull's blood and some of the goat's blood on all the horns of the altar. He will sprinkle some of the blood on the altar seven times with his finger to purify it from the Israelites' uncleanness.

Regulations for the Scapegoat
LV 16:10|LV 16:20-22

When Aaron has finished purifying the Most Holy Place, the Tabernacle, and the altar, he will present the live goat before the Lord. Lay both hands on its head and confess over it all the Israelites sins, wickedness, and rebellion, transferring them to the goat's head. Appoint an assistant to take the goat to a remote place in the desert, where it will carry upon itself all the people's sins. The assistant will then release the goat into the desert and it will make atonement for the people.

Conclusion of the Atonement Rituals
LV 16:23-28

Aaron must then enter the Tabernacle, take off the sacred linen clothing, bathe, and then put on his regular clothes. He must leave the sacred linen clothing in the Tabernacle and then come out and sacrifice the burnt offerings to make atonement for himself and for the people. He will also burn the fat of the sin offering on the altar.

The man who released the scapegoat must wash his clothes and bathe, and then he may return to the camp. Someone must take the remains of the bull and the goat offered for the sin offerings outside the camp and burn their hides, internal organs, and excrement. The man who burns them must wash his clothes and bathe, and then he may return to the camp.

Instructions for the Day of Atonement
LV 16:29-34

The tenth day of the seventh month is the day atonement will be made for the people, to cleanse you from all your sins before the Lord. Therefore you must practice self-denial and refrain from any work — this includes those that are native-born or foreign residents. You must observe the day as a Sabbath day of rest.

For generations to come, the priest anointed and ordained to succeed his father as High Priest must put on the sacred linen clothing and make atonement for the Most Holy Place, the Tabernacle, the altar, the priests, and all the members of the community. Atonement must be made once a year for all the sins of the Israelites.

These are permanent decrees.

And so it was done, as the Lord commanded Moses.

Sacrifices Must Be Offered at the Tabernacle
LV 17:1-9

The Lord gave Moses the following commands for Aaron, his sons, and all the rest of the Israelites: Any Israelite who offers to the Lord a bull, lamb, or goat anywhere other than the Tabernacle entrance will be considered guilty of bloodshed and must be cut off from the community. Any sacrifices they are currently making in the open fields must be brought to the Lord at the Tabernacle entrance. Give them to the priest, who will sacrifice them as peace offerings. He will splash the blood against the altar of the Lord and burn the fat as a pleasing aroma. The people must no longer offer sacrifices to the goat idols to whom they prostitute themselves. This must be a permanent law for them and for the generations to come. Burnt offerings and sacrifices must be performed at the Tabernacle entrance.

God Forbids Eating Blood
LV 3:17|LV 7:26-27|LV 17:10-14|LV 19:26a

If an Israelite or foreign resident eats blood, I will turn against them and cut them off from the community. The life of a creature is in the blood and it is the blood that makes atonement for one's life. That is why I have instructed you to pour it out on the altar.

Any Israelite or foreigner who hunts and kills a clean animal or bird must drain the blood and cover it with dirt; they must not eat the blood. This is a lasting command for the generations to come, wherever you live; you must not eat the blood of any bird or animal.

God Forbids Unlawful Sexual Relations
LV 18:1-20|LV 18:22-30|LV 20:10-21

The Lord gave Moses the following commands for the Israelites: You must not behave as they do in Egypt, where you used to live, and you must not behave as they do in the land of Canaan, where I am bringing you. Be careful to obey my laws, for the person who obeys them will live. I am the Lord your God.

Don't have sex with a close relative. I am the Lord:

Don't dishonor your father by having sex with your mother.

Don't have sex with your father's other wives; that would dishonor your father. Both the man and the woman must be put to death, and it will be their own fault.

Don't have sex with your sister — either your father's daughter or your mother's daughter, whether you grew up together or not. This would dishonor your sister. Both will be held responsible and must be publicly cut off from their people.

Don't have sex with your any of your granddaughters; that would be a disgrace.

Don't have sex with your stepsister; she is still your sister.

Don't have sex with your mother's or father's sister or your uncle's wife; she is your aunt and a close relative, and you dishonor both her and your uncle. Both parties will be held responsible and will die childless.

Don't have sex with your daughter-in-law. She is your son's wife. In this case both parties must be put to death. What they have done is perversion and they are responsible for their own death.

Don't have sex with your brother's wife; that would dishonor your brother. This is impure and both will remain childless.

Don't marry both a woman and her mother. All three parties must be burned in the fire to eliminate the wickedness among you.

Don't have sex with both a woman and her granddaughter; they're close relatives and that would be wicked.

Don't marry your wife's sister while your wife is still living; they would be rivals.

Don't have sex with a woman during her monthly period; she is ceremonially unclean. Both have exposed the source of her flow, and both must be cut off from their people.

Don't defile yourself by having sex with another man's wife. In this case both the man and the woman must be put to death.

Don't have sex with a man as one does with a woman; both men have done what is detestable and must be put to death. Their blood will be on their own heads.

Neither man nor woman must defile themselves by having sex with an animal; that's perversion. Both the animal and the humans must be put to death, and it will be their own fault.

You must keep my commands and avoid defiling yourselves by following the detestable customs of those who lived in the land before you. Neither Israelite nor foreign resident must do any of these detestable things. All these things are done by the people who live in the land I am bringing you to, and the land became defiled, so I will punish them for their sins and the land will vomit them out. And if you defile the land, it will vomit you out in the same way.

Those who practice any of these things must be cut off from their people. I am the Lord your God.

Laws Regarding Interactions With Others
LV 19:1-4|LV 19:9-18

The Lord gave Moses the following commands for the entire community of Israel:

Be holy because I, the Lord your God, am holy.

Each of you must respect your mother and father, and observe my Sabbaths.

Don't turn away from me to worship idols or fashion metal gods for yourselves.

When you harvest the crops of your land, leave some grain standing at the very edges of your field and leave whatever grain falls to the ground. Don't completely strip your vineyard of grapes or pick up the grapes that fall to the ground. Leave them for the poor people and foreign residents.

Don't steal, lie, cheat or take advantage of others.

Don't profane my name by using it to give weight to false statements.

Don't make hired workers wait until the next day for payment.

Don't make fun of deaf people or put an obstacle in front of the blind to make them stumble, but fear your God.

Judge everyone fairly when deciding legal cases; don't favor the poor or give preference to the rich.

Don't spread harmful gossip and don't be afraid to speak when someone's life is in danger.

Don't hold grudges or seek revenge; instead confront people directly regarding the offense so you won't also be guilty. Love your neighbor as yourself.

I am the Lord your God.

You must obey my commandments.

Don't mate two different kinds of animals, plant two kinds of seed in your field, or wear clothing made of two kinds of material.

If a man sleeps with a female bondservant who belongs to another man, he must compensate her master. But they won't be put to death, because she had not been fully redeemed or freed. The guilty man must bring a ram to the Tabernacle entrance as a guilt offering to the Lord. The priest will make atonement for him, and his sin will be forgiven.

When you enter the land of Canaan and plant fruit trees, the fruit is forbidden for three years and must not be eaten. In the fourth year, all the fruit must be dedicated as a holy offering of praise to the Lord but in the fifth year, you may eat the fruit. Do these things and your trees will bear more fruit.

Don't practice fortune-telling or witchcraft. Don't defile yourself by seeking out mediums or spiritists who consult the spirits of the dead.

Don't shave the hair at the sides of your head, trim your beard, or cut or tattoo yourselves as a way of mourning for the dead.

Don't disgrace your daughters by making them prostitutes, or the land will turn to prostitution and be filled with wickedness.

Observe my Sabbaths and have reverence for my sanctuary.

Show respect for the elderly.

Don't mistreat foreigners residing in your land. Treat them as you would a fellow Israelite and love them as yourself. Remember that you were once foreigners in Egypt.

Don't be dishonest when measuring length, weight, or volume. The containers used for measuring dry goods or liquids must be accurate.

I am the Lord your God, who brought you out of Egypt. You must fear me and obey all my commandments and regulations. I am the Lord your God.

Punishments for Sins Against God
LV 18:21|LV 20:1-8|LV 20:22-27

The Lord gave Moses the following commands: Israelites or foreign residents who sacrifice their children by fire to the god Molek must be stoned to death by the members of the community. And I myself will turn against them and cut them off from their people because they have defiled my sanctuary and profaned my holy name. If the members of the community ignore their sin and fail to stone them, I will turn against them and their family and cut them off from their people.

I will turn against and cut off from their people all those who prostitute themselves by following mediums and spiritists. Stone any man or woman who is a medium or spiritist among you; they are responsible for their own deaths."

Keep all my commandments; otherwise the land where I am bringing you will vomit you out. Don't adopt the customs of the nations who live there. I detest them because of their practices, so I am going to drive them out before you. But I'm giving it to you as an inheritance because I promised that you will possess their land, a land flowing with milk and honey. I am the Lord your God, who has set you apart from the nations.

This is why you must make a distinction between clean and unclean animals and between unclean and clean birds. Don't defile yourselves by anything that I have set apart as unclean.

Obey my commandments. Consecrate yourselves and be holy because I, the Lord your God, am holy, and I have set you apart from the nations as my own.

Priests Must Remain Holy
LV 21:1-33

Requirements for All Priests
LV 21:1-9|LV 21:24

The Lord gave Moses the following instructions for Aaron, his sons, and the rest of the Israelites:

Priests must not make themselves ceremonially unclean when their relatives die, except for their parents, children, brother, or an unmarried sister who is dependent upon them. They must not defile themselves for people related to them only by marriage.

Priests must not shave their heads, trim their beards, or cut their bodies. Because they present the special food offerings to the Lord, they must be set apart as holy to their God and must not profane my name.

They must not marry divorced women or women defiled by prostitution. A priest's daughter who defiles herself by becoming a prostitute disgraces her father, and she must be burned to death.

The priests are holy because I the Lord am holy, and it is I who sets you apart.

Requirements for the High Priest
LV 21:10-15

The High Priest has been dedicated to God by the anointing oil poured on his head and has been ordained to wear the priestly clothing. He must not leave his hair uncombed or tear his clothes in mourning. He must not defile the sanctuary or himself by leaving the sanctuary to enter a place where there's a dead body, not even for his mother or father. I am the Lord.

163

He must marry a virgin from his own clan. He must not marry a widow, a divorced woman, or a woman defiled by prostitution. In this way his offspring will be undefiled and will be qualified to serve me. I am the Lord, and I have set him apart as High Priest.

Priests Must Respect the Sacred Offerings
LV 21:16-23|LV 22:1-16

For the generations to come, no priests who have defects may offer food offerings to the Lord — whether they are blind, lame, disfigured, or deformed; have a crippled hand or foot; are hunchbacked or dwarfed; have an eye defect; have festering or running sores; or have damaged testicles. They may eat from the most holy offerings and the holy offerings, but they must not desecrate my sanctuary by going near the curtain or approaching the altar. I am the Lord, who makes them holy.

Priests who have a defiling skin disease, bodily discharge, or emission of semen may not eat the sacred offerings until they are cleansed. They will also be unclean if they touch something defiled by a corpse or touch any animal or person that makes them unclean, whatever the cause. They must not defile themselves by eating anything found dead or torn by wild animals. I am the Lord.

Those who touch any of these things will be unclean until evening and must not eat the sacred offerings until they have bathed. After the sun has set, they will be clean and may eat the sacred offerings, for this is their food.

For the generations to come, ceremonially unclean priests must stay away from the sacred offerings the Israelites dedicate to me, so they won't profane my holy name. Otherwise they will be cut off from my presence. I am the Lord.

The priests must carefully follow my instructions; otherwise they will be guilty and they'll die for treating the sacred offerings with contempt. I am the Lord, who makes them holy.

No one outside a priest's family may eat the sacred offering. The following are unauthorized:

* The priests' guests or hired workers
* A daughter who marries anyone other than a priest

However, the following may eat the sacred offering:

* Slaves purchased by the priest or born in his household
* A widowed or divorced daughter who has no children to care for her, and returns to live in her father's household

Anyone who accidentally eats the sacred offering must repay the priest its full value plus 20%. The priests must not allow the Israelites to bring guilt upon themselves by eating the sacred offerings, which require repayment. I am the Lord, who makes these offerings holy.

Acceptable Sacrifices
EX 23:19b|LV 22:17-33

Israelites or foreign residents who present a burnt offering to the Lord, either to fulfill a vow or as a voluntary offering, must present a bull, ram, or male goat without defect so it will be accepted on their behalf. Nothing with a defect will be accepted. Don't place any animal on the altar that is blind, crippled, or injured, or has warts, running sores, or scabs. The same applies to the peace offering.

As long as you live in the land, don't offer to the Lord an animal whose testicles have been damaged or removed, and don't accept such animals from foreigners as a sacrifice, because they won't be accepted on your behalf.

Animals from the herd or flock may be presented as a voluntary offering if they are deformed or have a stunted or elongated leg, but they aren't acceptable as fulfillment of a vow.

A newborn calf, lamb, or goat must remain with its mother for seven days. Afterward it will be acceptable as a food offering, but don't sacrifice a newborn and its mother on the same day. And don't cook a young goat in its mother's milk.

Sacrifices of thanksgiving to the Lord must follow the regulations so they will be accepted. Eat them on the same day and save no leftovers for the next day.

Keep my commandments. Don't disgrace my holy name; all of you must acknowledge me as holy. I am the Lord who set you apart and brought you out of Egypt to be your God.

Regulations for Observing Holy Festivals
LV 23:1-36|LV 23:39-44|NM 28:16-31|NM 29:1-40

Moses gave the Israelites the following instructions from the Lord:

These are the festivals of the Lord, and you must proclaim them at their appointed times as official days for gathering to worship (LV 23:1-2, 4, 44):

The Sabbath: You may work six days, but the seventh day is a day of sabbath rest to the Lord, a day of sacred assembly. Wherever you live, you must not do any work (LV 23:3).

The Passover and the Festival of Unleavened Bread: Celebrate the Lord's Passover beginning at twilight on the 14th day of the 1st month. On the 15th day, the Festival of Unleavened Bread begins: for 7 days you must eat bread made without yeast. Hold a sacred assembly on the 1st day and do none of your daily work.

Present a burnt offering as a special gift to the Lord. It will consist of 2 young bulls, 1 ram, and 7 one-year-old male lambs, all without defect. With each of the offerings, present a grain offering of the finest flour mixed with oil: 6 quarts with each bull; 4 quarts with the ram; and 2 quarts with each of the 7 lambs. Include a male goat as a sin offering to make atonement for yourselves.

Present these offerings every day for 7 days as a pleasing aroma to the Lord. They must be offered in addition to the daily burnt and liquid offerings. On the 7th day, hold another sacred assembly and do no daily work (LV 23:5-8|NM 28:16-25).

The Offering of Firstfruits: When you reap the harvest in the land I am going to give you, bring the first bundle of grain to the priest. On the day after the Sabbath, he will lift up the bundle before the Lord so it will be accepted on your behalf. On the same day, sacrifice a one-year-old lamb without defect as a burnt offering to the Lord, along with a grain offering consisting of four quarts of the finest flour mixed with olive oil. This food offering is a pleasing aroma to the Lord. Also present a quart of wine as a liquid offering. Don't eat any of the new grain, whether raw, roasted, or baked as bread, until the day you bring these offerings. This is a permanent law for the generations to come, wherever you live (LV 23:9-14).

The Harvest Festival (Festival of Weeks/Pentecost): Seven weeks after you offer the firstfruits of grain, which will be the 50th day after the 7th Sabbath, present another offering of new grain to the Lord. From wherever you live, bring two loaves made of 4 quarts of the finest flour, baked with yeast, as special firstfruits offerings to the Lord. Also present 7 one-year-old male lambs with no defects, 2 young bulls, and 1 ram. They will be a burnt offering to the Lord, along with the liquid offerings. With each of the offerings, present a grain offering of the finest flour mixed with oil: 6 quarts with each bull; 4 quarts with the ram; and 2 quarts with each of the 7 lambs. This special offering will be a pleasing aroma to the Lord.

Sacrifice 1 male goat for a sin offering to make atonement and 2 one-year-old lambs for a peace offering. The priest must lift up the lambs before the Lord as a special offering, along with the bread of the firstfruits. These are sacred offerings to the Lord for the priest. They must be offered in addition to the daily burnt, grain, and liquid offerings. Be sure the animals are without defect. On that same day, hold a sacred assembly and do no daily work. This must be a permanent law for the generations to come, wherever you live.

When you reap the harvest of your land, don't reap to the very edges of your field or gather the gleanings of your harvest. Leave them for the poor and foreign residents. I am the Lord your God (LV 23:15-22|NM 28:26-31).

The Festival of Trumpets: On the 1st day of the 7th month, hold a sacred assembly commemorated with trumpet blasts. Make it a day of sabbath rest and do no daily work. As an aroma pleasing to the Lord, offer a burnt offering of 1 young bull, 1 ram, and 7 one-year-old male lambs, all without defect. With each of the offerings, present a grain offering of the finest flour mixed with oil: 6 quarts with each bull; 4 quarts with the ram; and 2 quarts with each of the 7 lambs. Include a male goat as a sin offering to make atonement for yourselves. These must be offered in addition to the monthly and daily burnt, grain, and liquid offerings (LV 23:23-25|NM 29:1-6).

The Day of Atonement: The 10th day of the 7th month is the Day of Atonement. Hold a sacred assembly, practice self-denial, and don't do any work at all. As an aroma pleasing to the Lord, offer a burnt offering of 1 young bull, 1 ram, and 7 one-year-old male lambs, all without defect. With each of the offerings, present a grain offering of the finest flour mixed with oil: 6 quarts with each bull; 4 quarts with the ram; and 2 quarts with each of the 7 lambs. Include one male goat as a sin offering. They must be offered in addition to the sin offering of atonement and the daily burnt, grain, and liquid offerings.

This is the day when atonement is made for you before the Lord your God. Those who don't practice self-denial must be cut off from their people. I will destroy anyone who does any work on that day. It's a day of sabbath rest for you and you must observe your sabbath from the evening of the ninth day of the month until the following evening. This must be a permanent law for the generations to come, wherever you live (LV 23:26-32| NM 29:7-11).

The Festival of Shelters: On the 15th day of the 7th month, the Lord's Festival of Shelters begins. After you have gathered the crops of the land, Hold a sacred assembly. The first day is a day of sabbath rest and you must do no daily work.

Then take branches from luxuriant trees — from palms, willows, and other leafy trees — and rejoice before the Lord your God for seven days and present food offerings. All native-born Israelites must live in temporary shelters for seven days. In this way your descendants will know that I made you live in temporary shelters when I brought you out of Egypt. I am the Lord your God.

On the first day, present a burnt offering as a special gift, an aroma pleasing to the Lord. It will consist of 13 young bulls, 2 rams, and 14 one-year-old male lambs, all without defect. With each of the offerings, present a grain offering of the finest flour mixed with oil: 6 quarts for each of the 13 bulls; 4 quarts for each of the 2 rams; and 2 quarts for each of the 14 lambs. Include a male goat as a sin offering, in addition to the regular burnt, grain, and liquid offerings.

On the second day, offer 12 young bulls, 2 rams, and 14 one-year-old male lambs, all without defect. Also offer the prescribed grain and liquid offerings. Include a male goat as a sin offering, in addition to the regular burnt, grain, and liquid offerings.

On the third day, offer 11 bulls, 2 rams, and 14 one-year-old male lambs, all without defect. Also offer the prescribed grain and liquid offerings. Include a male goat as a sin offering, in addition to the regular burnt, grain, and liquid offerings.

On the fourth day, offer 10 bulls, 2 rams, and 14 one-year-old male lambs, all without defect. Also offer the prescribed grain and liquid offerings. Include a male goat as a sin offering, in addition to the regular burnt, grain, and liquid offerings.

On the fifth day, offer 9 bulls, 2 rams, and 14 one-year-old male lambs, all without defect. Also offer the prescribed grain and liquid offerings. Include a male goat as a sin offering, in addition to the regular burnt, grain, and liquid offerings.

On the sixth day, offer 8 bulls, 2 rams, and 14 one-year-old male lambs, all without defect. Also offer the prescribed grain and liquid offerings. Include a male goat as a sin offering, in addition to the regular burnt, grain, and liquid offerings.

On the seventh day, offer 7 bulls, 2 rams, and 14 one-year-old male lambs, all without defect. Also offer the prescribed grain and liquid offerings. Include one male goat as a sin offering, in addition to the regular burnt, grain, and liquid offerings.

On the eighth day, hold a sacred assembly to close out the festival and do no work, because this is also a day of sabbath rest. Present another burnt offering as a special gift, an aroma pleasing to the Lord. It will consist of 1 bull, 1 ram, and 7 one-year-old male lambs, all without defect. Also offer the prescribed grain and liquid offerings. Include a male goat as a sin offering, in addition to the regular burnt, grain, and liquid offerings.

Celebrate this as a festival to the Lord in the seventh month for seven days each year. This must be a permanent law for the generations to come (LV 23:33-36|LV 23:39-43|NM 29:12-38|NM 29:40).

The Daily Burnt Offerings
EX 29:38-46|NM 28:1-8

The Lord gave Moses the following instructions at Mount Sinai for the regular burnt offering: Make sure you present my food offerings on a daily basis at the appointed time. Each day you must bring 2 one-year-old lambs without defect as a regular burnt offering. Offer one lamb in the morning and the other in the evening, along with a grain offering consisting of 2 quarts of the finest flour mixed with a quart of oil from pressed olives. Also offer a quart of wine with each lamb and pour it out to the Lord at the sanctuary. In the evening offer the second lamb in the same way as the first, with its accompanying grain and liquid offerings. The aroma of these offerings is pleasing to me.

You and your descendants must offer these daily sacrifices at the Tabernacle entrance for all time to come. I will meet with my people and speak with you there in the place made holy by my glorious presence. Yes, I will make the Tabernacle and the altar holy, and I have set aside Aaron and his sons to serve me as priests. Then I will live among you as your God, and you will know that I am the Lord your God who brought you out of Egypt to dwell with you.

So Moses did everything as the Lord had commanded.

Sabbath Offerings
NM 28:9-10

Every Sabbath, offer 2 one-year-old lambs without defect, along with its liquid offering and a grain offering consisting of 4 quarts of the finest flour mixed with olive oil. This burnt offering is in addition to the regular burnt offering and its liquid offering.

Monthly Offerings
NM 28:11-15

Present a burnt offering to the Lord on the first day of each month: 2 young bulls, 1 ram, and 7 one-year-old male lambs, all without defect. They must be accompanied by grain offerings consisting of the finest flour mixed with olive oil: 6 quarts with each bull, 4 quarts with the ram, and 2 quarts with each lamb. The aroma of this burnt offering will be pleasing to the Lord.

Each burnt offering must also be accompanied by an offering of wine: 2 quarts with each bull; 1.5 quarts with the ram; and a quart with each lamb. Also present a male goat to the Lord as a sin offering. Offer these sacrifices on the first day of each month in addition to the daily burnt offerings.

Conclusion Regarding Holy Festivals
LV 23:37-38|NM 29:39

You must proclaim the Lord's appointed festivals as sacred assemblies for bringing food offerings to the Lord — the burnt offerings, grain offerings, peace offerings, sacrifices, and liquid offerings required for each day. Observe these festivals in addition to the Lord's Sabbath days and present the prescribed offerings to the Lord in addition to those you give as gifts, to fulfill vows, and as voluntary offerings.

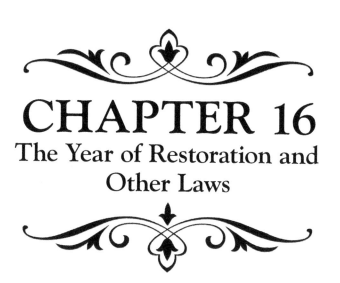

CHAPTER 16
The Year of Restoration and Other Laws

The Penalty for Blasphemy
LV 24:10-16|LV 24:23

There was a man whose father was Egyptian and whose mother was an Israelite named Shelomith, the daughter of Dibri the Danite. The man went out into the camp and got into a fight with another Israelite, and he blasphemed the Name of God with a curse. They brought him to Moses and put him in custody until they determined the Lord's will.

Then the Lord said to Moses: "Take the blasphemer outside the camp. All those who heard him must lay their hands on his head, and the entire community must stone him. Anyone who curses their God will be held responsible, and anyone who blasphemes the name of the Lord must be put to death, whether foreigner or native-born."

So Moses gave the order and the Israelites stoned the blasphemer outside the camp, as the Lord commanded.

The Penalty for Death
LV 24:17-22

Anyone who takes a human life must be put to death. Anyone who takes the life of someone's animal must make restitution — life for life. Anyone who injures another must suffer the same injury: a fracture for a fracture, an eye for an eye, and a tooth for a tooth. The same law applies to the foreigner and the native-born. I am the Lord your God.

The Sabbath Year
LV 25:1-7

The Lord gave Moses the following instructions at Mount Sinai: When you enter the land I am giving you, the land itself must observe a sabbath to the Lord. For six years, you may sow your fields, prune your vineyards, and gather the crops. But every seventh year, the land must have a year of sabbath rest to the Lord. Don't sow your fields or prune your vineyards. Don't store anything that grows by itself or gather the grapes of your unpruned vines. But whatever the land produces during the sabbath year may be eaten as daily food by your family, servants, hired workers, and temporary residents, as well as your livestock and the wild animals in the land.

The Year of Restoration
LV 25:8-55

Count off 7 sabbath years, for a total of 49 years. On the Day of Atonement, sound the trumpet throughout the land. Set apart the 50th year as a Year of Restoration, when families will receive back property they had to sell, and those sold as slaves will be allowed to return home. Don't plant any seed and don't store what grows by itself or gather the grapes of your unpruned vines. This Year of Restoration must be holy for you; eat only what you gather directly from the fields.

Don't take advantage of each other when selling or buying land. Determine the price based on the number of crops the land can produce before the next Year of Restoration. Increase the price if there are a lot of years left, and decrease it if only a few years are left, because what's really being sold is the number of crops the land can produce. Don't take advantage of each other, but fear the Lord your God.

Be careful to obey my laws, and the land will produce fruit so that you will have all you want to eat and you can live there in safety. You might wonder what you will eat in the 7th year if you don't plant or harvest crops. I will bless the land in the 6th year so that it will produce enough for 3 years. While you're planting during the 8th year, you will still be eating what you harvested in the 6th year, and it will last until the harvest comes in the 9th year.

You must never permanently sell the land, because it is mine and you live there as foreigners and temporary residents. Whenever land is sold, you must allow the original owner the first chance to buy it back.

If any of you become poor and sell your property, your nearest relative may buy it back. If no relative is able, you can buy it back yourself if you later become able to do so. Determine the value by calculating the years since the sale and paying the balance to the purchaser; you can then go back to your own property. But if neither you nor a relative is able to buy it back, the property will remain in the buyer's possession until the Year of Restoration. At that time it will be returned to you.

If you sell a house in a walled city, you retain the right to buy it back only up to a full year after its sale. But if you don't buy it back before then, the house will permanently belong to the buyer and the buyer's descendants. It must not be returned in the Year of Restoration. But houses in villages without walls around them should be treated as property in the open country. They can be bought back at any time and must be returned in the Year of Restoration.

The Levites always have the right to buy back their houses sold in the cities assigned to them. If they don't buy them back, their houses must be returned in the Year of Restoration, because the houses are their property among the Israelites. But the pastureland belonging to their cities must not be sold, because it belongs to them permanently.

If your fellow Israelites become poor and are unable to support themselves, help them as you would a foreigner and temporary resident, so they can continue to live among you. You must not charge interest when you lend them money and you must not sell them food at a profit. Fear the Lord your God, who brought you out of Egypt to be your God and to give you the land of Canaan.

If your fellow Israelites become poor and sell themselves to you, don't treat them like slaves but as hired workers or temporary residents; they will work for you until the Year of Restoration and then you must release them and their children so they can return to their own family and property. The Israelites are my own slaves who I brought out of Egypt; therefore they must not be sold as slaves. You can buy slaves from the nations around you, and you can buy the children of the temporary residents living among you, and they will become your property. You can leave them to your children as an inheritance and make them slaves for life, but you must fear your God and don't rule over any Israelite harshly.

If any of you become poor and sell yourself to rich foreigners or temporary residents, any of your relatives can buy you back or you can buy your own freedom if you earn enough money. The price paid must be based on the time period between the year of sale and the Year of Restoration, whatever it would cost to hire someone for that time period. The longer the time until the Year of Restoration, the more you will have to pay to buy your freedom. The price will be more if many years remain until the Year of Restoration, but will decrease if only a few years remain. Israelites sold to foreigners must be treated as workers hired on a yearly basis; make sure the foreign owners don't rule over them harshly.

Those who aren't bought back must be released along with their children in the Year of Restoration, because the Israelites are my own slaves who I brought out of Egypt. I am the Lord your God.

Instructions Regarding Vows to the Lord
LV 27:1-34

Evaluating the Price of a Vow
LV 27:1-8

The Lord gave Moses the following instructions: When a person is dedicated to the Lord as a special vow, that person may be set free by paying the following amounts, weighed according to the official standard:

Age	Value of a Male	Value of a Female
20-59	50 pieces of silver	30 pieces of silver
5-19	20 pieces of silver	10 pieces of silver
60 and above	15 pieces of silver	10 pieces of silver
1 month to 4 years	5 pieces of silver	3 pieces of silver

If those making the vow are too poor to pay the specified amount, present the person being dedicated to the priest, who will set an affordable price.

Regulations for Offering Animals as a Vow
LV 27:9-13

If you offer a ritually clean animal to the Lord as a vow, it is holy and you must not substitute it at all, whether for a good animal or a bad one. But if you do, both the original animal and its substitute will belong to the Lord. If you offer a ritually unclean animal as a vow, you must present the animal to the priest, who will judge its quality and set the price accordingly, and his decision will be final. If you want to buy back the animal, you must add an additional 20% to its value.

Regulations for Offering Property as a Vow
LV 27:14-25

If you dedicate your house to the Lord, the priest will judge its quality and set the price accordingly, and his decision will be final. If you want to buy the house back, you must add an additional 20% to its value and it will become yours again.

If you dedicate part of your family land to the Lord, set its value according to the amount of grain it would produce — 50 pieces of silver for every five bushels of barley. If you dedicate a field immediately after the Year of Restoration, the full price applies. But if you dedicate a field sometime after the Year of Restoration, the priest will reduce its price according to the years remaining until the next Year of Restoration. If you want to buy back the land, you must add an additional 20% to its value, and the field will be yours again. But if you don't buy it back or have sold it to someone else before first buying it back, you lose the right to buy it back. When the land is released in the Year of Restoration, it will permanently belong to the Lord and will be given to the priests.

If you dedicate to the Lord a field you purchased that isn't part of your family property, the priest will determine its value based on the number of years left until the next Year of Restoration. You must pay the price that same day, as a sacred gift to the Lord. The field will revert to the original owner or his descendants in the Year of Restoration. All prices must be set according to the official weight of silver, which is about 2 ounces.

Special Rules for Offering a Vow
LV 27:26-33

The following must not be offered as a vow to the Lord:

* **The firstborn of an animal**, because the firstborn already belongs to the Lord. Whether from the cattle or flock, it is the Lord's. Ceremonially unclean animals may be bought back at their set value, plus an additional 20%. If you don't buy it back, it can be sold at the price that was set.
* **Anything you own and have completely devoted to the Lord** — whether a human being, an animal, or family land; it belongs permanently to the Lord.
* **A person devoted to the Lord and condemned to death** — you cannot redeem them; they must be put to death.

10% of all the grain from the soil and the fruit from the trees belongs to the Lord. If you want to buy any of it back, you must pay its value, plus 20%. 10% of your herd and flocks belongs to the Lord. Don't examine the animals first and arrange it so that inferior animals are given, and don't make any substitutions. If you do, both the animal and its substitute will belong to the Lord.

Regulations for Vows Made by Women
NM 30:1-16

The Lord gave Moses the following instructions for the leaders of the tribes: When a man makes a vow to the Lord or makes a pledge under oath, he must not break his promise; he must do everything he said would.

When a young woman still living in her father's household makes a vow to the Lord or makes a pledge under oath and her father hears about it but doesn't object, then her vows and pledges will stand. But if her father forbids her, the Lord will forgive her for not fulfilling them.

Any vow or impulsive pledge made by a widow or divorced woman must be fulfilled.

If a woman makes a vow or impulsive pledge when she is already married or before she gets married, she must fulfill her vows unless her husband objects when he hears about it. But if her husband forbids her, she isn't required to fulfill them and the Lord will forgive her. Her husband has the right to confirm or annul any vow or pledge she makes. But if he doesn't object immediately, then he affirms her vows and pledges and she must fulfill them. But if he annuls them some time later, then he must bear the consequences of her failure to fulfill them.

Regulations for the Nazirite Vow
NM 6:1-21

The Lord gave Moses the following instructions for the Israelites: If a man or woman makes a special vow of dedication to the Lord to become a Nazirite, they must abstain from the following: wine and other fermented drink, vinegar made from wine or other fermented drink, grape juice, grapes, and raisins. As long as they are bound by the Nazirite vow, they must not eat anything that comes from the grapevine, not even the seeds or skins.

They must let their hair grow long and must not cut it until the time of their vow has been fulfilled. They have been set apart as holy to the Lord as long as they are Nazarites.

They must not go near a dead body. They must not make themselves ceremonially unclean even if their own parents or siblings die, because their hair is the symbol of their dedication to God and they are set apart to the Lord.

If someone dies suddenly near them, thus defiling their hair, they must wait seven days and then shave their head. Then they will be cleansed of their defilement. On the eighth day, they must bring two doves or two young pigeons to the priest at the Tabernacle entrance. The priest will offer one as a sin offering and the other as a burnt offering to make atonement for the Nazirite, for the guilt incurred for being near the dead body. That same day, they must reaffirm their commitment and let their hair start growing again. Because they became defiled, their previous days as a Nazarite don't count, and they will have to start over and make another Nazarite vow, bringing a one-year-old male lamb as a guilt offering.

When the Nazirite period of dedication is over. They must present their offerings to the Lord at the Tabernacle entrance: a one-year-old male lamb for a burnt offering, a one-year-old female lamb for a sin offering, and a ram for a peace offering, all without defect, along with the required grain and liquid offerings. They should also offer a basket of bread made with the finest flour and without yeast — thick loaves mixed with olive oil and thin wafers brushed with olive oil.

The priest must present all these before the Lord in the following order: the sin offering, burnt offering, basket of unleavened bread, the peace offering, and then the grain and liquid offerings.

Then at the Tabernacle entrance, the Nazirite must shave off the hair that symbolizes their dedication and put it in the fire under the peace offering.

Afterward the priest will give the Nazarite a boiled shoulder of the ram, and one thick loaf and a wafer from the basket, and then take them back and lift them up before the Lord. They are holy and belong to the priest, in addition to the breast that was lifted and the thigh that was offered. After that, the Nazirite may drink wine.

These are the required offerings for those taking a Nazirite vow. They may also vow to make additional offerings if they can afford it, but they must be sure to fulfill whatever vows they make.

The Test for an Unfaithful Wife
NM 5:11-31

The Lord gave Moses the following instructions for the Israelites: Suppose a man gets jealous and suspects his wife of cheating on him. Now she might be totally innocent; on the other hand, she might have been unfaithful but there were no witnesses to catch her in the act. In either case, he must take his wife to the priest, along with 2 quarts of barley flour as an offering on her behalf. He must not put olive oil or incense on it, because it's a jealousy offering, designed to bring the truth to light.

The priest will have her stand before the Lord. Then he will put holy water in a clay jar and add some dust from the Tabernacle floor, thus creating bitter water that brings a curse to those who are guilty. He will loosen her hair and place the jealousy offering in her hands, while he himself holds the bitter water.

Then the priest will put the woman under oath and say, "If you have not had sex with another man while married to your husband, you will not be harmed by the curse that this water brings. But if you're guilty, may your people know that the Lord's curse is upon you when he makes you infertile, causing your womb to shrivel and your abdomen to swell."

Then the woman must say, "Amen. May the Lord do so."

The priest must write these curses on a scroll and then wash the writing off into the bitter water. He will take the jealousy offering from her, lift it before the Lord, and burn a handful on the altar as a memorial offering. After that, he will have the woman drink the mixture. If she has been unfaithful, the water will cause bitter suffering. Her abdomen will swell and her womb will miscarry, and she'll become a curse among her people. The husband will be innocent of any wrongdoing, but she will bear the consequences of her sin. But if she is innocent, she will be found not guilty and will be able to have children.

Rewards for Obedience
LV 26:1-13

Don't make idols in your land or set up carved images, sacred pillars, or sculpted stones to bow down and worship. Observe my Sabbaths and have reverence for my sanctuary. I am the Lord your God.

Follow my decrees and be careful to obey my commands, and I will send rain in its season so that the ground will produce crops and the trees will produce fruit. Your fields will produce so much grain that you will still be threshing when it's time for the grape harvest and you will still be harvesting grapes when it's time to begin planting. You will have to clear out the old harvest to make room for the new, and you will have all you want to eat.

I will grant the land peace and you will live there safely, able to sleep with no fear. I will remove the wild animals. I will protect you from the sword of your enemies and you will slaughter them with your swords: 5 of you will defeat 100 and 100 will defeat 10,000.

I will bless you and make you fertile and give you many descendants. I will keep my covenant with you. I will live among you and be with you. I won't turn away from you. I will be your God and you will be my people. I am the Lord your God, who brought you out of Egypt so you would no longer be their slaves; I broke the bondage of slavery and enabled you to walk with your heads held high.

Punishments for Disobedience
LV 26:14-39

But if you reject my commandments and refuse to obey me, and so violate my covenant, I will bring disaster upon you — incurable diseases and fever that leads to blindness, and illness that will sap your strength. The seeds you plant will be in vain, because your enemies will eat the harvest. I will turn against you and allow your enemies to defeat you; those who hate you will rule over you, and you will flee even when no one is chasing you.

If you still won't obey me even after all this, I will punish you seven times over and break your stubborn pride. There will be no rain from the heavens above you, and the land beneath you will dry up and become hard like metal. Your strength will be spent in vain, because your soil won't produce its crops, nor will the trees produce their fruit.

If you continue to resist me and refuse to obey me, I will again increase your punishment seven times over, as your sins deserve. I will send wild animals and they will kill your children, destroy your cattle, and decrease your population so much that your roads will be deserted.

If these punishments don't cause you to return to me and you continue to be hostile toward me, I myself will be hostile toward you and punish you for your sins seven times over. I will bring war upon you for breaking the covenant, and when you withdraw into your cities for protection, I will send a plague to destroy you, and you will be captured by your enemies. When I cut off your food supply, ten women will only need one oven to bake bread, and they will ration it out in meager quantities so that when you eat, you won't be satisfied.

If you continue to be hostile toward me and refuse to obey me, my anger will burn against you and I will punish you for your sins seven times over. You will eat your own children. I will destroy your pagan shrines, tear down your incense altars, and pile your dead bodies on top of your lifeless idols, and I will despise you. I will reduce your cities to ruins and destroy your sanctuaries. I will not be pleased with the aroma of your offerings.

I will destroy the land so completely that your enemies who take it over will be shocked. I will scatter you among the nations and pursue you with my sword. Your land will be deserted and your cities will lie in ruins. While you are exiled in the land of your enemies, the land will finally rest and enjoy the sabbath years it missed while you lived there.

In the land of your enemies, I will make you so fearful that the sound of a windblown leaf will make you flee as though running from a sword. You will fall and stumble over one another, even though no one is pursuing you. You will be unable to stand up against your enemies. The land of your enemies will devour you and you will die there among them. Those of you who survive will waste away there because of your sins and the sins of your ancestors.

Repentance After Disobedience
LV 26:40-46|LV 27:34

But if you confess your sins and the sins of your ancestors regarding your unfaithfulness and hostility toward me, which caused me to send you into exile — when your stubborn hearts are humbled and you have paid for your sin, I will fulfill my covenant with Jacob, Isaac, and Abraham and remember my promise to give you the land.

But first you must leave the land to enjoy its sabbaths, thus paying for your sin of rejecting my laws. But while you're in exile, I won't completely abandon or destroy you, and thus break my covenant. For your sake I will remember the covenant with your ancestors who I brought out of Egypt in the sight of the nations to be their God. I am the Lord your God.

These are the laws and the regulations that the Lord established through Moses at Mount Sinai between himself and the Israelites.

CHAPTER 17
The Census

The Census of the Israelites
NM 1:1-51|NM 1:54|NM 7:2

While the Israelites were still in the Sinai Desert, a year after they had left Egypt, the Lord gave Moses the following instructions in the Tabernacle on the first day of the second month:

"You and Aaron must take a census of the whole Israelite community by their clans and families, listing every man by name, one by one. Count all the men age 20 and older who are fit for battle. The leaders of each tribe must help you, the same men who gave offerings at the Tabernacle dedication."

So Moses and Aaron gathered the leaders and called the whole community together and registered the people as the Lord had commanded.

Tribe	Leader Who Assisted in the Census	Number of Men 20 Years and Older Fit for Battle
Reuben (Israel's firstborn)	Elizur son of Shedeur	46,500
Simeon	Shelumiel son of Zurishaddai	59,300
Judah	Nahshon son of Amminadab	74,600
Issachar	Nethanel son of Zuar	54,400
Zebulun	Eliab son of Helon	57,400
Ephraim (Joseph's son)	Elishama son of Ammihud	40,500
Manasseh (Joseph's son)	Gamaliel son of Pedahzur	32,200
Benjamin	Abidan son of Gideoni	35,400
Dan	Ahiezer son of Ammishaddai	62,700
Asher	Pagiel son of Okran	41,500
Gad	Eliasaph son of Deuel	45,650
Naphtali	Ahira son of Enan	53,400

The total number of all the Israelites 20 years old and fit for battle was 603,550.

But the Levites weren't counted with the others because the Lord had said to Moses: "Don't include the tribe of Levi in the census with the other Israelites fit for battle. Instead, they are in charge of the Tabernacle of the covenant, its furnishings, and equipment. Whenever it's time to move, the Levites must take the Tabernacle down, carry it to the new location, and set it up. Anyone else who goes near it must be put to death."

So the Israelites did just as the Lord commanded Moses.

The Arrangement of the Tribal Camps
NM 1:52-53|NM 2:1-34

The rest of the Israelites must set up camp on the outskirts of the Tabernacle, some distance away, by tribe, displaying their own family banner. But the Levites must camp closely around the Tabernacle of the covenant to protect the Israelite community from the Lord's wrath.

Tribe	Leader of the Troops	Number of Men 20 Years and Older Fit for Battle	Camp Location
Judah	Nahshon son of Amminadab	74,600	On the east, toward the sunrise
Issachar	Nethanel son of Zuar	54,400	On the east, on one side of Judah
Zebulun	Eliab son of Helon	57,400	On the east, on the other side of Judah
TOTAL		186,400	
Reuben	Elizur son of Shedeur	46,500	On the south
Simeon	Shelumiel son of Zurishaddai	59,300	On the south, on one side of Reuben
Gad	Eliasaph son of Deuel	45,650	On the south, on the other side of Reuben
TOTAL		151,450	
Ephraim	Elishama son of Ammihud	40,500	On the west
Manasseh	Gamaliel son of Pedahzur	32,200	On the west, on one side of Ephraim
Benjamin	Abidan son of Gideoni	35,400	On the west, on the other side of Ephraim
TOTAL		108,100	

Tribe	Leader of the Troops	Number of Men 20 Years and Older Fit for Battle	Camp Location
Levi			Around the Tabernacle in the middle of the camp
Dan	Ahiezer son of Ammishaddai	62,700	On the north
Asher	Pagiel son of Okran	41,500	On the north, on one side of Dan
Naphtali	Ahira son of Enan	53,400	On the north, on the other side of Dan
TOTAL		157,600	

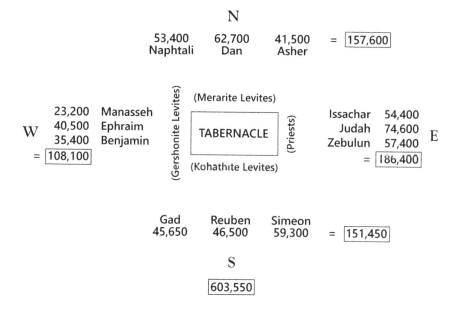

Judah and the two tribes assigned to its camp will set out first.

Reuben and the two tribes assigned to its camp will set out second.

The Levites will set out next, carrying the Tabernacle. They will set out in the same order as they encamp, each in their own place under their standard.

Ephraim and the two tribes assigned to its camp will set out next.

Dan and the two tribes assigned to its camp will set out last, under their standards.

So the total number of men in the camps, by their divisions, excluding the Levites, was 603,550, and the Israelites did everything just as the Lord had commanded Moses.

The Census of the Levites
NM 3:1-24|NM 3:27-30|NM 3:33-35|NM 3:38-51

This is the account of Aaron and Moses' family at the time the Lord spoke to Moses at Mount Sinai.

Nadab, Aaron's firstborn; Abihu; Eleazar; and Ithamar were anointed and ordained to serve as priests. But Nadab and Abihu died before the Lord when they offered unauthorized fire in the Sinai Desert, leaving behind no sons.

Eleazar and Ithamar served as priests during the lifetime of their father Aaron.

The Lord had said to Moses in the Sinai Desert, "Appoint the tribe of Levi to serve Aaron and his sons. They must serve the community by taking care of and guarding the Tabernacle and its equipment. But only Aaron and his sons must perform the duties of a priest; anyone else who tries to do so must be put to death.

"I've taken the Levites from among the Israelites in place of the first male offspring of every Israelite woman. The Levites are mine, for all the firstborn are mine. When I struck down all the firstborn in Egypt, I set apart for myself every firstborn in Israel, whether human or animal. I am the Lord. Now count all the male Levites a month old or older, by their families and clans."

So Moses counted them.

Levi had three sons: **Gershon, Kohath**, and **Merari**. They were the ancestors of the clans that bear their names.

Gershon had two sons: Libni and Shimei. The number of males in their clans was 7,500. Their camp was on the west, behind the Tabernacle. Their leader was Eliasaph son of Lael.

Kohath had four sons: Amram, Izhar, Hebron, and Uzziel. The number of males in their clans was 8,300. Their camp was on the south side of the Tabernacle. Their leader was Elizaphan son of Uzziel.

Merari had two sons: Mahli and Mushi. The number of males in their clans was 6,200. Their camp was on the north side of the Tabernacle. Their leader was Zuriel son of Abihail. These were the ancestors of the clans that bear their names.

Moses, Aaron, and Aaron's sons were camped to the east, toward the sunrise, in front of the Tabernacle. They were responsible for protecting the sanctuary on behalf of the Israelites. Anyone else who approached it would be put to death.

The total number of Levites counted was 22,000.

The Lord said to Moses, "Make a list of all the firstborn Israelite males who are a month old or more. In their place I'm claiming all the Levites as mine. I am the Lord. I'm also claiming the Levites' livestock as a substitute for all the Israelites' firstborn livestock."

So Moses counted all the firstborn of the Israelites, and the total was 22,273.

The Lord said, "The firstborn Israelites outnumber the Levites by 273, so you must buy them back. Collect five pieces of silver for each one, according to the official standard, and give the money to Aaron and his sons."

So Moses collected the money from the firstborn of the Israelites, which totaled 1,365 pieces of silver, each weighing about 2 ounces, according to the official standard. Then he gave it to Aaron and his sons.

So Moses did everything as commanded by the word of the Lord.

The Kohath Clan
NM 3:31-32|NM 4:1-20

The Lord gave Moses and Aaron the following instructions: All the men in the Kohath clan one month old and over are responsible for the care of the most holy things in the sanctuary: the Ark of the Covenant, table, lampstand, altars, utensils used in ministering, the curtain at the entrance of the Most Holy Place, and everything related to these items.

Now take a census of those age 30 to 50 who are qualified to serve in the Tabernacle; they will be responsible for transporting these items when the camp moves. But first, Aaron and his sons must go in and take down the inner curtain and cover the Ark of the Covenant with it. Cover the curtain with fine leather and then spread a cloth of solid blue on top of that. Finally, insert the carrying poles.

Spread a blue cloth over the table where the sacred bread is displayed and put the plates, dishes, bowls, and the jars for liquid offerings on top, as well as the bread itself. Spread a scarlet cloth over them, cover that with fine leather, and insert the carrying poles.

Use a blue cloth to cover the lampstand, lamps, wick trimmers, trays, and jars for the olive oil. Cover all of these items with fine leather and put the bundle on a carrying frame.

Spread a blue cloth over the gold altar of incense and cover that with fine leather. Then insert the carrying poles.

Wrap all accessories for the altar of incense in a blue cloth and cover that with fine leather, and then put them on a carrying frame.

Remove the ashes from the bronze altar and spread a purple cloth over it. Place on it all the utensils used for ministering at the altar, including the firepans, meat forks, shovels, and sprinkling bowls. Spread a covering of fine leather over this, and insert the carrying poles.

Eleazar son of Aaron is the chief leader over all the Levites. He must be in charge of the entire Tabernacle and everything in it, including its holy furnishings and articles, and those responsible for the sanctuary. He must handle the oil for the light, the fragrant incense, the regular grain offering, and the anointing oil.

You must ensure that the Kohath clans aren't wiped out from among the Levites. They must not carry the holy items in the Tabernacle until the priests have finished covering everything and the camp is ready to move. Aaron and his sons must go into the sanctuary and assign each man his task and transport duty. But the Kohath clan must not go in to look at the holy things or touch them, even for a moment, or they will die.

The Gershon Clan
NM 3:25-26|NM 4:21-28

All the men in the Gershon clan one month old and over are responsible for the Tabernacle and its inner, outer, and fine leather covers; the curtain at the entrance; the courtyard curtains that surround the Tabernacle and altar; the curtain at the courtyard entrance; the ropes; and everything else related to these items.

Now take a census of those age 30 to 50 who are qualified to serve in the Tabernacle; they will be responsible for transporting these items when the camp moves. Whether they are transporting items or doing other work, everything must be done under the priests' direction, specifically Aaron's son Ithamar.

The Merari Clan
NM 3:36-37|NM 4:29-33

All the men in the Merari clan one month old and over are responsible for the frames supporting the Tabernacle, its crossbars, posts, bases, all its accessories, as well as the courtyard posts with their bases, tent pegs, ropes, and everything else related to these items.

Now take a census of those age 30 to 50 who are qualified to serve in the Tabernacle; they will be responsible for transporting these items when the camp moves. Assign to each man what he must carry. They will work under the direction of Aaron's son Ithamar.

Number of Levites Qualified for Tabernacle Service
NM 4:34-49

So Moses, Aaron, and the leaders of the community counted all the Levites age 30 to 50 who were qualified to serve in the Tabernacle, by their clans and families. The Kohath clan totaled 2,750, the Gershon clan totaled 2,630, and the Merari clan totaled 3,200. So the combined total of all the clans was 8,580. And at the Lord's command through Moses, each was assigned his work and told what to carry.

The Purity of the Camp
NM 5:1-4

The Lord said to Moses, "Command the Israelites to send outside the camp anyone who has a defiling skin disease, has a discharge of any kind, or is ceremonially unclean because of a dead body, whether male or female. In this way they won't defile the camp, where I dwell among them."

So the Israelites sent them outside the camp as the Lord had instructed Moses.

CHAPTER 18
The Israelites' Departure
From Mount Sinai

The Cloud Above the Tabernacle
EX 40:36-38|NM 9:15-23

On the day the Tabernacle was set up, a cloud covered it continuously by day and fire lit up the cloud by night, so all the Israelites could see it. The cloud determined when the Israelites should move their camp and where they should set it up again. They stayed where they were as long as the cloud covered the tent, but when the cloud lifted, they followed it and camped wherever it stopped.

Whether the cloud remained over the Tabernacle for one night, a few days, a month, or a year, the Israelites didn't move until the cloud moved. They camped or traveled in obedience to the commands the Lord had given through Moses.

The Silver Trumpets
NM 10:1-10

The Lord said to Moses, "Make two trumpets of hammered silver to call the community together and move the camps. When long blasts are blown on both trumpets, the whole community must assemble at the Tabernacle entrance. If just one is blown, only the leaders need to assemble. When short blasts are sounded, the tribes camped on the east will move out. When short blasts are sounded, the tribes camped on the south will move out. The priests must be the ones to blow the trumpets; this is a permanent law for the generations to come.

"When your enemies attack you in your own land and you go to war, sound the alarm on the trumpets and the Lord your God will come to your aid and rescue you from your enemies. Also, when you celebrate the annual and monthly New Moon festivals, sound the trumpets when offering your burnt and peace offerings. They will remind me of my covenant with you; I am the Lord your God."

The Israelites Leave Sinai
NM 10:11-36

In the 2nd year, on the 20th day of the 2nd month, the cloud lifted from the Tabernacle. So the Israelites left the Sinai Desert for the first time since they had arrived there, following the instructions the Lord had given through Moses. Whenever they set out, division by division, they went in the following order:

Judah's troops went first, carrying their banner, led by Nahshon son of Amminadab; Nethanel son of Zuar led the tribe of Issachar; and Eliab son of Helon led the tribe of Zebulun. Then the Tabernacle was taken down, and the Gershon and Merari clans marched next, carrying the Tabernacle with them.

Reuben's troop went next, carrying their banner, led by Elizur son of Shedeur; Shelumiel son of Zurishaddai led the tribe of Simeon; and Eliasaph son of Deuel led the tribe of Gad. Next came the Kohath clan, carrying the sacred objects of the Tabernacle. The Tabernacle would be set up at the new location before they arrived.

Ephraim's troop went next, carrying their banner, led by Elishama son of Ammihud; Gamaliel son of Pedahzur led the tribe of Manasseh; and Abidan son of Gideoni led the tribe of Benjamin.

Finally, Dan's troop followed, serving as the rear guard for all the units, carrying their banner. Ahiezer son of Ammishaddai led the tribe of Dan; Pagiel son of Okran led the tribe of Asher; and Ahira son of Enan led the tribe of Naphtali.

Now Moses' brother-in-law, Hobab — the son of Moses' father-in-law Jethro — was with them. Moses said to Hobab, "We're on our way to the land the Lord promised us. Come with us and we'll treat you well, for the Lord has promised to bless us."

"No," Hobab replied, "I'm going back to my own land and family."

But Moses said, "Please don't leave us. Be our guide; you know where we should camp in the desert. If you come with us, we'll share with you all the blessings the Lord gives us."

So they left Sinai, the mountain of the Lord, and traveled for three days, and the Lord's Ark of the Covenant preceded them to show them where to camp. The cloud of the Lord hovered over them whenever they set out from the camp, and they continued traveling until the cloud eventually stopped in the Paran Desert.

Whenever the Ark set out, Moses said, "Arise, O Lord! May your enemies be scattered and may they flee before you." Whenever the Ark stopped, he said, "Return, Lord, to the countless thousands of Israel."

The Lord Sends Fire Upon the Camp
NM 11:1-3

But the people soon began to complain about their hardships. The Lord's anger burned against them and he sent fire to destroy the outer edges of the camp. The people cried out to Moses and when he prayed to the Lord, the fire died down. So that place was called Taberah, because the fire from the Lord had burned among them.

The Lord Sends Quail at Kibroth-Hattaavah
NM 11:4-6|NM 11:10-34

Now some foreigners who had left Egypt with the Israelites began to crave other food, causing the Israelites to also start complaining. "If only we could have some meat!" they said. "In Egypt we freely ate fish, cucumbers, watermelons, herbs, onions, and garlic. But now we've lost our appetite; we never see anything but this manna!"

Moses heard family after family whining as they stood at their tent entrances. The Lord was very angry, and Moses was distressed. He asked the Lord, "Why did you bring this trouble on your servant? What have I done to deserve the responsibility of taking all these people to the land you promised their ancestors? I didn't conceive or give birth to them, so why ask me to carry them as a nurse carries a baby? Where am I supposed to get meat for them all? They keep whining and asking for meat, but I can't be responsible for all these people by myself; the burden is too heavy. If this is how you're going to treat me, please go ahead and kill me. Take pity on me and spare me this misery!"

The Lord replied, "Assemble 70 men who are considered leaders among the people and bring them to the Tabernacle. I will come down and speak to you there. I will take some of the Spirit I have given you and also give some to them. They will share the responsibility of the people with you so you won't have to do it alone.

"Tell the people that I have heard their complaints. They must purify themselves to prepare for tomorrow. If they want meat, then meat they shall have! But they won't eat it for just 1 or 2 days, not even 5, 10, or 20 days, but for a whole month. They will eat it until it comes out of their nostrils and they hate it. They have complained that they regret leaving Egypt, and in so doing they have rejected the Lord, who lives among you."

But Moses said, "Here I am among all these people, and 600,000 foot soldiers. How can you feed them meat for a whole month! It wouldn't be enough even if all the flocks and cattle were slaughtered or if all the fish in the sea were caught."

"Is the Lord's arm too short?" the Lord replied. "You will soon see whether or not my words come true."

So Moses told the people what the Lord had said and assembled the leaders at the Tabernacle. Then the Lord came down in the cloud and spoke with him, and he took some of the Spirit on Moses and gave it to the leaders. When the Spirit rested on them, they prophesied, but only that one time.

Now two of the leaders, Eldad and Medad, had remained in the camp. However, the Spirit also rested on them and they prophesied there in the camp. So a young man ran and told Moses.

Joshua son of Nun, who had been Moses' assistant since his youth, said, "Moses, my lord, stop them!"

But Moses replied, "Do you see this as a threat to my leadership? I wish that all the Lord's people were prophets and that the Lord would put his Spirit upon them!" Then Moses and the leaders returned to the camp.

Then the Lord sent a wind to blow quail in from the sea, piling them up three feet deep all around the camp, as far as a day's walk in every direction. All that day and night and all the next day, the people gathered quail. They gathered at least 50 bushels and spread them out around the camp to dry.

So the people gorged themselves on the meat. But before they had finished eating it all, the Lord's anger burned against them, and he struck them with a severe plague. Therefore the place was named *Kibroth-Hattaavah* (which means *graves of greed*) because there they buried the people who had craved meat.

Miriam and Aaron Oppose Moses
NM 11:35|NM 12:1-16

From Kibroth-Hattaavah the people traveled to Hazeroth and stayed there for some time.

Now Moses was a very humble man, more humble than anyone else on earth. But Miriam and Aaron began to speak against Moses because he had married a Cushite. "Does the Lord speak only through Moses?" they asked. "Doesn't he also speak through us?"

And the Lord heard them. Suddenly he said to Moses, Aaron, and Miriam, "All of you come to the Tabernacle."

When they did, the Lord came down in a pillar of cloud to the Tabernacle entrance and summoned Aaron and Miriam. They stepped forward and he said, "Listen carefully: When there are prophets among you, I, the Lord, reveal myself in visions and speak to them in dreams, but it's different with my servant Moses. I have put him in charge of my people Israel, and he is the one I trust. I speak with him face to face, clearly and not in riddles. He sees the form of the Lord, so why weren't you afraid to speak against him?"

So the Lord's anger burned against them, and then he left.

When the cloud lifted from above the tent, Miriam had a defiling skin disease — her skin had become white as snow. Then Aaron said to Moses, "Please, my lord, don't hold this sin against us that we so foolishly committed. Don't let her be like a stillborn infant whose flesh is half eaten away when it comes from its mother's womb."

So Moses cried out to the Lord, "God, please heal her!"

The Lord replied to Moses, "If her father had chastised her by spitting in her face, wouldn't she be defiled? So confine her outside the camp for seven days; after that you can bring her back."

So Miriam was confined outside the camp for seven days. After she was brought back, the Israelites left Hazeroth and camped in the Paran Desert.

The Israelites Explore Canaan
NM 13:1-25

The Lord said to Moses, "Send a leader from each tribe to explore the land of Canaan, which I'm giving to the Israelites."

So Moses sent the following leaders out from the Paran Desert to explore the land:

Shammua son of Zakkur from the tribe of Reuben

Shaphat son of Hori from the tribe of Simeon

Caleb son of Jephunneh from the tribe of Judah

Igal son of Joseph from the tribe of Issachar

Joshua son of Nun from the tribe of Ephraim (Moses had changed his name from Hoshea to Joshua.)

Palti son of Raphu from the tribe of Benjamin

Gaddiel son of Sodi from the tribe of Zebulun

Gaddi son of Susi from the tribe of Manasseh (a tribe of Joseph)

Ammiel son of Gemalli from the tribe of Dan

Sethur son of Michael from the tribe of Asher
Nahbi son of Vophsi from the tribe of Naphtali
Geuel son of Maki from the tribe of Gad.

Then Moses said, "Go up through the Negev and into the hill country. See what the land is like and whether the people who live there are strong or weak, few or many. Is the land good or bad? Are their cities walled or unprotected? Is the soil fertile or poor? Does it have many trees?" It was the season when grapes were beginning to ripen, so Moses added, "Do your best to bring back some of the land's fruit."

So the men explored the land from the Desert of Zin as far as Rehob, toward Lebo Hamath. They went up through the Negev and arrived at Hebron, which had been built seven years before Zoan in Egypt. There at Hebron, a race of giants lived: Ahiman, Sheshai, and Talmai. These clans were the descendants of Anak.

When the men arrived at the Valley of Eshkol, they cut off a branch bearing a single cluster of grapes and two of them carried it on a pole between them, along with some pomegranates and figs. That place was called the Valley of Eshkol because of the cluster of grapes they had cut off there. At the end of 40 days, they had finished exploring the land.

The Spies Report on the Exploration
NM 13:26-33

The men returned to Kadesh in the Paran Desert and showed everyone the fruit of the land. They gave Moses their report, saying, "The land does flow with milk and honey and here is some of the fruit. But the people who live there are powerful, and the cities are large and well-fortified. We even saw descendants of Anak! The Amalekites live in the Negev; the Hittites, Jebusites, and Amorites live in the hill country; and the Canaanites live along the Mediterranean Sea and the Jordan River."

But Caleb silenced them and said, "We should go take possession of the land, for we can certainly do it."

But the men who had gone with him said, "No, we can't attack them, because they're stronger than we are. The land devours anyone who lives there. The people are giants — they're the descendants of Anak who come from the Nephilim. We felt as small as grasshoppers, and we must have looked the same to them!"

The People Rebel
NM 14:1-45

That night all the Israelites wept aloud and complained against Moses and Aaron. "It would have been better if we had died in Egypt or even in this desert!" they said. "Why is the Lord bringing us to this land? We will die in battle and our wives and children will be captured. Wouldn't it be better for us to return to Egypt? We should choose a leader and go back."

Then Moses and Aaron fell with their faces to the ground in front of the whole community. And Joshua and Caleb tore their clothes in sorrow and said, "The land we explored is excellent, flowing with milk and honey. If the Lord is pleased with us, he'll lead us into that land and give it to us. But don't rebel against the Lord. And don't be afraid of the people who live there, because we'll devour them. They have no protection, but the Lord is with us."

But the whole community threatened to stone them. Then the glorious presence of the Lord appeared to all the Israelites at the Tabernacle and said to Moses, "How long will these people treat me with contempt and refuse to believe in me, even with all the miracles they've seen me perform? I will strike them down and destroy them with a plague, but I will make you into a greater and stronger nation."

Moses said to the Lord, "You brought these people up from Egypt by your power. But if you destroy them, the Egyptians will hear about it and tell the inhabitants of Canaan. Lord, they have already heard that these are your people and that we see you face to face. They know that your cloud hovers over them and that you lead them in a pillar of cloud by day and a pillar of fire by night. But if you kill them all, the nations will say, 'The Lord couldn't bring his people into the land he promised them, so he slaughtered them in the desert.'

"Now Lord, please display your power. You said, 'The Lord is slow to anger, abounding in love, and forgiving sin and rebellion. Yet he doesn't fail to punish the guilty; he punishes the children for the sin of the parents to the third and fourth generation.' Now according to your unfailing love, forgive them, just as you've done time and time again since they left Egypt."

The Lord replied, "I have forgiven them, as you requested. But as surely as I live and as surely as my glory fills the whole earth, not one of these people will enter the land I promised to their ancestors. They saw my glory and the miracles I performed in Egypt and in the desert. They have disobeyed me, treated me with contempt, and tested my patience over and over again. Now don't go toward the land where the Amalekites and Canaanites are living in the valleys. Tomorrow you must turn around and go back into the desert toward the Red Sea."

Then the Lord gave Moses and Aaron the following message for the Israelites, "How long will you wicked people complain against me? As surely as I live, I will do to you exactly what you said: You will die in this desert — not one of those age 20 or older who was included in the census will occupy the land I promised. But my servant Caleb son of Jephunneh has a different attitude and has remained faithful to me. I will bring him into the land and his descendants will inherit it. Joshua son of Nun will also enter the land.

"You claimed your children would be captured in the land, but they are the ones I will allow to enjoy the land you've rejected. You will die and your bodies will be scattered in this desert. Your children will wander in the desert for 40 years, suffering for your unfaithfulness, until the last of you die here. Because you explored the land for 40 days, you will wander in the desert for 40 years, suffering the consequences of your sins, and you will know what it's like to have me against you. I, the Lord, have spoken, and I will surely do these things to this wicked community that has gathered together against me. You will meet your end in this desert; here you will die."

So the Lord sent a plague to strike down the 10 men who had explored the land and spread a bad report, and they died there before the Lord. Of the 12 men who explored the land, only Joshua and Caleb survived.

When Moses reported all this to the Israelites, they were overcome with grief. Early the next morning, they decided to head toward the hill country of Canaan. "We have surely sinned!" they said. "Now we're ready to enter the land the Lord promised."

But Moses said, "Why are you disobeying the Lord's command? Don't go; you won't succeed, because the Lord isn't with you. When you face the Amalekites and the Canaanites in battle, they'll defeat you and you will die. You turned away from the Lord and now he won't be with you."

But they defiantly went anyway, even though neither Moses nor the Ark of the Covenant left the camp. Then the Amalekites and the Canaanites attacked them and defeated them, and chased them back all the way to Hormah.

A Sabbath-Breaker Is Put to Death
NM 15:32-36

One day a man was gathering wood on the Sabbath day. Some of the Israelites saw him and brought him to Moses, Aaron, and the whole community. They kept him in custody because they weren't sure what to do with him.

"He must die," the Lord said to Moses. "The whole community must stone him outside the camp."

So they did as the Lord commanded.

Tassels on Clothing
NM 15:37-41

The Lord gave Moses the following instructions for the Israelites: For the generations to come, you must sew tassels onto the corners of your clothing, and attach a blue cord to each tassel. They will help you remember and obey all the Lord's commands. You will be dedicated to me and won't be unfaithful, following your own wishes and desires. I am the Lord, who brought you out of Egypt to be your God.

Korah, Dathan, and Abiram Rebel
NM 16:1-50

Now some of the Israelites rebelled against Moses: They were:

- **Korah son of Izhar**, a descendant of Levi's son Kohath
- **250 of Korah's followers** — They were Israelite leaders who were well known to the community
- **Dathan and Abiram**, sons of Eliab, of the tribe of Reuben
- **On son of Peleth**, also of the tribe of Reuben

Korah and his followers went to Moses and Aaron. "You've gone too far!" Korah said. All the members of the community have been set apart by the Lord, and he is with them. So why do you exalt yourselves above us?"

Moses fell with his face to the ground to pray. Then he replied, "Tomorrow the Lord will reveal who belongs to him. He will allow that man to approach him, and the man he chooses will be his priest.

It is you Levites who have gone too far! Isn't it enough that the God of Israel has set you apart from the rest of the Israelites to serve the community at the Lord's Tabernacle? But now you want the priesthood too! Who is Aaron that you should complain against him? You're really complaining against the Lord."

Then Moses summoned Dathan and Abiram. "No, we won't come!" they said. "You brought us out here to kill us here in the desert. It's bad enough that you brought us out of Egypt, a land flowing with milk and honey, claiming you'll bring us into another land flowing with milk and honey. But you haven't done that or given us any property of our own, and now you want to rule over us too! You're misleading these people, and we refuse to come!"

Moses became very angry and said to the Lord, "Don't accept any of their offerings. I haven't taken so much as a donkey from them, nor have I mistreated any of them."

Then Moses said to Korah, "You, your 250 followers, and Aaron must appear before the Lord tomorrow. Fill your fire pans with burning coals and incense and present them before the Lord."

So the next day each of them did as instructed and stood with Moses and Aaron with their firepans at the Tabernacle entrance. Meanwhile Korah had stirred up the whole community against Moses and Aaron, so many of them gathered outside around their tents.

Then the glorious presence of the Lord appeared to them and the Lord said to Moses and Aaron, "Stand back away from this community, so I can destroy them at once."

But Moses and Aaron fell with their face to the ground and cried out, "O God who gives breath to all living things, will you punish the entire community because of one man's sins?"

"Then tell everyone to move away from the tents of Korah, Dathan, and Abiram," the Lord replied.

So Moses got up and went to the tents of Dathan and Abiram, and the leaders followed him. He warned the community, "Move away from the tents of these wicked men! Don't touch anything belonging to them, or you'll be swept away because of their sins."

So they moved away from the tents. Dathan and Abiram were standing at their tent entrances with their wives and children.

Then Moses said, "The Lord will demonstrate that he has sent me to do these things and that it wasn't my idea. If these men die a natural death, then the Lord didn't send me. But if the Lord does something unheard of and allows the earth to swallow them up with everything they own, sending them down alive into the realm of the dead, then you will know that these men have treated the Lord with contempt."

As soon as he finished speaking, the ground split open and swallowed the men and their households, along with all those associated with Korah. They went down alive into the realm of the dead, with everything they owned, and they vanished, screaming as the earth closed over them.

The Israelites heard them screaming and ran away, shouting, "The earth is going to swallow us too!"

Fire also came out from the Lord and consumed the 250 men who were offering incense near the Tabernacle.

Then Lord said to Moses, "Tell Aaron's son Eleazar to remove the firepans from the men's charred remains and scatter the coals some distance away. The firepans are holy because they were presented to the Lord, even though the men who held them sinned and lost their lives. Hammer the firepans into sheets to cover the altar as a warning to the Israelites."

So Eleazar the priest collected the bronze firepans and had them hammered into thin sheets to cover the altar, as the Lord had directed. This reminded the Israelites that no one except a descendant of Aaron should burn incense before the Lord. If they did, they would die like Korah and his followers.

The next day the whole Israelite community complained against Moses and Aaron, "You've killed the Lord's people."

At that moment, Moses and Aaron turned toward the Tabernacle and suddenly the cloud covered it and the glorious presence of the Lord appeared. So they went to the front of the Tabernacle.

The Lord said to Moses, "Get away from these people; I will destroy them on the spot!"

But Moses and Aaron fell with their faces to the ground.

Then Moses said to Aaron, "Quickly put incense and burning coals from the altar into your firepan, and then take it out to the community to make atonement for them. Wrath has come out from the Lord and a plague has started."

So Aaron did as Moses said and ran into the midst of the community. The plague had already started, but Aaron offered the incense and made atonement for the people. He stood between the living and the dead, and the plague stopped spreading. But 14,700 people died, not counting those who had died with Korah. Then Aaron returned to Moses at the Tabernacle entrance.

The Budding of Aaron's Staff
NM 17:1-13

The Lord said to Moses, "Get a staff from the leader of each tribe and write each man's name on it. Write Aaron's name on the staff for the tribe of Levi, because there must be one staff for the leader of each tribe. Place the staffs in the Tabernacle in front of the Ark of the Covenant, where I meet with you. Buds will sprout on the staff of the man I choose, and I will end this constant complaining against you."

So the leaders gave Moses the 12 staffs and Moses placed them before the Lord in front of the Ark of the Covenant, along with Aaron's staff.

The next day Moses entered the tent and saw that not only had Aaron's staff produced buds, it had produced blossoms and almonds too! Then Moses brought all the staffs out and took them to the Israelites. They looked at them, and each leader took his own staff back.

The Lord said to Moses, "Now put Aaron's staff inside the Ark of the

Covenant with the Ten Commandments as a warning to those rebellious Israelites. They will die unless their complaints against me stop."

So Moses did just as the Lord commanded him.

Then Israelites said to Moses, "We're doomed! Any of us who even comes near the Tabernacle of the Lord will die, won't we?"

Priests and Levites Responsible for the Tabernacle
NM 18:1-7|NM 18:22-23a

The Lord gave Aaron the following instructions: You and your descendants and the other Levites are responsible for any violations connected with the sanctuary, and you and your descendants alone are responsible for any violations connected with the priesthood. Your fellow Levites can assist you and your descendants when you minister, but you must make sure they don't go near the sacred objects or the altar. If they do, they will die and so will you. No one other than the Levites may come near you. They must join you in the work and keep guard over the Tabernacle, and they will bear the responsibility for any violations committed against it. This is a permanent law for the generations to come.

Follow these instructions so my wrath won't fall on the Israelites again. I have given the Levites to you as a special gift, dedicated to the Lord for service at the Tabernacle, but only you and your sons may serve as priests for service at the altar and behind the veil. I have given you the work of the priesthood as a gift. From now on the Israelites must not go near the Tabernacle, or they will be put to death.

The Priest and Levite Offering Portions
NM 18:8-21|NM 18:23b-32

Then the Lord gave Aaron the following instructions: I have put you in charge of the offerings presented to me. When the Israelites present the holy offerings to me as gifts, whether grain, sin, or guilt offerings, the portion not burned in the fire belongs to you and your sons as your permanent share. Every male must eat it as a most holy offering.

I'm also giving to you as your permanent share the special harvest offerings the Israelites lift before the altar: the best of the olive oil, wine, and grain. Everyone in your household who is ceremonially clean may eat them, both your sons and daughters.

Everything in Israel permanently dedicated to the Lord also belongs to you. The first male offspring of both human and animal offered to the Lord will be yours, but you must buy back your firstborn sons and the firstborn of unclean animals when they're a month old. The redemption price is set at five pieces of silver, according to the official standard.

But the firstborn of cows, sheep, or goats are holy and belong to me; you must not buy them back. Instead, splash their blood against the altar and burn their fat as a food offering, an aroma pleasing to the Lord. You can eat the meat from these animals just as you can eat the breast and right thigh that are lifted up as a special offering.

I am giving all these sacred offerings to you and your family as your permanent share. This is an everlasting covenant, preserved as salt, between you and the Lord. The priests will not receive an allotment of property or land among the Israelites, because I am your special possession.

As payment for their service at the Tabernacle, I'm giving the Levites all the tithes that the Israelites offer to the Lord. This is why they won't receive an allotment of property or land; I am their special possession among the Israelites.

Then Lord gave Moses the following instructions for the Levites: When you receive the tithe from the Israelites, you must present a tenth of the best and holiest part of everything as the Lord's portion. This offering will be considered the equivalent of grain offered from your own threshing floor or wine from your own winepress. This is the Lord's sacred offering, and you must give it to Aaron. After you give your portion, you and your family may eat the rest of it wherever you like, just as the Israelites eat part of their grain and wine offerings.

Be sure not to defile the Israelites' sacred gifts. If you eat any before giving the Lord his portion, you will die. But you won't be punished as long as you first offer the best part to the Lord.

CHAPTER 19
The Israelites in Moab

Water From the Rock at Meribah
NM 20:1-13|NM 33:38b|DT 1:2

It only takes *11 days* to travel from Mount Sinai to Kadesh-Barnea, but it wasn't until the first month of the *40th year*, that the whole Israelite community returned once again to the Paran Desert, which was in the region of Zin. The Israelites stayed at Kadesh, and there Miriam died and was buried.

Now the community had no water, and they confronted Moses and Aaron and said, "It would have been better if we had died in front of the sacred tent with the others! Why did you bring us and our livestock out of Egypt to die here in the desert? This is a terrible place! There is no grain, figs, grapevines, or pomegranates, and no water to drink!"

Moses and Aaron left them and went to the Tabernacle entrance and fell with their face to the ground to pray, and the glorious presence of the Lord appeared. The Lord said, "Moses, take Aaron's staff from the covenant box and then you and Aaron gather the community together. Go speak to that rock and it will pour out water for the community and their livestock."

So Moses took the staff from the Lord's presence, and they gathered the community together in front of the rock. Moses spoke to them in anger and said, "Listen, you rebels, do we need to bring water out of this rock for you?" Then he struck the rock twice with the staff. Water gushed out, and the community and their livestock satisfied their thirst.

But the Lord said to Moses and Aaron, "Because you didn't trust in me enough to acknowledge me as holy to the Israelites, you won't bring them into the land I promised them."

This place was known as Meribah because the Israelites argued with the Lord there and he demonstrated his holiness to them.

Edom Denies Israel Passage
NM 20:14-21

Moses sent messengers from Kadesh to the king of Edom with the following message: "You know about all the hardships that your brother Israel has faced. Our ancestors went to Egypt and lived there many years. The Egyptians mistreated us, but we cried out to the Lord and he heard our cry, sending an angel to bring us out of Egypt.

"Now we're here at Kadesh on the edge of your territory. Please let us pass through your land. We won't go into your fields and vineyards or drink water from your wells. We'll stay on the main road and won't veer off from it until we've passed through your territory."

"No," the Edomites replied, "if you try to pass through, we'll attack you."

"But we'll stay on the main road," the Israelites replied. "And if we or our animals drink your water, we'll pay for it. We only want to pass through, that's all."

"No," they answered again, "you can't pass through."

Then Edom marched out against them with a large and powerful army. Since they refused to let the Israelites pass, they turned and went a different way.

The Death of Aaron
NM 20:22-29|NM 33:38-39

In the 40th year after the Israelites left Egypt, the Israelites left Kadesh and arrived at Mount Hor. There near the border of Edom, the Lord said to Moses and Aaron, "Aaron won't enter the land I'm giving the Israelites, because both of you rebelled against my command about the water at Meribah. Take Aaron and his son Eleazar up the mountain and remove Aaron's clothing and put them on Eleazar, for Aaron will join his ancestors and die there."

So on the 1st day of the 5th month, Moses did as the Lord commanded. They ascended Mount Hor as the whole community watched. Moses removed Aaron's priestly clothing and put them on Eleazar, and then Aaron died there on top of the mountain at age 123. Then Moses and Eleazar came down. When the Israelites learned that Aaron had died, they mourned for him 30 days.

The Israelites Defeat Arad
NM 21:1-3|NM 33:40

The Canaanite king of Arad, who lived in the Negev, heard that the Israelites were approaching on the road to Atharim. So he attacked them and captured some of them. Then the Israelites vowed to the Lord, "If you allow us to conquer these people, we'll completely destroy their cities and everything in them and dedicate them unconditionally to you."

So the Lord granted their request and allowed them to completely destroy the Canaanites and their cities, and that's why the place was named *Hormah*, which means *place of destruction*.

The Bronze Snake
NM 21:4-9

They traveled from Mount Hor along the road to the Red Sea to go around Edom, but the people grew impatient on the way. They spoke against God and Moses, saying, "Why did you bring us out of Egypt to die in the desert? There's nothing to eat or drink, and we can't stand any more of this miserable manna!"

So the Lord sent venomous snakes to bite the people, and many of them died. So they said to Moses, "We sinned when we spoke against the Lord and against you. Please pray to the Lord to take these snakes away."

So Moses prayed for them.

Then the Lord said to Moses, "Make a bronze image of a snake and put it up on a pole; anyone who is bitten can look at it and live."

So Moses did as instructed, and anyone bitten was healed if they looked at the bronze snake.

The Journey to Moab
NM 21:10-20

The Israelites continued traveling and camped at Oboth. Then they camped in Iye-Abarim, in the desert east of Moab, toward the sunrise, and then in the Zered Valley. After that they crossed the Arnon River and camped on the north side in the desert bordering the territory of the Amorites. That's why the *Book of the Lord's Battles* speaks of: ". . . the city of Waheb in the area of Suphah, the valleys of the Arnon River, and the valleys that extend to the city of Ar and toward the border of Moab."

From there they continued on to Beer. A well was there and the Lord said to Moses, "Gather the people together and I'll give them water."

Then the Israelites sang this song: "Spring up, O well! Let's sing about the well that the princes and nobles dug with their scepters and staffs."

Then they traveled from the desert to Mattanah, from Mattanah to Nahaliel, from Nahaliel to Bamoth, and from Bamoth to the valley in Moab where the top of Mount Pisgah overlooks the desert.

The Israelites Defeat Sihon and Og
NM 21:21-35|DT 1:4

The Israelites sent messengers to Sihon, king of the Amorites: "Please let us pass through your land. We won't go into your fields and vineyards or drink water from your wells. We'll stay on the main road and won't veer off from it until we have passed through your territory."

But Sihon wouldn't let them pass through his territory. He assembled his entire army and marched out into the desert. When he reached Jahaz, he attacked the Israelites. But they defeated the enemy with their swords and took possession of their land from the Arnon River to the Jabbok River. But they only went as far as the Ammonite border, because it was protected. The Israelites captured all the Amorite cities and settled in them, including Heshbon and its surrounding villages. Heshbon was the capital from which King Sihon ruled. He had defeated the former king of Moab and captured his land as far as the Arnon River.

That's why the poets sang:

> Come to Heshbon, King Sihon's city; let it be rebuilt and restored. Fire went out from Heshbon, a blaze from the city of Sihon. It consumed the city of Ar in Moab and destroyed the hills of the Arnon River.

> How terrible for you, people of Moab! You are destroyed, worshipers of Chemosh! Your god has given up his sons as fugitives and his daughters as captives to Sihon, the Amorite king. But we completely defeated Moab, all the way from Heshbon to Dibon, and wiped them out as far away as Nophah and Medeba.

So Israel settled in the land of the Amorites.

Moses sent spies to Jazer, and the Israelites captured it and the surrounding cities and drove out the Amorites living there. Then they turned and took the road to Bashan, where Og was king. He ruled the cities of Ashtaroth and Edrei. King Og marched out with his whole army to battle them at Edrei.

The Lord said to Moses, "Don't be afraid, for I will give you victory over him, his army, and his land. You will defeat him as you did King Sihon."

So they killed him, his sons, and his whole army, leaving no survivors, and they took possession of his land.

Balak Summons Balaam
NM 22:1-20

Then the Israelites traveled to the plains of Moab and camped along the Jordan across from Jericho.

Now Balak son of Zippor, who was king of Moab at that time, saw how the Israelites had defeated the Amorites, and Moab was filled with dread because there were so many people. So the Moabites said to the leaders of Midian, "This mob is going to destroy everything around us, like a bull devouring grass in the field."

So King Balak sent a message to Balaam son of Beor, who was living in his native land at Pethor near the Euphrates River: "A nation has come out of Egypt; they're spreading out everywhere and will soon take over the land. Now come and put a curse on them, because they're too powerful for me. Perhaps then I'll be able to defeat them and drive them out of the land, for I know that whoever you bless is blessed, and whoever you curse is cursed."

The leaders of Moab and Midian left, taking with them the fee to pay Balaam for the curse. When they reached Balaam, they delivered Balak's message.

"Spend the night here," Balaam said, "and I'll report back to you with the Lord's answer."

So the Moabite leaders stayed with him.

God appeared to Balaam and asked, "Who are these men?"

So Balaam told God about the message Balak had sent to curse Israel.

"Don't go with them," God said. "You must not put a curse on those people, because they have my blessing."

The next morning Balaam got up and said to Balak's officials, "Return to your land, for the Lord refuses to let me go with you."

So the Moabite officials returned and told Balak, "Balaam refused to come with us."

Then Balak sent other leaders, more numerous and more distinguished than the first. They gave Balaam this message: "Don't let anything prevent you from coming, because I'll reward you generously and do whatever you say. Come and put a curse on these people for me."

But Balaam replied, "Even if Balak gave me all the silver and gold in his palace, I couldn't do anything to go against the command of the Lord my God. Now spend the night here and I'll see if the Lord has anything else to say."

That night God said to Balaam, "Go with these men since they have come for you, but do only what I tell you."

Balaam's Donkey Speaks
NM 22:21-41

Balaam got up in the morning, saddled his donkey, and went with the Moabite officials. His two servants were with him. But God was very angry, and the angel of the Lord stood in the road to block Balaam's way. When

Balaam's donkey saw the angel of the Lord standing in the road with a drawn sword, it turned off the road into a field, and Balaam beat it to get it back on the road.

Then the angel of the Lord stood in a narrow path between two vineyards, with a wall on each side. So the donkey pressed close to one of the walls, crushing Balaam's foot against it, and Balaam beat the donkey again.

Then the angel moved ahead and stood in a narrow place where there was no room to pass in either direction, so the donkey stopped and lay down. Balaam lost his temper and beat it with his staff. Then the Lord gave the donkey the ability to speak, and it said to Balaam, "What have I done to make you beat me these three times?"

Balaam said, "You've made a fool of me! If I had a sword, I'd kill you right now."

The donkey replied, "I'm your donkey and you've ridden me all this time. Have I ever done this before?"

"No," Balaam said.

Then the Lord allowed Balaam to see the angel standing in the road with his sword, so he bowed with his face to the ground.

The angel of the Lord asked him, "Why did you beat your donkey? I am blocking your way because your path is one of destruction. The donkey saw me and turned away from me each time. If it hadn't, I certainly would have killed you by now and spared the donkey."

Balaam said, "I've sinned. I didn't realize you were standing in the road. Now if you're displeased, I'll go back."

"No, go with the men, but speak only what I tell you." So Balaam went with Balak's officials.

When Balak heard that Balaam was coming, he went out to meet him at the Moabite city on the Arnon border, at the edge of his territory. Balak said to Balaam, "I sent you an urgent message. Why didn't you come sooner? Don't you believe I'll reward you?"

"Well, I'm here now," Balaam replied. "But I can't say whatever I please. I must say only what God tells me to."

Then Balaam went with Balak to Kiriath-Huzoth, where Balak slaughtered cattle and sheep and fed Balaam and his officials. The next morning Balak took Balaam up to Bamoth-Baal, where he could see the outskirts of the Israelite camp.

Balaam said, "Build me seven altars here and prepare seven bulls and seven rams."

Balak did as Balaam said, and the two of them offered a bull and a ram on each altar.

Then Balaam said to Balak, "Stay here with your offering while I go see if the Lord will meet with me. I'll tell you whatever he reveals to me." Then he went to the top of a barren hill.

God met him there and Balaam said, "I built seven altars and sacrificed a bull and a ram on each."

And the Lord gave him a message for Balak.

So Balaam went back and found Balak standing beside his offering, with all the Moabite officials.

Then Balaam delivered this message: "Balak, king of Moab, brought me from Aram, from the eastern mountains. 'Come, curse Jacob for me,' he said; 'come and announce Israel's doom.' But how can I curse those God hasn't cursed? How can I condemn those the Lord hasn't condemned? From the rocky peaks I can see them, from the hills I can watch them. I see a people who live alone, set apart from other nations. Who can count Jacob's descendants or number even a fourth of them? They are as numerous as dust! Let me die the death of the righteous, and may my final end be like theirs!"

Balak said to Balaam, "What have you done to me? I brought you to curse my enemies, but you've done nothing but bless them!"

"I must speak what the Lord tells me," Balaam replied.

Then Balak said to Balaam, "Let's try another place where you can see some of them. Curse them from there."

So Balak took him to the field of Zophim on top of Mount Pisgah, and he built seven altars and offered a bull and a ram on each.

Balaam said to Balak, "Stay here beside your offering while I go meet with God."

The Lord met with Balaam and sent him back with another message for Balak.

Balaam returned and Balak was standing beside his offering, with the Moabite officials.

"What did the Lord say?" Balak asked.

Then Balaam gave this message: "Arise, Balak, son of Zippor; listen and hear what I have to say. God is not a man, that he should lie, nor a human, that he should change his mind. Does he speak and then not act? Does he promise and not fulfill? I received a command to bless; God has blessed and I can't reverse it.

"There's no misfortune planned for Jacob, no trouble in store for Israel. The Lord their God is with them, and they proclaim him as their King. With the strength of a wild ox, God brought them out of Egypt. No magic curse can touch Jacob; no witchcraft can be used against Israel. Now people will say about Jacob and Israel, 'See what wonders God has done!' The people rise up like a lioness, refusing to rest until it devours its prey and drinks the blood of its victims."

Then Balak said to Balaam, "If you won't curse them, at least don't bless them!"

"Didn't I tell you I must do whatever the Lord says?" Balaam answered.

Balaam's 3rd Message
NM 23:27-30|NM 24:1-9

Then Balak said to Balaam, "I'll take you to another place. Perhaps God will let you curse them from there."

So Balak took Balaam to the top of Mount Peor, overlooking the desert.

Just as before, Balak built seven altars and offered a bull and a ram on each altar.

Since Balaam realized that the Lord intended to bless Israel, he didn't seek omens as he had before, but turned to face the desert. When he saw Israel encamped tribe by tribe, the Spirit of God came upon him and he said:

"This is the prophecy of Balaam son of Beor, the prophecy of one whose eyes see clearly, the prophecy of one who hears the words of God, who sees a vision from the Almighty, who falls into a trance with his eyes uncovered:

"How beautiful are your tents, Jacob; how lovely are your dwelling places, Israel! Like valleys they spread out, like gardens beside a river, like aloes planted by the Lord, like cedars beside the waters. They and their descendants will prosper like an orchard beside a stream. Their king will be greater than Agag; their kingdom will be exalted. God brought them out of Egypt with the strength of a wild ox. They devour hostile nations and break their bones in pieces, piercing them with their arrows. Like a lion they crouch and lie down, like a lioness — who dares to arouse them? May those who bless Israel be blessed and those who curse them be cursed!"

Then Balak's anger burned against Balaam. He pounded his fist against his hand and said, "I asked you to curse my enemies — instead you have blessed them three times! Now get out of here and go home! I promised to generously reward you, but the Lord has kept you from your reward!"

Balaam said, "Like I told your messengers, even if you give me all the silver and gold in your palace, I can't do anything of my own accord, good or bad, to go beyond the command of the Lord. I must say only what the Lord tells me to. Now I'm going to return to my people, but let me warn you of what the Israelites will do to your people in the future.

"This is the prophecy of Balaam son of Beor, the prophecy of one whose eyes see clearly, the prophecy of one who hears the words of God, who has knowledge from the Most High, who sees a vision from the Almighty, who falls into a trance with his eyes uncovered:

"I see him, but not now; I behold him, but in the distant future. A star will rise out of Jacob; a scepter will emerge out of Israel. He'll crush the foreheads of Moab, the skulls of all the people of Sheth. Edom will be conquered, along with its enemy, Seir, but Israel will be victorious. A ruler will arise out of Jacob and destroy the cities' survivors."

Then Balaam had a series of three visions and said:

"Amalek is the greatest of all nations, but its destiny is utter destruction."

"The dwelling place of the Kenites is secure, safe as a nest set high on a cliff. But Assyria will take you captive and you will be destroyed."

Then he spoke his final message, "Alas! Who can survive when God plans destruction? Invaders will sail from the shores of Cyprus and conquer Assyria and Eber, but they too will be utterly destroyed."

Then Balaam returned home, and Balak also left.

While Israel was staying in Shittim, the men began to have sexual intercourse with Moabite women. The women invited them to pagan sacrificial feasts, and the people ate the meal and worshiped the god of Moab, Baal of Peor. So the Lord's anger burned against them.

The Lord said to Moses, "Execute all the people involved and expose them before the Lord in broad daylight, so that my fierce anger will turn away from the Israelites."

So Moses said to Israel's judges, "Kill everyone under your authority who worshiped Baal of Peor."

Then an Israelite man brought a Midianite woman into his tent right in front of Moses and the whole community, while they were weeping at the Tabernacle entrance. Now Phinehas, who was Eleazar's son and Aaron's grandson, saw them enter. He went and got a spear, entered the tent, and drove the spear right through the man and into the woman's stomach. Then the plague against the Israelites stopped, but it had already killed 24,000 people.

The Israelite who was killed with the Midianite woman was Zimri son of Salu, the leader of a family from the tribe of Simeon. The Midianite woman was Cozbi daughter of Zur, the leader of a Midianite clan.

The Lord said to Moses, "Phinehas has appeased my passionate anger against the Israelites, so I didn't destroy them as I had intended. Tell him I'm making my covenant of peace with him. He and his descendants will be my priests forever because, in his zeal for his God, he made atonement for the Israelites' sin."

Then the Lord said to Moses, "The Midianites are now Israel's enemies, so you must destroy them. They deceived you into worshiping Baal at Peor and defiled the camp in the incident involving Cozbi."

CHAPTER 20
The Second Census and Land Assignments

The Second Census
NM 26:1-65|NM 33:50-56|NM 36:1a

After the plague ended, the Lord said to Moses and Eleazar the priest, "Take a census of the whole Israelite community by families — all those age 20 or older who are fit for military service."

So on the plains of Moab by the Jordan across from Jericho, Moses and Eleazar instructed the leaders to take the census, as the Lord commanded.

These were the descendants of Israel, by tribe, who left Egypt:

Reuben (the firstborn son of Israel): There were 43,730 men from Reuben's tribe, consisting of the clans of Hanoch, Pallu, Hezron, and Carmi.

    Pallu's son was Eliab, and Eliab's sons were Nemuel, Dathan, and Abiram. Dathan and Abiram were the community leaders who had conspired with Korah and against Moses and Aaron, rebelling against the Lord. The earth swallowed them up, along with Korah, whose 250 followers were consumed by fire as a warning. But Korah's sons didn't die.

Simeon: There were 22,200 men from Simeon's tribe, consisting of the clans of Nemuel, Jamin, Jachin, Zerah, and Shaul.

Gad: There were 40,500 men from Gad's tribe, consisting of the clans of Zephon, Haggi, Shuni, Ozni, Eri, Arod, and Areli.

Judah: There were 76,500 men from Judah's tribe, consisting of the clans of Shelah, Perez, Zerah, Hezron, and Hamul. Judah's sons Er and Onan had died in Canaan.

Issachar: There were 64,300 men from Issachar's tribe, consisting of the clans of Tola, Puvah, Jashub, and Shimron.

Zebulun: There were 60,500 men from Zebulun's tribe, consisting of the clans of Sered, Elon, and Jahleel.

Joseph's sons:

Manasseh: There were 52,700 men from Manasseh's tribe, consisting of the clans of Machir, his son Gilead, and his six grandsons: Iezer, Helek, Asriel, Shechem, Shemida, and Hepher. Zelophehad son of Hepher had no sons, but he had five daughters: Mahlah, Noah, Hoglah, Milcah, and Tirzah.

Ephraim: There were 32,500 men from Ephraim's tribe, consisting of the clans of Shuthelah, Becher, Tahan, and Eran the son of Shuthelah.

Benjamin: There were 45,600 men from Benjamin's tribe, consisting of the clans of Bela, Ashbel, Ahiram, Shephupham, and Hupham — as well as the clans of Ard and Naaman, Bela's two sons.

Dan: There were 64,400 men from Dan's tribe, consisting of the clan of Shuham.

Asher: There were 53,400 men from Asher's tribe, consisting of the clans of Imnah, Ishvi, and Beriah, and consisting of the two clans of Heber and Malchiel, the sons of Beriah. Asher's daughter was Serah.

Naphtali: There were 45,400 men from Naphtali's tribe, consisting of the clans of Jahzeel, Guni, Jezer, and Shillem.

So the total number of Israelite men fit for battle was 601,730.

Levi: The tribe of Levi included the clans of Gershon, **Kohath**, and Merari, as well as the clans of Libni, Hebron, Mahli, Mushi, and Korah.

Now **Kohath** was the ancestor of **Amram**, whose wife was Jochebed, a descendant of Levi born in Egypt. Their children were **Aaron**, Moses, and their sister Miriam.

Aaron was the father of Nadab, Abihu, Eleazar, and Ithamar. But Nadab and Abihu died when they offered unauthorized fire before the Lord.

All the male Levites a month old or older numbered 23,000. They weren't counted with the other Israelites because they received no inheritance among them.

So Moses and Eleazar counted the people, and not one person that had been counted by Moses and Aaron in the Sinai Desert was still alive. The Lord had said they would all die in the desert, except Caleb son of Jephunneh and Joshua son of Nun, and it happened just as he said.

Then the Lord gave Moses the following instructions for the Israelites: "When you cross the Jordan into Canaan, drive out all the inhabitants of the land. Destroy all their carved images and cast idols, and demolish all their high places. I've given you this land, so take possession of it and settle there. Divide the land among the tribes based on the number of people in each, so that the larger tribes have more land and the smaller tribes have less. Distribute each inheritance by drawing lots, and I will show you what land to give each tribe.

"But if you fail to drive out the inhabitants of the land, they will be as troublesome as splinters in your eyes and thorns in your sides. And then I will do to you what I plan to do to them."

Zelophehad's Daughters Request Property
NM 27:1-11

Now Zelophehad and his daughters, Mahlah, Noah, Hoglah, Milkah, and Tirzah, were from the tribe of Manasseh. The daughters approached Moses, Eleazar, the leaders, and the whole community at the Tabernacle entrance and said, "Our father died in the desert, but he died for his own sin; he wasn't one of Korah's followers, who rebelled against the Lord. He had no sons, but why should our father's name disappear from his clan? Give us property among our father's relatives."

So Moses brought their case before the Lord. "Yes, they are right," the Lord said. "Give each of them part of the land that their father would have inherited.

"Tell the Israelites: If a man dies and leaves no son, give his inheritance to his daughter. If he has no daughter, give his inheritance to his brothers. If he has no brothers, give his inheritance to his father's brothers. If his father had no brothers, give his inheritance to the nearest relative in his clan. This is a legal requirement for the Israelites, just as I, the Lord, have commanded you."

Joshua Appointed Moses' Successor
NM 27:12-23

Then the Lord said to Moses, "Climb the Abarim mountains so you can see the land I am giving the Israelites. Afterward you will die just as your brother Aaron did, because when the community rebelled at the waters of Meribah Kadesh in the Desert of Zin, neither of you trusted in me enough to acknowledge me as holy to the Israelites."

Moses replied, "O Lord God, who gives breath to all living things, please appoint someone to lead the community. Give them someone who can lead them in battle so your people won't be like sheep without a shepherd."

"Joshua son of Nun has the spirit of leadership in him," the Lord said. "Have him stand before Eleazar the priest and the entire community; lay hands on him and commission him to lead the people. Give him some of your authority so the Israelites will obey him. But when direction from the Lord is required, Eleazar will obtain decisions for him using the Urim to seek the Lord's counsel. In this way Eleazar will direct Joshua and the community regarding when they should go to battle and when they should retreat."

So Moses laid his hands on Joshua and commissioned him before Eleazar and the whole community, as the Lord commanded.

Vengeance on the Midianites
NM 31:1-24

The Lord said to Moses, "Take vengeance on the Midianites on the Israelites' behalf. After that, you will join your ancestors in death."

So Moses said to the people, "Choose 1,000 men from each tribe to go to battle against the Midianites and carry out the Lord's vengeance." So Moses sent 12,000 armed men into battle, as the Lord commanded. Phinehas, son of Eleazar the priest, went with them, carrying some articles from the sanctuary and the trumpets for signaling.

They attacked Midian and killed the men, including Balaam son of Beor and the five kings of Midian: Evi, Rekem, Zur, Hur, and Reba. They captured the women and children and took all the cattle, flocks, and property as plunder. Then they burned all the cities where the Midianites lived, as well as their camps. They brought everything they had taken, including the people and animals, to Moses, Eleazar, and the Israelite community while they were camped on the plains of Moab beside the Jordan River, across from Jericho.

Moses, Eleazar, and the other leaders met the army outside the camp. But Moses was angry with the commanders of the army. "Why did you allow the women to live?" he asked. "They followed Balaam's advice and enticed the Israelites to be unfaithful to the Lord at Peor, causing a plague to strike the Lord's people. Now kill all the boys and all the women except the virgins; you can keep them for yourselves.

"Those who have killed anyone or touched a corpse must stay outside the camp for seven days. On the third and seventh days, you must purify yourselves and your captives, as well as any clothing and anything made of leather, goat hair, or wood."

Then Eleazar said to the soldiers who had returned from battle, "Gold, silver, bronze, iron, tin, lead, and anything else that can stand it must be put through fire, and then purified with the water of cleansing, as the Lord commanded Moses. Use the water of cleansing for anything else that can't withstand fire. Wash your clothes on the seventh day. You will then be clean and can return to the camp."

Dividing the Spoils
NM 31:25-54

The Lord said to Moses, "You, Eleazar, and the family leaders of each tribe must count all the people and animals that were captured. Divide the spoils equally between the soldiers and the rest of the community. From the soldiers' portion, first give the Lord his share: one out of every 500, whether people or animals. Give them to Eleazar as an offering to the Lord. From the Israelites' half, select one out of every 50 and give them to the Levites, who are responsible for the Lord's Tabernacle."

So Moses and Eleazar did as the Lord commanded and made a list of everything that had been taken from the Midianites, which totaled 675,000 sheep and goats, 72,000 cattle, 61,000 donkeys, and 32,000 virgins.

Each half included 337,500 sheep and goats, 36,000 cattle, 30,500 donkeys, and 16,000 virgins. From the half that belonged to the soldiers, Moses gave 675 sheep and goats, 72 cattle, 61 donkeys, and 32 virgins to Eleazar to be dedicated to the Lord. From the half that belonged to the Israelites, Moses selected one out of every 50 animals and women and gave them to the Levites.

Then the commanders of the army went to Moses and said, "Your servants have counted the soldiers under our command, and no one is missing. So we are bringing the gold articles, armbands, bracelets, rings, earrings, and necklaces we acquired. We are giving them to the Lord as payment for our lives and to make atonement for ourselves."

The items that each soldier had taken weighed about 420 pounds. Moses and Eleazar accepted the gold from the commanders and presented them as a gift to the Lord, bringing them into the Tabernacle as a memorial of what they had done.

The Transjordan Tribes
NM 32:1-42|DT 3:13b|DT 3:14

The tribes of Reuben and Gad had large herds and flocks. They saw that the lands of Jazer and Gilead had good pastures, so they approached Moses, Eleazar, and the other leaders. "The Lord has helped us capture this land," they said, "and Ataroth, Dibon, Jazer, Nimrah, Heshbon, Elealeh, Sebam, Nebo, and Beon have pastures for all our livestock. If you are pleased with your servants, don't make us cross the Jordan; give us this land as our possession."

Moses said, "Do you expect the rest of the Israelites to go to war while you just sit here? Why are you discouraging them from crossing over? Your ancestors did the same thing when I sent them from Kadesh-Barnea up to the Valley of Eshkol to explore the land, and they discouraged the Israelites from entering. The Lord's anger burned against Israel that day. He swore that no one age 20 or older who had left Egypt would see the land the Lord had promised to Abraham, Isaac, and Jacob. Only Caleb son of Jephunneh the Kenizzite and Joshua son of Nun remained faithful. So the Lord made that whole generation wander in the desert 40 years, until they all died.

"And now, you brood of sinners, here you are behaving just like them and making the Lord even angrier. If you turn away from following him, he'll once again leave all these people in the desert, and you'll be responsible for their destruction."

They replied, "We want to build pens here for our livestock and fortified cities for our families. They will live here, protected from the inhabitants of the land, but we'll still go to battle with the other tribes until they have claimed the land. We won't return to our homes until each tribe has received its inheritance. We won't claim any land on the other side of the Jordan, because our inheritance will be here on the east side."

"Ok," Moses said, "if you assist the tribes in battle until the Lord has driven out his enemies, then you will fulfill your obligation to the Lord and to Israel. Then you can return to this land and it will be your possession. But if you fail to keep your promise, you'll be sinning against the Lord, and you will certainly be punished. Go ahead and build cities for your families and pens for your flocks, but make sure you keep your promise."

"We, your servants, will do as our lord commands," the men of Reuben and Gad replied. "Our families, flocks, and cattle will remain here in the cities of Gilead, but we'll cross over to fight for the Lord."

Then Moses said to Eleazar, Joshua, and the leaders of the tribes, "If the tribes of Reuben and Gad keep their promise, give them the land of Gilead as their possession. But if they fail to keep their promise, they must accept land with the rest of you in Canaan."

The tribes of Gad and Reuben replied, "We are your servants and we'll do what the Lord commands. We'll cross over into Canaan for battle, but we'll inherit the property on this side of the Jordan."

So Moses gave to the tribes of Gad, Reuben, and half the tribe of Manasseh the kingdom of Sihon king of the Amorites and the kingdom of Og king of Bashan — the whole land with its cities and surrounding territory.

The tribe of Gad rebuilt Dibon, Ataroth, Aroer, Atroth-Shophan, Jazer, Jogbehah, Beth-Nimrah, and Beth-Haran as fortified cities, and built pens for their flocks. And the tribe of Reuben rebuilt Heshbon, Elealeh, and Kiriathaim, as well as Nebo and Baal-Meon. They changed the names of some of the cities they rebuilt.

The descendants of Machir, Manasseh's son, captured Gilead and drove out the Amorites. So Moses gave Gilead to them and they settled there. And Nobah captured Kenath and its surrounding villages and named the area Nobah, after himself.

Jair, another descendant of Manasseh, conquered the whole Argob region of Bashan, as far as the border of Geshur and Maacah. Bashan was known as the land of the Rephaim. Jair captured many cities in Gilead and changed the name of that region to *Havvoth-Jair* (which means *villages of Jair*).

Stages in Israel's Journey
NM 33:1-38a|NM 33:41-49

At the Lord's command, Moses kept a written record of the Israelites' progress after he and Aaron led them out of Egypt, tribe by tribe. This is a record of their journey:

The Israelites left the Egyptian city of Rameses on the 15th day of the 1st month, the day after the first Passover. They marched out triumphantly in full view of the Egyptians, who were burying their firstborn. The Lord had struck them down, demonstrating his power over Egypt's gods.

After the Israelites left Rameses, they camped at Sukkoth and from there they moved their camp to Etham, on the edge of the desert. Then they turned back to Pi-Hahiroth, east of Baal-Zephon, and camped near Migdol. They left Pi-Hahiroth and crossed the Red Sea. They traveled for three days in the Etham Desert and camped at Marah.

Next they camped at Elim, where there were 12 springs of water and 70 palm trees. They left Elim and camped by the Red Sea and then camped in the Desert of Sin. From there they camped at Dophkah, Alush, and Rephidim, where they had no water. They left Rephidim and camped in the Sinai Desert, and from there they camped in the following places: Kibroth-Hattaavah, Hazeroth, Rithmah, Rimmon-Perez, Libnah, Rissah, Kehelathah, Mount Shepher, Haradah, Makheloth, Tahath,

Terah, Mithkah, Hashmonah, Moseroth, Bene-Jaakan, Hor-Haggidgad, Jotbathah, Abronah, Ezion-Geber, and finally Kadesh, in the Zin Desert.

From Kadesh they camped at Mount Hor, on the border of Edom, where Aaron died.

From Mount Hor they traveled toward Moab and camped at the following places on the way: Zalmonah; Punon; Oboth; Iye-Abarim in the territory of Moab; Dibon-Gad; Almon-Diblathaim, near Mount Nebo in the Abarim Mountains; and finally on the plains of Moab beside the Jordan River, across from Jericho. Along the Jordan River, they camped from Beth-Jeshimoth as far as Abel-Shittim.

The Boundaries of Canaan
NM 34:1-29

The Lord gave Moses the following instructions for the Israelites: When you enter Canaan, the land allotted to you must have these boundaries on each side:

The southern border will extend from the Zin Desert along the border of Edom. It will begin on the east at the southern end of the Dead Sea. Then it will run south toward Scorpion Pass, continue on to Zin, and end south of Kadesh-Barnea. Then it will go to Hazar-Addar and on to Azmon, where it will turn toward the Brook of Egypt and end at the Mediterranean Sea.

The western border will be the Mediterranean Sea.

The northern border will begin at the Mediterranean Sea and run eastward to Mount Hor, then to Lebo-Hamath and continue to Zedad, then to Ziphron, and end at Hazar-Enan.

The eastern border will begin at Hazar-Enan and run south to Shepham. It will then go to Riblah on the east side of Ain and continue along the eastern hills of the Sea of Galilee, then south along the Jordan River, ending at the Dead Sea.

Then Moses said to the Israelites, "Assign this land as an inheritance to the nine and a half tribes by drawing lots, as the Lord commanded. Remember that the tribes of Reuben, Gad, and half of Manasseh already received their land east of the Jordan River, across from Jericho."

Then the Lord said to Moses, "Eleazar and Joshua must divide the land with the help of one leader from each tribe." These are the tribes and their leaders who were to assign the inheritance to the Israelites:

Judah: Caleb son of Jephunneh
Simeon: Shemuel son of Ammihud
Benjamin: Elidad son of Chislon

Dan: Bukki son of Jogli
Manasseh (son of Joseph): Hanniel son of Ephod
Ephraim (son of Joseph): Kemuel son of Shiphtan
Zebulun: Elizaphan son of Parnach
Issachar: Paltiel son of Azzan
Asher: Ahihud son of Shelomi
Naphtali: Pedahel son of Ammihud

Assigned Cities for the Levites
NM 35:1-5|NM 35:6b-8

Then the Lord gave Moses the following instructions: From the Israelites' portion, give the Levites 48 cities to live in and pasturelands for all their livestock. The cities must be assigned in proportion to each tribe's inheritance. Take many cities from a tribe that has many, but few from one that has few.

The pasture land will extend 1,500 feet from the city wall in each direction. Outside the city, measure 3,000 feet in every direction—north, south, east, and west, with the city in the center.

Cities of Refuge
NM 35:6a|NM 35:9-34

Six of the cities you give the Levites will be cities of refuge. These are cities where a person may flee if they accidentally kill someone. There they will be protected from relatives seeking revenge. They must not be put to death before standing trial for murder before the community. Assign three cities of refuge on this side of the Jordan and three in Canaan. These cities of refuge are both for Israelites and foreign residents.

But anyone who uses a weapon of iron, stone, or wood to kill someone is guilty of murder.

If anyone hates someone and with malicious intent pushes that person, throws an object at him, or punches him, and he dies, it is murder. The guilty party must be put to death by the victim's nearest relative as soon as he finds him.

But suppose there is no hostility and no harm is intended and someone accidentally kills a person, whether by pushing him, throwing something at him, or dropping a heavy stone on him. Then the community must rule in favor of the accused and protect him from the victim's relative who is seeking revenge. The person accused of murder can return to the city of refuge and must stay there until the death of the High Priest.

But if the accused leaves the city of refuge before the High Priest dies, and is found outside the city, the person seeking revenge may kill him without being guilty of murder. Only after the death of the High Priest may the accused return to his own property.

This a permanent law for the generations to come, wherever you live.

No one can be executed as a murderer unless two or more witnesses testify that he is guilty. One witness is not enough.

Don't accept payment to spare the life of a murderer. He deserves to die and must be put to death. Don't accept payment to allow the accused to leave a city of refuge and return to his own land before the death of the High Priest. These rules ensure that the land is not defiled. Murder pollutes the land, and atonement can be made only by the death of the murderer. Don't defile the land where you live, for I, the Lord, also live among the Israelites.

Land Must Not Pass Between Tribes
NM 36:1-12

One day the family leaders from the Gilead clan of the Manasseh tribe went to Moses and the other leaders. "Sir," they said, "the Lord commanded you to divide the land by lot and to give our brother Zelophehad's inheritance to his daughters. But if they marry men from other tribes, their inheritance will be taken from us and given to the tribe they marry into, and the total land allotted to us will be reduced. Even in the Year of Restoration, the land wouldn't return to us, because it will permanently belong to the tribe they married into."

So Moses gave the Israelites the following command from the Lord: "Joseph's descendants are right. Zelophehad's daughters may marry anyone they please as long as they marry within their own tribe. The same is true for any women who inherit land. No land must pass from one tribe to another, it must remain the property of the tribe who received it. In this way the Israelites will keep the property of their ancestors.

So Zelophehad's daughters — Mahlah, Tirzah, Hoglah, Milkah, and Noah — did as the Lord commanded and married their cousins on their father's side. So their inheritance remained within the tribe of Manasseh.

THE SERMONS OF MOSES

MOSES' FIRST SERMON

CHAPTER 21
Reflections on Israel's Journeys

Prologue to Moses' First Sermon
NM 36:13|DT 1:1|DT 1:3|DT 1:5|DT 4:44-47

40 years after they left Egypt, the Israelites stayed for a while on the plains of Moab by the Jordan across from Jericho. There the Lord had given various commands and regulations to the Israelites through Moses.

The Lord had defeated the Amorite kings Sihon and Og. There in the land that had belonged to King Sihon, the Israelites camped in the Jordan Valley near Suph, opposite Beth-Peor, in the desert east of the Jordan River. The city of Paran was in one direction, and the cities of Tophel, Laban, Hazeroth, and Dizahab were in the other direction.

On the 1st day of the 11th month, Moses addressed the Israelites. These are the words he spoke, reminding them of all the Lord's commands:

The Command to Leave Mount Sinai
DT 1:6-8

When we were at Mount Sinai, the Lord our God said we had stayed there long enough. So we broke camp as he directed and went into the hill country of the Amorites and their neighbors, the Canaanites, which included the Jordan Valley, the hill country, the western foothills, the Negev, the coastal plain, and Lebanon — all the land as far as the great Euphrates River. The Lord gave us this land that he promised to your ancestors — Abraham, Isaac, and Jacob — and to their descendants. And he instructed us to take possession of the land.

The Appointment of Leaders
DT 1:9-18

The Lord your God, the God of your ancestors, increased your numbers and made you as numerous as the stars in the sky. And I pray that he would multiply you a thousand times more and bless you as he promised! But because there were so many of you, I couldn't bear your problems, burdens, and disputes all by myself. So I told you to choose from each tribe some wise, understanding, and respected men whom I would appoint as leaders. And you agreed that my plan was a good one.

So I appointed the men to have authority over you. Some of them became military commanders in charge of groups of thousands, hundreds, fifties, and tens. Others became judges, and I gave them the following instructions: Judge fairly when you listen to their disputes, whether the case involves Israelites or foreign residents. Judge everyone on the same basis, regardless of their status. Don't be intimidated by anyone, for the decisions you make come from God. If any case is too hard for you, bring it to me and I will handle it.

After this I gave you the Lord's commands.

Spies Sent to Canaan
DT 1:19-25

So we left Mount Sinai as the Lord our God commanded us. You remember that vast and terrifying desert we traveled through on the way to the hill country of the Amorites. Finally, we reached Kadesh-Barnea. Then I told you we had reached the land the Lord our God is giving us and instructed you to go take possession of it. The Lord, the God of your ancestors, commanded it, so I urged you not to hesitate or be afraid.

Then you asked me to send men to explore the land and bring back a report about the cities and the best plan of attack. I agreed and selected 12 men, one from each tribe, and they explored the hill country as far as the Valley of Eshkol. They brought back some of the land's fruit and reported that the land the Lord our God is giving us is good.

Rebellion Against the Lord
DT 1:26-46

But you rebelled against the Lord's command and refused to enter the land. You stayed in your tents and complained, saying, "The Lord hates us, so he brought us out of Egypt to deliver us to the Amorites so they can destroy us. The men terrified us when they said the people are stronger and taller than we are, and the cities are large, with walls up to the sky. They even saw giants — the descendants of Anak! How can we go now?"

But I told you not to be terrified or afraid of them. The Lord your God will lead you, and he will fight for you, as you saw with your own eyes in Egypt and in the desert. He has carried you safely all the way to this place, just as a father carries his son. He led you in fire by night and in a cloud by day, showing you the way to go and where to camp. But still you didn't trust in the Lord your God, and he heard your complaints and became angry. He solemnly swore no one from that evil generation would see the good land he promised your ancestors. However, Caleb followed the Lord wholeheartedly, so the Lord will give him and his descendants part of the land he explored.

The Lord even became angry with me because of you and won't allow me to enter the land either. Instead, he told me to encourage my assistant, Joshua. He will enter the land and lead Israel as they take possession of it.

The Lord also said your children, who were still too young to know right from wrong, would enter the land and take possession of it — the very children you said would be taken captive.

So he told us to turn around and go back through the desert toward the Red Sea.

Then you confessed you had sinned against the Lord and decided to go up and fight, as the Lord your God had originally commanded. So all of you strapped on weapons, thinking it would be easy to go attack the hill country.

But the Lord said not to go up and fight, because he wouldn't be with you, and your enemies would defeat you. But you arrogantly rebelled against the Lord's command and marched up into the hill country. The Amorites who lived there attacked you, chasing you like a swarm of bees from Seir all the way to Hormah, and they defeated you. You came back and wept before the Lord, but he paid no attention to you and denied your requests. And so you stayed in Kadesh for a long time.

Wanderings in the Desert
DT 2:1-23

After a while we turned around and headed back into the desert toward the Red Sea, as the Lord had directed. For many years we wandered around the mountain range of Seir, until the Lord said we had wandered enough and told us to turn north. We were getting ready to pass through the land of our relatives, Esau's descendants who live in Seir. (The Horites used to live in Seir, but the Lord destroyed them. Esau's descendants drove them out and settled in their region, and they have lived there to this day. In the same way, the Israelites later drove out the Canaanites when the Lord gave them their land.) The Lord warned us that they would be afraid of us, but we should not start a war with them. He has given Esau and his descendants the hill country of Seir and therefore wouldn't give us even a square foot of their land. If we ate any of their food or drank their water, we were instructed to pay them in silver.

Remember that the Lord your God has blessed you in everything you have done. He has watched over you every step of the way as you traveled through this vast desert these 40 years, and you have lacked nothing.

So we bypassed the land of our relatives, avoiding the road through the Arabah Valley that runs from Elath and Ezion-Geber, and turning north along the desert route toward Moab.

Then the Lord instructed us not to bother or attack the Moabites. He wouldn't give us any part of their land because he had given it to Lot's descendants.

(Before the Lord gave the land to the Moabites, a numerous and powerful group of people lived there. They were as tall as the Anakim, another race of giants. The Moabites called them Emim, although others referred to both the Anakim and the Emim as Rephaim.)

The Lord instructed us to cross the Zered Valley. 38 years passed from the time we left Kadesh-Barnea until we crossed the Zered Valley. By then, the entire generation of men old enough to fight in battle had died, as the Lord had said they would. The Lord struck them down until he completely eliminated them from the community.

When the last of them had died, the Lord instructed us to cross Moab's border at Ar. He told us not to bother or attack the Ammonites. He wouldn't give us any part of their land because he had given it to Lot's descendants.

(Before the Ammonites conquered the land, the Rephaim had lived there, but the Ammonites called them Zamzummim. They were also numerous and powerful, and as tall as the Anakim. The Lord destroyed them and the Ammonites drove them out and settled there. The same thing happened when the Philistines from Caphtor destroyed the Avvim, who lived in villages as far south as Gaza, and settled in their place.)

Two Amorite Kings Defeated
DT 2:24-37|DT 3:1-11|DT 4:48

After we had passed through Moab, the Lord commanded us to cross the Arnon River. He promised to allow us to attack King Sihon and give us his land. From that day, he promised to make the nations throughout the earth terrified of us. They would tremble with fear at the mention of our name. So I sent messengers from the Kedemoth Desert to King Sihon offering peace, saying, "Let us pass through your country as Esau's descendants did in Seir and the Moabites did in Ar. We'll stay on the main road and won't veer off into your land. Sell us food and water and we'll pay the appropriate price in silver. We just need to cross the Jordan into the land the Lord our God is giving us."

But King Sihon refused and the Lord your God made him stubborn and rebellious so we could defeat him, as we have already done. The Lord told us to go ahead and take possession of the land because he was giving it to us. Sihon and his army battled us at Jahaz, and the Lord our God helped us defeat him, his sons, and everyone else in his army. We captured and destroyed all the cities and completely destroyed the men, women, and children, leaving no survivors. But we kept the livestock and anything else of value for ourselves. With the Lord's help, we captured all the cities from the Arnon River all the way to Gilead, including the city of Aroer on the edge of the valley and the city in the middle of the valley. Not one city had walls that were too strong for us.

The Lord our God gave us all of these cities. But as he commanded, we didn't go near the land of the Ammonites, the land along the Jabbok River, or the land around the cities in the hill country.

Next we turned north toward the region of Bashan, where King Og ruled. He and his whole army attacked us at Edrei. The Lord said not to be afraid, because he had given us victory over the king, his army, and his land. He would help us defeat him as we had defeated King Sihon.

So we took all Bashan as far as Salekah and Edrei, all 60 cities of Og's kingdom — which included all the cities on the plateau — the region of Gilead, and the Argob region. The cities were fortified with high walls and barred gates, but many of the villages were unwalled. We took all the livestock and other items of value for ourselves, but we completely destroyed each city, including the men, women, and children, leaving no survivors.

(King Og was the last survivor of the Rephaim. His coffin was made of iron and was more than 13 feet long and 6 feet wide. It's still located in the Ammonite city of Rabbah.)

So we took from these two Amorite kings the land east of the Jordan River, all the way from the city of Aroer on the edge of the Arnon River to Mount Hermon. (The Sidonians call Mount Hermon "Sirion" and the Amorites call it "Senir.")

The Division of the Land
DT 3:12-13a|DT 3:15-22|DT 4:49

When we took possession of the land east of the Jordan, I assigned the tribes of Reuben and Gad half the hill country of Gilead and its cities. This included the territory extending from Gilead down to the territory north of Aroer by the Arnon River. The middle of the river formed the southern border. The northern part of their land extended to the Jabbok River, which formed the Ammonite border.

I assigned the other half of Gilead and all of King Og's kingdom, Bashan, to half the tribe of Manasseh. And I assigned the northern half of Gilead to the descendants of Machir, Manasseh's son.

On the west, the territory of the three tribes extended to the Jordan River, from Lake Galilee in the north to the Dead Sea in the south, and to the foot of Mount Pisgah in the east.

And then I told the three tribes: "The Lord your God has given you this land east of the Jordan. Leave your wives, children, and your large herds of cattle here in the cities assigned to you, but arm all your able-bodied men for battle. You must lead the way across the Jordan in helping your fellow Israelites conquer the land. After the Lord gives them victory, you may return to your homes."

And then I said to Joshua, "You saw with your own eyes everything the Lord your God did to King Sihon and King Og. He will do the same to all the kingdoms across the Jordan. So don't be afraid of them; the Lord himself will fight for you."

Moses Forbidden to Cross the Jordan
DT 3:23-29|DT 4:21

The Lord was angry with me because of you, and he solemnly swore that I wouldn't cross the Jordan and enter the fertile land he's giving you as your inheritance. I pleaded, "Sovereign Lord, you've only just begun to show your greatness and power to me, your servant. For what god in heaven or on earth can do the mighty things you do? Please allow me to cross over the Jordan and see the fertile land, the beautiful hill country, and the Lebanon mountains."

But the Lord wouldn't grant my request. "That's enough," he said. "Don't bring it up again. Now go to the top of Mount Pisgah and look to the north, south, east, and west. Take a good look, because you're not going to cross the Jordan River. Joshua will be the one to lead these people across and enable them to inherit the land. So give Joshua his instructions and encourage and strengthen him."

Afterward we stayed in the valley near Beth-Peor.

Moses Urges Obedience
DT 4:1-14

Now people of Israel, listen to these laws and regulations. Obey them so that you will live and take possession of the land that the Lord, the God of your ancestors, is giving you. Don't add to or subtract from the commands I'm giving you. You saw with your own eyes how the Lord your God destroyed everyone who worshiped Baal at Mount Peor, but all who remained faithful to the Lord your God are still alive today.

I have given you the laws as the Lord my God instructed. No other nation is so great as to have such righteous laws as those I'm giving you today. Follow them faithfully when you enter the land, and then all the nations will hear about your obedience and say, "Surely this great nation is wise and intelligent." Do you know what makes us greater than other nations? Our God is near to us and answers when we call upon him.

Remember the day the Lord told me to gather you together so you could hear his words and learn to revere him as long as you live in the land. You stood before the Lord your God at the foot of Mount Sinai while it blazed with fire to the very heavens, with black clouds and deep darkness. When the Lord spoke to you out of the fire, you heard only his voice but saw no form. And he declared to you his covenant, the Ten Commandments, which he commanded you to follow, and then he wrote them on two stone tablets. And he directed me to teach you the decrees and laws to follow in the land that you're crossing the Jordan to possess. But watch out and be careful. Make sure you don't forget the things your eyes have seen; don't let the memories fade as long as you live. Teach them to your children and grandchildren.

Warning Against Worshiping Idols
DT 4:15-20|DT 4:22-31

When the Lord spoke to you from the fire at Mount Sinai, you saw no visible form of any kind; you heard only his voice. Therefore, be very careful so that you don't corrupt yourselves. Don't make any idols or images of any shape, whether man or a woman, animals on earth, birds in the air, crawling creatures, or fish in the waters below. And when you look up to the sky and see the heavenly array — the sun, the moon, and the stars — don't be tempted to worship them. The Lord your God has provided them for the benefit of every nation under heaven. But the Lord set you apart and brought you out of Egypt, out of the iron furnace, to be his people.

I won't be crossing the Jordan River, because I will die here, but you will cross over and take possession of that fertile land. And when you do, be sure not to forget the covenant the Lord your God made with you; don't make any idols in any form, for the Lord your God is like a consuming fire, destroying everything in its path. He is a jealous God and will tolerate no rivals.

Soon you will cross the Jordan River and live in the land, and you will have children and grandchildren. After many years have passed, you might forget the Lord's commands and start worshipping idols, even though you know he considers this evil, and you will provoke the Lord to anger. Today

I call heaven and earth as witnesses against you that you won't live long if you do this, because the Lord will wipe you out and scatter you among the nations, where only a few of you will survive. While you're there you'll worship gods of wood and stone, gods that can't see, hear, eat, or smell.

In the future when you're suffering all these things, then you'll return to the Lord your God and obey him. And if you seek him with all your heart and with all your soul, you'll find him. For the Lord your God is merciful and won't abandon or destroy you. He won't forget the covenant he made with your ancestors.

The Lord Is God
DT 4:32-40

Has any other people heard the voice of God speaking out of the fire and lived? Has any god ever tried to take for himself one nation out of another nation, by testings, by signs and wonders, by war, by a mighty hand and an outstretched arm, or by great and awesome deeds, as the Lord your God did in Egypt?

When the Lord brought you out of Egypt, he took you from one nation and made you his own nation. You saw with your own eyes how he made the Egyptians suffer, using plagues and war, miracles and wonders, and other terrifying events. What other god has ever dared to do such a thing? At Mount Sinai you heard him speaking from the midst of the fire, and yet you are still alive! What other people have ever experienced this? Search throughout history, from the time God created humans until now. Search from one end of the heavens to the other, and you'll find that no one has ever heard of a god doing the things the Lord your God has done for you.

But the Lord showed you these things so you would know that he alone is God. He spoke from heaven and allowed you to hear his voice from out of the fire to discipline you. He loved your ancestors and chose you to be his people, so he brought you out of Egypt by his great power. Now you're facing nations larger and stronger than you, but the Lord has already started driving them out of their land so he can give it to you.

Remember today and never forget that the Lord is God, whether in heaven above or on the earth below. There is no other god. Obey the Lord's commands that I'm giving you today, and all will go well with you and your descendants. You will live a long time in the land the Lord your God is giving you, and it will belong to you forever.

MOSES' SECOND SERMON

CHAPTER 22
The Ten Commandments and Laws
Related to the 1st and 2nd Commandments

Worship Only God

Reminder of the Ten Commandments
DT 5:1-31

Moses summoned Israel again and said: Listen to the laws and regulations I'm giving you today; learn them and obey them. The Lord our God made a covenant with our ancestors at Mount Sinai, but he didn't make the covenant only with them, he made it with all of us who are here today. And this is what the Lord said:

I am the Lord your God, who brought you out of Egypt, out of the land of slavery.

1. Do not worship any other god but me.
2. Do not carve out idols in the image of anything in heaven above, on the earth beneath, or in the waters below. Do not bow down to them or worship them, because I, the Lord your God, am a jealous God, punishing the children for the sin of the parents to the third and fourth generation of those who hate me, but showing love to a thousand generations of those who love me and keep my commandments.
3. Do not misuse the name of the Lord your God; anyone who misuses my name will not go unpunished.
4. Observe the Sabbath day by keeping it holy, as the Lord commanded. You can do all your work in six days, but the seventh day must be dedicated to the Lord your God as a day of rest. Neither you, your children, your servants, your livestock, nor foreign residents

may do any work on the Sabbath. Your servants need rest just as you do. Remember that you were slaves in Egypt and the Lord freed you with a mighty hand and an outstretched arm; therefore he has commanded you to observe the Sabbath.

5. Honor your father and mother so you may have long life and so all will go well with you in the land I'm giving you.
6. Do not commit murder.
7. Do not commit adultery.
8. Do not steal.
9. Do not give false testimony against your neighbor.
10. Do not covet your neighbor's house, land, wife, servants, livestock, or anything else that belongs to your neighbor.

After the Lord proclaimed them in a loud voice from out of the fire, the cloud, and the deep darkness, he wrote only these ten commandments on two stone tablets and gave them to me.

The Lord spoke to you there face to face, but when you heard the voice and the mountain was ablaze with fire, your tribe leaders and elders said to me, "The Lord our God has shown us his glory and majesty. Today we have seen that it's possible for people to live even if God speaks with them. But this great fire will consume us and we'll certainly die if we hear his voice again. Why should we take the risk? Has anyone ever heard the voice of the living God from the fire, as we did, and survived? You go and listen to everything the Lord our God says and tell us whatever he tells you. We'll listen and obey."

The Lord heard you and said to me, "I agree with them. If only they would always have hearts that would fear me and always keep my commands, so that they and their descendants will prosper forever! Tell them to return to their tents. You stay here with me and I will give you all the laws they should follow in the land I'm giving them."

So I stood between him and you to give you his word, because you were afraid of the fire and didn't want to approach the mountain.

The Golden Calf
DT 9:7-29|DT 10:4b

Don't ever forget how you made the Lord your God angry in the desert. You've been rebellious against the Lord from the day you left Egypt until now. At Mount Sinai you made him angry enough to destroy you. I ascended the mountain to receive the tablets of stone containing the Lord's covenant with you, and I stayed there 40 days and 40 nights, eating and drinking nothing. The Lord inscribed on the tablets with his own finger the commandments he proclaimed to you out of the fire.

Then he gave me the tablets and said, "Go down at once, because your people whom you brought out of Egypt have become corrupt. They turned quickly away from my commands and made an idol. These people are stubborn indeed! Leave me alone so I can destroy them and blot out their name from the face of the earth. And I'll make you into a stronger and more numerous nation than they are."

So I descended the mountain while it was ablaze with fire, carrying the Ten Commandments. When I saw that you had made an idol in the shape of a calf, I threw the two tablets down, breaking them to pieces right before your eyes. I burned that sinful calf, crushed it and ground it to powder as fine as dust, and threw the dust into a stream that flowed down the mountain.

You also made the Lord angry at Taberah, Massah, and Kibroth-Hattaavah. At Kadesh-Barnea you didn't trust him enough to obey him and take possession of the land. You have rebelled against the Lord ever since I've known you!

When you made the calf, you sinned against the Lord your God, doing what was evil in his sight. I was afraid because he was angry enough to destroy you, and Aaron too. But once again I prayed to the Lord for 40 days and 40 nights, fasting and praying for you and Aaron. "Sovereign Lord," I prayed, "remember your servants Abraham, Isaac, and Jacob. Don't destroy your people, who belong to you. You rescued them and brought them out of Egypt with a mighty hand. Overlook their stubbornness, their wickedness, and their sin. If you destroy them, the Egyptians will say, 'Their God was unable to take them into the land he promised them; he hates them so much that he brought them into the desert to die.'"

And the Lord granted my request.

The Second Set of Tablets
DT 10:1-4a|DT 10:5-11

Then the Lord said to me, "Chisel out two more stone tablets and make a wooden Ark. Ascend the mountain and I'll write the same commandments that were on the tablets you broke. Then put the tablets in the Ark."

So I did as the Lord commanded. I made the ark out of acacia wood and chiseled out two stone tablets. I ascended the mountain with them, and the Lord wrote the Ten Commandments and gave them to me. Then I descended the mountain and put the tablets in the Ark, and they're still there now.

Again I stayed on the mountain 40 days and 40 nights. The Lord had granted my request because it wasn't his will to destroy you. So he told

THE CHRONOLOGICAL WORD TRUTH LIFE BIBLE

me, "Go and lead the people on their way, so they can possess the land I promised to their ancestors."

Remember on the day you made the calf, the Lord set apart the tribe of Levi to carry the Ark of the Covenant, to minister before the Lord, and pronounce blessings in his name, as they still do today. That's why the Levites have no share or inheritance among their fellow Israelites; the Lord is their inheritance, as the Lord your God told them.

Aaron didn't die that day at Mount Sinai. Remember after we traveled from the wells of Bene-Jaakan, Aaron died and was buried at Mount Hor in the vicinity of Moserah. His son Eleazar succeeded him as priest. Then we traveled to Hor-Haggidgad and on to Jotbathah, a land flowing with streams of water.

Love and Obey the Lord Your God
DT 5:32-33|DT 6:1-25|DT 7:11-15|DT 8:1-20|DT 11:1-17

Hear, O Israel, the Lord our God is God alone. Love the Lord your God with all your heart and with all your soul and with all your strength. Keep all these commandments in your hearts and teach them repeatedly to your children. Talk about them always, whether at home or out on the road, whether going to bed at night or getting up in the morning. Tie them as symbols on your hands and your foreheads. Write them on the doorframes of your houses and on the gates of your cities.

Remember today that it was you and not your children who experienced the discipline of the Lord your God. When he brought you out of Egypt, out of the land of slavery, you saw his majesty, his power, the miracles, and everything thing he did to Pharaoh and his whole country. You saw what he did to the Egyptian army; he overwhelmed its horses and chariots with the waters of the Red Sea as they pursued you, completely destroying them.

Both you and your children saw what the Lord did for you in the desert until you arrived here. You saw how he punished Dathan and Abiram, sons of Eliab the Reubenite. The earth swallowed them up right before your eyes, with their households, their tents, and every living thing that belonged to them. You have seen with your own eyes all the great things the Lord has done.

He led you through the desert these 40 years, through the vast and dreadful desert, a thirsty and waterless land with poisonous snakes and scorpions. He did this to test your heart to see whether you'd obey his laws. He brought you water out of hard rock. He caused you to be hungry and then fed you with manna, a food neither you nor your ancestors had known, to humble you and teach you that man doesn't live on bread alone

238

but on every word that comes from the mouth of the Lord. Your clothes didn't wear out and your feet didn't swell during these 40 years.

The Lord, the God of your ancestors, instructed me to give you these commands to observe in the land when you cross the Jordan. Therefore faithfully observe all the commands I'm giving you today; serve him with all your heart and all your soul, so you will have the strength to take over the land when you cross the Jordan. The Lord is bringing you into a good land; it's not like Egypt, where you came from. There you planted your seed and had to pump water with your foot.

But the land you're entering drinks from heaven, because the Lord will send rain in its season, both autumn and spring rains. It's a fertile land that will produce wheat and barley, vines and fig trees, pomegranates, olive oil, new wine, honey, and grass for your cattle. It's a land with brooks, streams, and deep springs gushing out into the valleys and mountains; a land where bread will be in abundance and you'll lack nothing; a land where the rocks are filled with iron, and copper is abundant in the hills, a land flowing with milk and honey.

The Lord your God, the God of your ancestors — Abraham, Isaac, and Jacob — is giving to you and your descendants a land with large, prosperous cities you didn't build, houses stocked with goods you didn't purchase, wells you didn't dig, and vineyards and olive trees you didn't plant. It's a land the Lord your God cares for, and his eyes are continually upon it throughout the year. So when you have eaten all you want and are satisfied, be careful not to forget the Lord, who brought you out of Egypt, out of the land of slavery.

Carefully follow the commands of the Lord your God in every detail, walking in obedience and honoring him. And then you and your descendants will fear the Lord as long as you live. You will live long and prosperous lives in the land and he will give you many children and increase your cattle and flocks, just as he promised. And in the end, all will be well with you.

You'll be more blessed than any other nation; neither you nor your livestock will be infertile. The Lord will protect you from every sickness and spare you from the horrible diseases afflicted on Egypt; instead, he'll inflict them on your enemies.

Fear the Lord your God and serve him. If you make any vows, make them in his name alone. Don't follow the gods of the nations around you, for the Lord your God, who lives among you, is a jealous God and will tolerate no rivals. If you're not careful, you'll be enticed away from the Lord to worship other gods, and the Lord's anger will burn against you. He'll shut up the heavens so that it won't rain and the ground will be so dry it will yield no produce. He'll wipe you off the face of the earth and you will quickly die even though the Lord has given you good land.

Don't test the Lord your God as you did at Massah. Keep his commands and do what is right in the Lord's sight, and then you will prosper in the land and the Lord will cast out all your enemies living there.

Understand that as a parent disciplines his children, so the Lord your God disciplines you. When you've eaten and are satisfied, praise the Lord your God for the good land he has given you. Be careful not to forget the Lord; otherwise you will become proud because you will eat and be satisfied, you will build fine houses and settle down, your cattle and flock will grow large, your silver and gold will increase, and everything you have will be multiplied. You might begin to think you acquired all this wealth by your own strength, but remember the Lord your God is the one who gives you the ability to produce wealth. In this way he confirms the covenant he made with your ancestors.

In the future, your children may ask why the Lord our God gave all these laws. Tell them: "We were Pharaoh's slaves in Egypt, and with our own eyes we saw him perform miracles and inflict terrible plagues on Egypt, Pharaoh, and his whole household. He brought us out from Egypt to give us the land he promised to our ancestors. The Lord commanded us to obey all these laws and to fear him, so that we will live and always prosper. And when we obey all these laws, as the Lord our God has commanded, we will be counted as righteous."

Don't ever forget the Lord your God; make sure you obey him! If you worship other gods, I assure you today that you will surely be destroyed, just like the nations the Lord destroyed before you.

Driving Out the Nations
DT 7:1-10|DT 7:16-26|DT 9:1-6 |DT 11:22-25|DT 11:31-32|DT 12:1-3|DT 12:29-31

Listen Israel, soon you will cross the Jordan to take possession of the land the Lord your God is giving you. When you have settled there, be sure to faithfully obey all the laws I'm setting before you today. If you do, then the Lord will drive out the Hittites, Girgashites, Amorites, Canaanites, Perizzites, Hivites, and Jebusites — seven nations larger and stronger than you.

The land has large cities with walls up to the sky. The people are Anak's descendants — they're giants! You've heard the saying, "Who can defeat the Anakites?"

You might wonder how you can drive out nations so much stronger than you, but don't be afraid of them. Remember everything the Lord your God did to Egypt and its king. You saw with your own eyes the miraculous power he used to bring you out. The same way he destroyed Egypt, he will destroy the nations you fear. They will try to hide from you, but he will cause them to be filled with terror and kill them all. Don't be afraid of them, because the Lord your God is among you.

He is a great and awesome God and will drive out those nations little by little, as you advance. You won't be able to eliminate them all at once, because the wild animals would multiply too quickly. When you attack them, the Lord your God will throw them into complete confusion until they're destroyed. He'll put their kings under your power and you'll erase their names from the face of the earth. No one will be able to stand against you, because you'll destroy them all.

Be assured today that the Lord your God will go ahead of you and destroy them like a devouring fire. Every place you set your foot will be yours: extending from the desert to Lebanon and from the Euphrates River to the Mediterranean Sea. No one will be able to stand against you. As the Lord your God promised, he will cause people to be terrified of you everywhere you set foot in the land. When he subdues them, you'll drive them out and quickly annihilate them, as the Lord promised.

When the Lord your God delivers the nations to you and allows you to defeat them, you must destroy them. Don't pity them and don't be curious about how they serve their gods, because you will copy them and they will trap you. You must not worship the Lord your God the way they worship their gods, because they do all kinds of detestable things the Lord hates, such as burning their children as sacrifices to their gods.

You must completely destroy these nations, showing no mercy. Don't make peace treaties with them. Don't allow your daughters to marry their sons or allow your sons to marry their daughters, because they'll turn your children away from me to serve other gods. Then the Lord's anger will burn against you and immediately destroy you.

Completely destroy all the places where they worship their gods — on high mountains, hills, and under every green tree. Tear down their pagan altars, smash their sacred pillars, and chop down and burn their Asherah poles and idols. In this way you will completely erase the names of their gods. Be careful to follow these laws in the land that the Lord, the God of your ancestors, is giving you, as long as you live there.

Burn all their idols and don't desire the silver and gold that covers them. If you keep them for yourselves, they will ensnare you. They are detestable to the Lord your God and you must not bring anything detestable into your house. If you do, you will be cursed along with the idols. Idols are disgusting and you must totally detest them.

The Lord your God has chosen you out of all the nations on the face of the earth and set you apart to be his people, his treasured possession. He didn't choose you because you were more numerous than other nations, for you were the fewest of them all. He chose you because he loved you and wanted to keep his promise to your ancestors. You're not taking possession of the land because of your own righteousness; indeed, you people are very stubborn. No, it's not because of your righteousness but because of the wickedness of these nations. The Lord your God will drive them out to fulfill his promise to your ancestors — Abraham, Isaac, and Jacob.

This is why he brought you out with a mighty hand and rescued you from the cruel hand of Pharaoh, who made you his slaves in Egypt. Remember that the Lord your God is the only God, and he is faithful, keeping his covenant and showing his love to a thousand generations of those who love him and keep his commandments. But he won't hesitate to punish and destroy those who hate him.

The Designated Place of Worship
DT 12:4-28|DT 12:32|DT 14:23

You haven't yet reached the resting place the Lord your God is giving you, so right now everyone does as they please, but don't continue doing so. When you cross the Jordan and settle in the land, he'll give you rest from all your enemies around you so you can live in safety. You must not worship the Lord your God the way they worship their gods, and you must not offer sacrifices anywhere you please. Instead, the Lord will choose a place from among your tribes where his name will be honored, and that's where you must seek the Lord and bring everything commanded: burnt offerings and sacrifices; tithes of your grain, new wine, and olive oil; special gifts; possessions you vowed to the Lord; voluntary offerings; and the firstborn of your livestock. There you, your children, and your servants can eat and rejoice in the presence of the Lord your God because he has blessed you. Don't eat any of these items in your own city — you must eat them at the designated place in the presence of the Lord your God. Invite the Levites living among you to celebrate with you, because they have no land of their own. Be careful not to neglect the Levites as long as you live in the land. Do these things and you will learn to fear the Lord your God.

Now sometimes you'll want to slaughter an animal just for food and not as a sacrifice. In that case, you can kill and eat the animal where you live, just as you would if you hunted a deer or gazelle. Even people who are ceremonially unclean can eat this meat, and everyone can freely eat as much as the Lord has blessed them with. But you must not eat the blood, because the blood represents life, and you must not eat the life with the meat; let it drain out on the ground like water.

But for your sacrifices, present both the meat and the blood at the altar of the Lord your God. Pour out the blood beside the altar, but you may eat the meat. Be sure to obey all these laws, and then all will go well with you and your descendants because you'll be doing what's right in the Lord's eyes.

Make sure you do all I command you; don't add anything to it or take anything away from it.

Worshiping Other Gods
DT 13:1-18|DT 16:21-22|DT 17:2-7

Someday prophets or dream interpreters may come along who can perform miracles and predict the future. But if they then suggest worshiping other gods, pay them no attention. The Lord your God is testing you to determine whether you love him with all your heart and all your soul. You must follow and honor him. Keep his commands and obey him; serve him and cling to him. And that prophet or dream interpreter who tried to turn you away from his commands must be put to death for encouraging rebellion against the Lord your God, who brought you out of Egypt and rescued you from the land of slavery. You must purge this evil from among you.

Even if your siblings, your children, your beloved spouse, or your closest friend encourage you to worship the gods of the nations around you, whether near or far, from one end of the land to the other, don't yield to them. Show them no pity and don't protect them; they must be stoned to death. You must throw the first stone, and then the rest of the community will follow. In this way all the Israelites will be afraid, and no one will do such an evil thing again.

When you enter the land and begin settling in the cities, you might hear that some wicked people are encouraging those in their city to worship other gods. First investigate to find out if this detestable thing is true. If so, you must completely destroy the city and all who live there: both the people and the livestock. Gather all their possessions into the middle of the public square and completely burn them, along with the city, as a whole burnt offering to the Lord your God. That city must remain in ruins forever and never be rebuilt, and you must keep none of the condemned things. Then the Lord will turn from his fierce anger, show you mercy, and have compassion on you. He'll increase your numbers, as he promised your ancestors — because you have obeyed the Lord your God by keeping all his commands and doing what's right.

When you build an altar to the Lord your God, don't erect a wooden symbol of the goddess Asherah beside it, and don't set up a sacred pillar, for God hates these.

When you settle in the cities the Lord is giving you, someone might do what is evil in the sight of the Lord your God and violate his covenant. They might worship other gods or the sun, moon, or stars. If so, you must conduct a thorough investigation. If you find that this detestable thing has been done in Israel, stone the person to death at the city gate. But remember that the testimony of two or three witnesses is required to put a person to death; one witness is not enough. Those who witnessed the event must throw the first stone, and then the rest of the people will follow. You must purge the evil from among you.

Fear the Lord
DT 10:12-22|DT 11:18-21|DT 11:26-30

And now, Israel, the Lord your God asks only that you fear him, walk in obedience, love him, serve him with all your heart and all your soul, and observe all his commands that I'm giving you today. This is for your own good.

Everything belongs to the Lord your God — the highest heavens, the earth, and everything in it. Yet the Lord loved your ancestors and chose you, their descendants, above all the nations. Therefore circumcise your hearts and don't be stubborn any longer. For the Lord is God of gods and Lord of lords. He is the great God, mighty and awesome, who shows no favoritism and accepts no bribes. He defends orphans and widows, and loves foreign residents, providing them food and clothing. You must also love foreigners because you yourselves were foreigners in Egypt.

Fear the Lord your God and serve him. Hold fast to him and make vows only in his name. He alone deserves your praise because he's your God, who performed great and awesome miracles that you saw with your own eyes. Seventy of your ancestors went down into Egypt, but now the Lord your God has made you as numerous as the stars in the sky.

Fix these words in your hearts and minds. Tie them as symbols on your hands and your foreheads. Write them on the doorframes of your houses and on the gates of your cities. Teach them to your children and talk about them always, whether at home or out on the road, whether going to bed at night or getting up in the morning. Then you and your descendants will live a long time in the land the Lord swore to give your ancestors, as long as the heavens are above the earth.

Today I'm setting before you a blessing and a curse — a blessing if you obey the Lord's commands, a curse if you disobey and worship other gods you've never worshiped before. When the Lord your God brings you into the land, you must proclaim the blessings on Mount Gerizim and the curses on Mount Ebal. As you know, these mountains are west of the Jordan River, in the land of the Canaanites who live in the Jordan Valley, near Gilgal, not far from the oaks of Moreh.

CHAPTER 23
Laws Related to the 3rd & 4th Commandments

Honoring God's Name by Maintaining Purity & The Sabbath Year and Associated Festivals

Clean and Unclean Food
DT 14:1-21

You have been set apart as holy to the Lord your God and he has chosen you to be his treasured possession out of all the nations on the face of the earth. Don't cut yourself or shave the front of your head to mourn for the dead.

Don't eat anything the Lord has declared unclean. These are some of the animals you may eat: cattle, wild sheep and goats, deer, gazelles, and antelopes. You may eat any animal that has divided hoofs and chews the cud, but don't eat camels, rabbits, and rock-badgers. These animals chew the cud but don't have divided hoofs, so they're ceremonially unclean for you. Pigs are also unclean; they have divided hoofs but don't chew the cud. Don't eat their meat or touch their carcasses.

You may eat any water creature that has fins and scales. But anything that doesn't have fins and scales is unclean for you.

You may eat any clean bird. But don't eat eagles, vultures, buzzards, falcons, crows, ostriches, owls, hawks, seagulls, pelicans, storks, herons, cormorants, hoopoes, and bats. You may eat any clean winged creature, but don't eat any flying insects, because they're all unclean.

Don't eat anything you find already dead. You can give it to foreign residents or sell it to other foreigners.

Don't cook a young goat in its mother's milk.

The Law of the Tithe
DT 14:22|DT 14:24-29

Be sure to set aside a tenth of your livestock and everything your fields produce each year, and bring them to the place the Lord designates. But if that place is too far away and the Lord has blessed you so much that you can't carry your tithe, then exchange it for silver and use that to buy whatever you like: livestock, wine, or anything else. Then you and your household can rejoice and eat there in the presence of the Lord your God.

At the end of every third year, store all the tithes for that year in your cities so that Levites, foreigners, orphans, and widows living among you will have food to eat, and then the Lord your God will bless you in all you do.

Dedicating Firstborn Animals
DT 15:19-23|DT 17:1

Set apart for the Lord your God every firstborn male of your livestock. Don't put the cattle to work or shear the sheep. Each year you and your family must eat them in the presence of the Lord your God at the designated place of worship. If an animal has a defect, is lame or blind, or has a serious flaw, you must not sacrifice it to the Lord your God. Such offerings are detestable to him. Instead, eat them in your own city. Anyone, whether ceremonially unclean or clean, may eat it, just as you would eat a gazelle or deer. But remember not to eat the blood; instead, pour it out on the ground.

The Year for Canceling Debts
DT 15:1-11

At the end of every seventh year, you must cancel all loans made to a fellow Israelite, because the Lord has declared the debt canceled. But you may require repayment from a foreigner. If you fully obey all the commands I'm giving you, no one will have to be poor, because the Lord your God will richly bless you in the land he's giving you. You will lend to many nations but borrow from none. You will rule over many nations but none will rule over you.

But there will always be poor people in the land; therefore I command you not to be stingy; freely lend them whatever they need. Don't be tempted to avoid helping them because you know it's almost the year for canceling debts. If they appeal to the Lord, you'll be found guilty of sin, so give generously from the heart and then the Lord your God will bless you in all you do.

If any of your fellow Israelites sell themselves to you, set them free in the seventh year. But don't send them away empty-handed; give to them generously from what the Lord your God has blessed you with: flocks, grain, and wine. Remember that you were slaves in Egypt and the Lord your God freed you. But if your servants love you and your family and don't want to leave, push an awl through their earlobe into the door, and they will become your servant for life. Don't consider it a hardship to set your servant free, because you received six years of service for half the cost of hiring someone to do the work. Obey and the Lord your God will bless you in everything you do.

Celebrate the Passover of the Lord your God in the month of Abib, because that's the month he brought you out of Egypt. Go to the designated place of worship and sacrifice an animal from the herd or flock for the Passover meal. Eat all of the meat of the Passover sacrifice that same night; don't eat bread made with yeast and don't leave any until morning. For seven days eat unleavened bread.

You must not sacrifice the Passover anywhere except the Lord's designated place of worship. Sacrifice it in the evening, the time of your departure from Egypt. Roast it and eat it there and then return to your tents in the morning. For the next six days, eat unleavened bread, which will help you remember your hasty escape from Egypt all the days of your life. No yeast must be found in the land at all for seven days. On the seventh day, come together to worship the Lord your God and do no work.

Count seven weeks from the beginning of the grain harvest. Celebrate the Festival of Weeks to the Lord your God by giving a voluntary offering in proportion to how he has blessed you. Rejoice before the Lord your God at the designated place of worship with your family, servants, the Levites, foreigners, orphans, and widows living among you. Remember that you were slaves in Egypt, and carefully follow these laws.

After you finish the grain and grape harvests, celebrate the Festival of Tabernacles for seven days at the designated place of worship. For the

Lord your God will bless you in all your harvest and in all the work of your hands, and your joy will be complete.

Conclusion Regarding Festivals
DT 16:15-17

These are the three yearly festivals: The Festival of Unleavened Bread, the Festival of Weeks, and the Festival of Tabernacles. All the men must worship the Lord your God at the designated place of worship. No one should appear before the Lord empty-handed. Each of you must bring a gift in proportion to the way the Lord your God has blessed you. Be joyful at your festivals and celebrate them with your family, servants, the Levites, foreigners, orphans, and widows living among you. But be sure you don't worship anywhere but at the designated place of worship.

CHAPTER 24
Laws Related to the
5th Commandment

Life in the Land

Appointing Judges
DT 16:18-20

Appoint judges and officials for each tribe in every city the Lord your God is giving you, and they must judge the people fairly. Don't distort justice by accepting a bribe; it blinds the eyes of the wise and corrupts the words of the righteous. Justice must always prevail so that you may live and possess the land the Lord your God is giving you.

Handling Difficult Cases
DT 17:8-13

Some cases might be too difficult for the local judges, such as murder, lawsuits, or assaults. Take such cases to the Lord's designated place of worship. The priests and judge in office at that time will give you a verdict, and you must completely abide by their decisions. Anyone who shows contempt for the judge or for the priest who ministers to the Lord your God must be put to death. In this way you will purge the evil from Israel. Everyone will be afraid and they'll be sure to obey the court's decisions in the future.

Requirements for a King
DT 17:14-20

When you have settled in the land the Lord your God is giving you and decide you want a king to rule over you like the rest of the nations, be sure to appoint a king chosen by the Lord your God. He must be an Israelite, not a foreigner. He must not build up a large number of horses

251

for his army or make the people return to Egypt to buy more, because the Lord has told you not to ever go back there. He must not marry multiple women, or his heart will be led astray, and he must not accumulate large amounts of silver and gold.

When he begins to rule, he must write a copy of God's law on a scroll, taken from the original kept by the Levitical priests. He must keep it with him and read it as long as he lives so that he may learn to fear the Lord his God and carefully obey these laws. This will prevent him from becoming proud and thinking he is better than his fellow Israelites and that he can disregard the law. If he obeys the Lord, he and his descendants will reign a long time in Israel.

The Food Share for Priests and Levites
DT 18:1-8

The priestly tribe of Levi will receive no land of their own as the other tribes do. They will live on the food offerings presented to the Lord as their share. They will have no inheritance, because their inheritance is the privilege of being the Lord's priests, as he promised them.

When the people sacrifice cattle or sheep, the priests' share includes the shoulder, internal organs, and the meat from the jaw. You must give them the firstfruits of your grain, new wine, and olive oil, and the first part of the wool from shearing your sheep. Give them these gifts because the Lord your God has chosen them and their descendants out of all your tribes to forever minister in his name.

If a Levite earnestly desires to leave his home and go serve at the designated place of worship, he is welcome to serve the Lord there. He must receive the same food share as the priests who serve there permanently, even though he has received money from the sale of his family possessions.

Occult Practices Forbidden
DT 18:9-13

When you enter the land the Lord your God is giving you, don't imitate the detestable habits of the other nations. Let no one be found among you who sacrifices their children in the fire, practices divination or sorcery, interprets omens, engages in witchcraft or casts spells, or consults the dead. Anyone who does these things is detestable to the Lord. You must be blameless before the Lord your God. These detestable practices are the reason the Lord will cast those nations out of their land.

The Future Office of Prophet
DT 18:14-22

Even though the other nations in the land listen to those who practice sorcery or divination, the Lord your God forbids you to do such things. He will raise up for you a prophet like me from your fellow Israelites, and he's the one you must listen to. Remember this is what you asked of the Lord your God when we were gathered at Mount Sinai. You didn't want to hear his voice or continue seeing the blazing fire, because you were afraid you would die.

The Lord said to me, "Their request is wise. I will appoint them a prophet like you from among the Israelites. I'll put my words in his mouth and he will tell them everything I command him. I myself will punish anyone who doesn't heed the words that the prophet speaks in my name. But if a prophet presumes to speak in my name anything I haven't commanded, or speaks in the name of other gods, he must be put to death."

You may wonder how you can know whether a message has been spoken by the Lord. This is how: If the Lord has spoken, the prophecy will come true. But if the prophecy doesn't come true, then the Lord hasn't spoken. That prophet has spoken on his own authority, so he doesn't deserve your respect.

CHAPTER 25
Laws Related to the
6th Commandment

Murder, Death, War, and the Preservation of Life

The Cities of Refuge
DT 4:41-43|DT 19:1-14

When the Lord your God has destroyed the nations in the land he's giving you, and you've settled there, set aside three cities of refuge. Divide the land into three regions, with one city in the middle of each, so that it can be easily reached from anywhere in the land. People can escape to any of these cities if they accidentally murder someone and there was no hostility between them.

For example, two men may be cutting wood together in the forest and one of them swings his ax, the head flies off, and it kills his friend. That man may save his life by escaping to one of the cities of refuge. Otherwise, the family member seeking revenge might pursue him in a rage. If the city is too far away, he will be caught and killed, even though he doesn't deserve death.

The Lord your God will give you all the land he promised your ancestors if you love him forever and obey the laws I'm giving you. When that happens, choose three more cities as a place of refuge. These cities are necessary to prevent you from executing innocent people in the land the Lord your God is giving you.

But those filled with hostility who deliberately ambush someone and commit murder are not protected. If they flee to a city of refuge, the city elders will send for them, and they will be handed over to die to the family member seeking revenge. Show no pity. You must purge from Israel the guilt of shedding innocent blood so that it may go well with you.

Don't move your neighbor's boundary marker to enlarge your own property. Your predecessors set them up previously in the land the Lord your God is giving you to possess.

Moses had already set aside three cities of refuge east of the Jordan:
* Bezer in the desert plateau for the tribe of Reuben
* Ramoth in Gilead for the tribe of Gad
* Golan in Bashan for the tribe of Manasseh

The Importance of Honest Witnesses
DT 19:15-21

One witness isn't enough to convict someone accused of a crime. Cases must be established only by the testimony of two or three witnesses.

If a witness tries to harm someone by making a false accusation, both parties must go to the one place of worship and be judged by the priests and judges in office at the time. The judges must investigate thoroughly. If the witness proves to be a liar, he must be punished for giving false testimony against a fellow Israelite. Give him the same punishment you would have given to the accused if found guilty. You must purge the evil from among you. The rest of the people will hear about it and be afraid to ever do such an evil thing again. Show no pity. You must repay life for life, eye for eye, tooth for tooth, hand for hand, and foot for foot.

The Cursed Body on a Tree
DT 21:22-23

If a criminal is executed and you hang his body on a tree, don't leave the body there overnight. Bury it the same day, because anyone hung on a tree will bring God's curse upon the land. You must not defile the land the Lord your God is giving you.

Instructions for Going to War
DT 20:1-20

When you go to war against your enemies, you will see an army with horses and chariots greater than yours, but the Lord your God, who brought you up out of Egypt, will be with you. Before you go into battle, the priest will come forward and say, "Listen, Israel, today you're going into battle, but don't be afraid; don't panic or be terrified, for the Lord your God is with you and he's the one who will fight for you against your enemies and give you victory."

Then the officers will say to the army: "Did any of you build a new house you haven't yet had a chance to live in? If so, go home, or you might die in battle and someone else might move in. Did you plant a vineyard without the opportunity to enjoy it? Go home, or you might die in battle and someone else might enjoy it. Did you just become engaged? Go home, or you might die in battle and someone else might marry your fiancé. Is anyone afraid? Go home so you won't make your fellow soldiers afraid too."

When the officers finish speaking, they will appoint commanders over the army.

When you march up to attack a city, make its people an offer of peace. If they accept and open their gates, all the people will be subject to forced labor and will work for you. If they refuse to make peace and engage you in battle, lay siege to that city. When the Lord your God delivers it into your hand, kill all the men and take the women, children, livestock, and everything else for yourselves. Do the same for all the cities that are some distance away from you and are not part of the nearby nations.

However, for the nearby nations — the Hittites, Amorites, Canaanites, Perizzites, Hivites, and Jebusites — you must completely destroy anything that breathes, as the Lord your God has commanded. Otherwise, they'll teach you to sin against the Lord and follow all the detestable things they do in worshiping their gods.

When you lay siege to a city and the war drags on, don't cut down the trees, because you can eat their fruit. Don't treat the trees as enemies you need to attack. However, you may cut down trees that aren't fruit trees and use them to build the equipment needed to attack the city until it falls.

Atonement for an Unsolved Murder
DT 21:1-9|DT 22:8

When you are in the land the Lord your God is giving you, someone may be found murdered in a field, but you don't know who's responsible. The elders and judges will measure the distance from the body to the neighboring cities. Then the elders of the city nearest the body will select a young cow that has never been put to work. The elders and the priests will take it down to a valley that has never been plowed or planted and that has a stream running through it. The priests must go too because the Lord your God has chosen them to minister and pronounce blessings in his name. They must decide all cases of dispute and assault.

The elders will break the cow's neck and wash their hands over it. Then they will declare, "We didn't murder this person and we didn't see who did. But since the victim was innocent, please forgive your people, the Israelites, who you rescued from Egypt. Lord, don't hold us responsible."

If you do what's right in the Lord's sight, you will cleanse the guilt of shedding innocent blood from the community and won't be held responsible.

When you build a new house, be sure to put a rail around your roof so you won't bring the guilt of bloodshed on your house if someone falls from the roof.

Marrying a Captive Woman
DT 21:10-14

When the Lord gives you victory in battle against your enemies and you take captives, you might be attracted to one of the women and want to marry her. But first you must bring her home and have her shave her head, trim her nails, and change her clothes. Allow her to mourn her parents for a full month, and then you can marry her. But if she doesn't please you, let her go wherever she wishes. You must not sell her or treat her as a slave, since you dishonored her.

The Rights of the Firstborn
DT 21:15-17

Suppose a man has two wives and he loves one more than the other. When the man dies, the older son must be given the rights of the firstborn, even if he's the son of the woman the man loves least. When he divides his property, he must not show favoritism to the son of the wife he loves most; he must give his firstborn a double portion because that share belongs to him.

Punishment for a Rebellious Son
LV 20:9|DT 21:18-21

Suppose someone has a stubborn and rebellious son who refuses to obey even when his parents discipline him. His parents must take him to the elders at the city gate and say, "Our son is stubborn and rebellious and won't obey us. He spends all his time drinking and partying." Then all the men of the city must stone him to death. You must purge the evil from among you so all Israel will hear about it and be afraid.

Those who curse their parents must be put to death, and it will be their own fault.

Protecting Animal Life
DT 22:1-4|DT 22:6-7

If you see someone's cow or sheep out wandering around, don't ignore it but be sure to take it back to its owner. If they don't live near you or if you don't know who owns it, take it home with you and keep it until they come looking for it. Then give it back. Do the same if you find clothing or anything else someone has lost.

If you see that someone's animal has fallen down under a heavy load, help the owner get it to its feet; don't ignore it.

As you walk along the road, you might see a bird's nest in a tree or on the ground. You can take any chicks or eggs you find, but don't take the mother if she's in the nest with them; let her go, so that it will go well with you and you will have a long life.

CHAPTER 26
Laws Related to the 7th, 8th, & 9th Commandments

Separation From Impurity, Theft, & Respect for Others

The Importance of Maintaining Purity
DT 22:5|DT 22:9-12|DT 24:8-9

Women must not wear men's clothing, and men must not wear women's clothing; the Lord your God detests anyone who does this.

Don't plant two kinds of seed in your vineyard; if you do, both the crops you plant and the fruit of the vineyard will be defiled.

Don't hitch both an ox and a donkey to your plow.

Don't wear clothes made of both wool and linen.

Wear tassels on the four corners of your outer garment.

I've given the priests instructions for handling defiling skin diseases, so be sure to do exactly as they say. Remember what the Lord your God did to Miriam along the way after you left Egypt.

Marriage Regulations
DT 22:13-30|DT 24:1-5

Suppose a man marries a woman but is displeased with her, so he accuses her of not being a virgin. Then the young woman's parents must take their daughter's blood-stained sheet to the city gate. Her father will say to the elders, "I allowed my daughter to marry this man, and now he's accusing her of not being a virgin. But here is the proof of my daughter's virginity."

Then the elders must punish the husband by fining him 100 pieces of silver. The money will be given to the young woman's father because her husband has ruined the reputation of an Israelite virgin. She will continue to be his wife, and he must not divorce her as long as he lives.

But if the charge is true and there's no proof of her virginity, the men of her city must bring her to the door of her father's house and stone her to death. She has done an outrageous thing in Israel by being promiscuous before marriage.

If a man sleeps with another man's wife, both the man and the woman must die.

If a man is caught in town having sex with an engaged woman and she didn't scream for help, stone both of them to death at the city gate. The man is guilty because he slept with another man's wife and the woman is guilty because she didn't call for help, even though she was inside the city with people nearby.

But if an engaged woman is raped out in the country, only the man will be put to death, because the woman is innocent and has done nothing wrong. It must be assumed that she screamed, but there was no one to rescue her. This case is the same as an unwitnessed murder.

If a man rapes a woman who isn't engaged, he must marry her and pay her father the bride-price of 50 pieces of silver. He can never divorce her as long as he lives, because he violated her.

A man must not marry his father's wife; this dishonors his father.

You must purge all evil from among you.

Suppose a man marries a woman and later doesn't want her because there's something about her he doesn't like. So he gives her a certificate of divorce and sends her away. If she later marries another man and that man divorces her or dies, she can't marry her first husband again, because she has been defiled and a remarriage would be offensive to the Lord. You must not bring guilt upon the land the Lord is giving you.

Don't send a man to war or give him other public duties if he has recently gotten married. Allow him to stay at home for one year and make his wife happy.

Exclusion From the Community
DT 23:1-8

None of the following people may enter the Lord's community:

* A man whose testicles are crushed or whose male organ has been cut off

* Anyone born of a forbidden marriage, or their descendants, not even in the 10th generation.

* Ammonites, Moabites, or any of their descendants, not even in the 10th generation. Remember they didn't give you food or water when you left Egypt, and they hired Balaam son of Beor from

Pethor, in Aram-Naharaim, to pronounce a curse on you. But the Lord your God refused Balaam's request and turned the curse into a blessing because he loves you. Don't make a peace treaty with them as long as you live.

But the Edomites are your relatives and you must not despise them. And don't despise the Egyptians, because you lived as foreigners in their country. The third generation of Egyptian children may enter the Lord's community.

Personal Hygiene in the Camp
DT 23:9-14

Keep your camp pure, even during times of war. Any man unclean because of an emission of semen during the night must go outside the camp and remain there. That evening he must wash himself and at sunset he may return to the camp.

Designate a place outside the camp where you can relieve yourself, and dig a hole to cover up your excrement. Your camp must be holy, for the Lord your God moves about there to protect you and deliver your enemies to you. He must not see anything indecent that causes him to turn away from you.

Prostitution Forbidden
DT 23:17-18

No Israelite, whether man or woman, must become a temple prostitute. And you must not bring the earnings of a prostitute into the house of the Lord your God to pay a vow, because the Lord your God detests both prostitutes and their wages.

The Law for Escaped Slaves
DT 23:15-16

Slaves who escape from their master and take refuge with you should remain free. Don't hand them over to their master and don't be cruel to them. Let them live among you in whatever city they choose.

Respect for Another's Possessions
DT 23:19-25|DT 24:6-7

You may charge a foreigner interest, but don't charge a fellow Israelite interest, whether on money, food, or anything else. Then the Lord your God will bless everything you do in the land you're entering to possess.

If you make a vow to the Lord your God, be sure to pay it, for he will certainly demand it from you. Otherwise, you will be guilty of sin. You must be sure to do whatever you promised because you made your vow freely. Remember that if you refrain from making a vow, you can't be guilty of breaking it.

You may eat all the grapes you want if you're in your neighbor's vineyard, but don't put any in your basket. You may pick kernels with your hands from your neighbor's grainfield, but don't use a sickle to cut their standing grain.

Don't take a pair of millstones — not even the upper millstone — as security for a debt. The borrower needs them to grind his grain, and that would be taking away his livelihood.

Anyone who kidnaps a fellow Israelite and treats them like a slave or sells them must die. You must purge the evil from among you.

Fair Treatment of Others
DT 24:10-22|DT 25:1-4

When you make a loan, don't go into the person's house to pick up the item he's offering as security; wait outside and let him bring it out to you. If he's poor and gives you his garment, don't keep it overnight. Return it by sunset so he can sleep in it. He will be grateful and the Lord your God will consider your actions righteous.

Don't take advantage of hired workers who are poor and needy, whether they are fellow Israelites or foreign residents. Pay them each day before sunset, because they're counting on it. Otherwise they may cry out to the Lord against you, and you'll be guilty of sin.

Parents must not be put to death for crimes committed by their children, nor children put to death for crimes committed by their parents; each will die for their own sin.

Don't deprive foreigners and orphans of their rights. Don't take a widow's garment as security for a loan. Remember that you were slaves in Egypt and the Lord your God rescued you.

When you're harvesting your crops and forget a bundle of grain in the field, don't go back to get it. When knocking down olives from your trees, don't go back a second time to pick those that you missed. When you harvest the grapes in your vineyard, don't go back over the vines to pick what you left. Leave all the leftovers for foreigners, orphans, and widows so that the Lord your God may bless you in everything you do. Remember that you were slaves in Egypt; that's why I'm giving you these commands.

Don't muzzle an ox to keep it from eating while it treads out grain.

Take all disputes to court and the judges will decide the case, acquitting the innocent and condemning the guilty. If the guilty person is sentenced to be beaten, the judge will make him lie face down and have him beaten in his presence. The number of lashes depends on the crime committed, but must not exceed 40 lashes. Any more than that would publicly humiliate him.

CHAPTER 27
Laws Related to the
10th Commandment

Respect for the Property of Others

Respect for What Belongs to Others
DT 25:5-16

If brothers are living together and one of them dies without a son, his widow must not marry outside the family. Her brother-in-law must fulfill his duty and marry her. The first son she bears will be considered the legal son of the dead brother so that his name won't be erased from Israel.

But if he doesn't want to marry her, the woman must go to the city gate and let the elders know that he won't fulfill his duty. The elders will try to reason with him, but if he continues to refuse, his brother's widow will approach him in the presence of the elders, take off one of his sandals, spit in his face, and say, "This is what happens to the man who refuses to provide children for his brother." From then on his family will be known in Israel as "The Family of the Unsandaled."

If two men are fighting and a wife tries to rescue her husband by grabbing the other man's genitals, cut off her hand. Show her no pity.

Don't cheat people by having two sets of weights and measures, one to receive more when you make a purchase and the other to give less when you are selling. You must weigh and measure things honestly so that you may live long in the land the Lord your God is giving you. The Lord detests anyone who is dishonest.

The Lord's Firstfruits and Tithes
DT 26:1-15

Soon you will take possession of and settle in the land the Lord your God is giving you. Gather the firstfruits of each crop you harvest, put them in a basket, and take it to the Lord's designated place of worship. Say to the priest on duty, "With this gift I acknowledge that I have entered the land the Lord my God promised our ancestors."

The priest will place the basket in front of the altar. Then you will say in the Lord's presence: "My father was a wandering Aramean who took his family to live in Egypt. There were only a few people when they moved there, but they eventually became a large and powerful nation. The Egyptians mistreated us and made us work as slaves. But we cried out to the Lord, the God of our ancestors, and he heard our cries and saw our misery, hardship, and oppression. He brought us out of Egypt with a mighty hand and an outstretched arm, terrifying the Egyptians with great signs and wonders. He brought us here and gave us this land flowing with milk and honey. And now I bring the firstfruits of the produce that the Lord has given me."

Then bow down in the presence of the Lord your God and worship him. Then you, the Levites, and the foreign residents can celebrate all the good things the Lord has given to you.

Every year you must give 10% of your produce to the Lord, but the third year is the year of the special tithe. Give the tithe to the Levites, foreigners, orphans, and widows. In this way they will have enough to eat. Then say to the Lord your God: "I haven't forgotten your commands; I've completely obeyed them. I took this special tithe from my house and distributed it just as you said. I didn't eat any of it while I was in mourning, touch it while unclean, or give it as an offering for the dead. Please look down from heaven, your holy dwelling place, and bless your people Israel. You promised our ancestors that you would give us a land flowing with milk and honey, and you have kept your promise."

Follow the Lord's Commands
DT 25:17-19|DT 26:16-19

Today the Lord your God has declared that you are his people, his treasured possession, and commands you to carefully obey these laws with all your heart and soul. You have acknowledged that the Lord is your God and agreed to obey him. Keep your promise and the Lord will make you greater than any other nation, and you will receive praise and honor. You will be a nation set apart to the Lord your God, just as he promised.

Remember how the Amalekites treated you when you left Egypt; they didn't fear God. They attacked you when you were exhausted from your journey, and killed everyone who was lagging behind. So when the Lord your God has given you the land and gives you rest from all your enemies, you must blot out the name of Amalek from the face of the earth. Don't forget to do this!

The Altar on Mount Ebal
DT 27:1-8

Moses and the elders of Israel commanded the people: Obey all the commands I'm giving you today. Soon you will cross the Jordan into a land flowing with milk and honey, just as the Lord, the God of your ancestors, promised. On the day you cross over, go to Mount Ebal, set up some large stones, and coat them with plaster. Write very clearly all these laws on the stones. Then build an altar of stones to the Lord your God, but don't use an iron tool; use stones that can be used without being cut. Offer burnt offerings on the altar to the Lord your God. Sacrifice peace offerings and eat them and celebrate in the Lord's presence.

Curses From Mount Ebal
DT 27:9-26

Then Moses and the priests said: Listen, Israel, and be silent! Now you belong to the Lord your God, so you must obey him and follow his laws that I'm giving you today.

When you cross the Jordan, the tribes of Simeon, Levi, Judah, Issachar, Joseph, and Benjamin will stand on Mount Gerizim to hear the blessings, and the tribes of Reuben, Gad, Asher, Zebulun, Dan, and Naphtali will stand on Mount Ebal to hear the curses.

Then the Levites will shout out:

"Cursed is anyone who makes an idol of stone, wood, or metal and secretly worships it. The Lord hates idolatry."

Then all the people will say, "Amen!"

"Cursed are those who dishonor their parents."

Then all the people will say, "Amen!"

"Cursed are those who move their neighbor's boundary stone."

Then all the people will say, "Amen!"

"Cursed are those who lead a blind person in the wrong direction."

Then all the people will say, "Amen!"

"Cursed are those who deprive foreigners, orphans, or widows of their rights."

Then all the people will say, "Amen!"

"Cursed is the man who sleeps with his father's wife, dishonoring his father's bed."

Then all the people will say, "Amen!"

"Cursed are those who have sex with an animal."

Then all the people will say, "Amen!"
"Cursed is a man who sleeps with his sister or half-sister."
Then all the people will say, "Amen!"
"Cursed is a man who sleeps with his mother-in-law."
Then all the people will say, "Amen!"
"Cursed are those who secretly commit murder."
Then all the people will say, "Amen!"
"Cursed are those who accept money to murder an innocent person."
Then all the people will say, "Amen!"
"Cursed is anyone who doesn't obey these laws."
Then all the people will say, "Amen!"

Blessings for Obedience
DT 28:1-14

Faithfully obey the commands of the Lord your God and he will make you greater than all the nations on earth. He will:

* Bless your cities and your fields
* Bless you with many children, crops, cattle, and flocks
* Bless your grain basket and bowl for kneading bread
* Bless you both at home and at work

The Lord will defeat your enemies when they attack you. They'll attack you from one direction but flee from you in seven.

The Lord will fill your barns with grain. The Lord your God is giving you the land and will bless you in everything you do.

Obey the Lord's commands completely and don't worship other gods, and he will set you apart as his own people, as he promised. Then everyone on earth will see that the Lord has chosen you, and they'll be afraid of you. The Lord will give you prosperity in the land he promised to your ancestors, blessing you with many children, numerous livestock, and abundant crops.

The Lord will open the storehouse of the heavens, and send rain in its season to bless all the work of your hands. You'll lend to many nations but borrow from none. The Lord will make you the head, not the tail; you will always be on the top and never at the bottom.

Curses for Disobedience
DT 28:15-68

But if you reject the Lord your God and fail to faithfully obey his commands, all these curses will overtake you:

* You'll be cursed in your cities and your fields.
* Your grain basket and bowl for kneading bread will be cursed.

- Your children, crops, cattle, and flocks will be few.
- You'll be cursed both at home and at work.

The Lord will curse everything you do. He will send disaster and confusion until you are completely destroyed and none of you is left in the land. He will send terrible diseases, fever, swelling, and mildew. These disasters will pursue you until you die. The Lord will make the sky as unyielding as a bronze roof to keep out the rain, and the ground as hard as iron. Your crops will be scorched by the hot east wind or ruined by mildew.

The Lord will give your enemies victory over you. You'll attack them from one direction but flee from them in seven, and you'll be a horrible sight to all the kingdoms on earth. When you die, no one will scare away the birds and wild animals that will eat your carcasses. The Lord will make you suffer diseases that will cause sores, itchy patches, or boils like those the Egyptians had, and there will be no cure. You will become insane and go blind. You will be so confused that you'll have to feel your way around like someone stumbling around in darkness. Everything you do will be unsuccessful; you'll be constantly oppressed and robbed, and no one will rescue you.

You'll be engaged to marry a woman, but another will rape her. You'll build a house, but you won't live in it. Your ox will be slaughtered before your eyes, but you'll eat none of it. Your donkey will be stolen from you and won't be returned. Your sheep will be given to your enemies, and no one will rescue them. Your children will be given as slaves to a foreign nation. You'll strain your eyes looking for them day after day, powerless to lift a hand. A foreign nation will eat the crops your labor produced, and you'll suffer constant oppression and abuse. All the tragedy you see will drive you mad. The Lord will cover your knees and legs with incurable, painful boils that spread from the soles of your feet to the top of your head.

The Lord will exile you and the king you chose to a foreign nation where you and your ancestors have never lived. There you'll worship other gods of wood and stone. You'll become an object of horror, ridicule, and mockery among the nations where the Lord will send you.

You'll plant much but harvest little, because locusts will devour your crops. You'll plant and cultivate vineyards but you won't begin to drink the wine or gather the grapes, because worms will destroy the vines. Olive trees will grow everywhere throughout your land, but you won't have any oil, because the olives will fall off before they ripen. You'll have children but you will lose them, because they'll be taken as prisoners of war. Swarms of locusts will take over all your trees and crops.

The foreigners living among you will become more wealthy and powerful, but you'll become more poor and powerless. They'll have money to lend to you, but you'll have none to lend to them. They'll be the head, but you'll be the tail.

All these curses will pursue, attack, and destroy you because you didn't obey the commands of the Lord your God. They'll be evidence of God's judgment upon you and your descendants forever. Because you didn't serve the Lord your God joyfully in times of prosperity, he will send enemies to attack and enslave you. Then you will live in poverty with nothing to eat, drink, or wear. The Lord will put an iron yoke on your neck until he has destroyed you.

He will bring a distant nation against you from the ends of the earth, whose language you won't understand. They will swoop down upon you like an eagle. They'll be ruthless and show no respect for the elderly or pity for the young. They'll devour the offspring of your livestock and the crops of your land, leaving you no grain, new wine, or olive oil, and you will perish. They'll attack your cities until all the walls in your land, which you trusted to protect you, are knocked down.

When your enemies are attacking your cities, even the men who are the most gentle and kind will become so desperate for food that they will eat the children that the Lord your God has given them. They'll even refuse to share the meal with their own brother, beloved wife, or other children.

A sensitive and kind woman may have grown up in such luxury that she never had to put her bare foot on the ground. But she will become so desperate for food that she will secretly eat both her newborn baby and the afterbirth, without sharing any with her beloved husband or her other children.

Carefully obey all the laws written in this book, and revere the glorious and awesome name of the Lord your God. If you don't, the Lord will punish you and your descendants with severe and incurable diseases, including the dreadful diseases you experienced in Egypt, and even sicknesses and disasters not recorded in this Book of the law. You will have no relief from them and you will be destroyed.

You became as numerous as the stars in the sky, but if you disobey the Lord your God, only a few of you will be left. Just as the Lord delighted in making you prosper and multiply, so he will delight in ruining and destroying you, and you'll be uprooted from the land you're entering to possess.

Then the Lord will scatter you among all nations, from one end of the earth to the other. There you'll worship other gods of wood and stone that are unfamiliar to you and your ancestors. You'll find no peace among these nations, and nowhere to call your own. The Lord will overwhelm you with anxiety, failing eyesight, and despair.

You will constantly be in danger, filled with terror day and night, living in constant fear of death. Everything you see will make your heart pound with fear; every morning you'll wish for evening and every evening you'll wish for morning. The Lord will send you back to Egypt even though he never intended for you to return there. You'll offer to sell yourselves to them as slaves, but no one will purchase you.

MOSES' THIRD SERMON

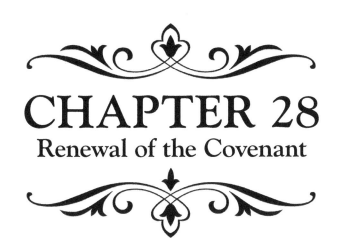

CHAPTER 28
Renewal of the Covenant

These are the terms of the covenant the Lord commanded Moses to make with the Israelites in Moab, in addition to the covenant he'd made with them at Mount Sinai.

Moses summoned all the Israelites and said:

You've seen everything the Lord did in Egypt to Pharaoh, his officials, and his entire country. You saw with your own eyes his terrible plagues and miracles. For 40 years the Lord led you through the desert, but your clothes and sandals didn't wear out. You didn't have bread, food, wine, or beer, but he provided special food so you would acknowledge him as your God. But the Lord hasn't yet allowed you to fully understand the things you've experienced.

When we first arrived here, King Sihon of Heshbon and King Og of Bashan attacked us, but we defeated them. We took their land and gave it to the tribes of Reuben, Gad, and half the tribe of Manasseh.

Faithfully obey the terms of this covenant so that you may prosper in everything you do. Today all of you are standing in the presence of the Lord your God — your leaders and officials, men, women, and children, and even the foreign residents who cut our wood and carry our water. You're here to enter the covenant the Lord your God is making with you today. This will establish you as his people and confirm that he is your God, just as he promised you and your ancestors, Abraham, Isaac, and Jacob. This covenant is being made not only with those of you standing here in the Lord's presence, but also with your descendants.

You remember how we lived in Egypt and the countries we passed through on the way here. You saw their detestable images and idols of wood and stone, of silver and gold. Make sure no man or woman, no clan or tribe, turns away from the Lord our God to worship their gods. That would be like a root that produces bitter and poisonous fruit.

Make sure none of you hear the words of this solemn covenant and convince yourself that you'll be ok if you stubbornly decide to do whatever you please. Your private sin will have public consequences. The Lord will not forgive you; instead, his anger and passion will burn against you. All the curses written in this book will fall upon you, and the Lord will blot out your name from the face of the earth. The Lord will single you out from all the tribes of Israel and pour out on you all the curses listed in this covenant.

Your descendants and the foreigners who come from distant lands will witness the disasters and suffering the Lord has brought upon your land. It will be a burning waste of salt and sulfur — with nothing planted and nothing growing, not even a blade of grass. It will be like the destruction of Sodom and Gomorrah, and Admah and Zeboyim, which the Lord destroyed in fierce anger. All the nations will ask why the Lord's fierce anger has done this to the land.

And the answer will be: These people abandoned the covenant of the Lord, the God of their ancestors, the covenant he made with them when he brought them out of Egypt. They went off and worshiped other gods, gods they didn't know, gods he hadn't given them. Therefore the Lord's anger burned furiously against this land, and he brought on it all the curses written in this book. He uprooted them from their land and banished them to another land, where they still live today.

There are some things the Lord our God has kept secret, but he has revealed his laws, and we and our descendants must obey them forever.

Prosperity After Turning to the Lord
DT 30:1-10

When you are scattered in faraway countries, you will realize that the Lord is punishing you and that the curses he promised have been fulfilled. But if you and your descendants return to him with all your heart and all your soul, and begin obeying his laws, then the Lord will have mercy on you. He will bring you back from the nations where he scattered you, even if you are scattered to the farthest corners of the earth, and he will make you more prosperous and numerous than your ancestors.

He will remove the curses from you and put them on those who hate and persecute you. The Lord your God will give you and your descendants obedient hearts so you will once again obey his commands. You will love him with all your heart and continue to live in the land. Then he will make you prosperous in everything you do: You will have many children, numerous livestock, and abundant crops. Obey the commands written in this Book of the Law with all your heart and soul, and the Lord will once again delight in making you prosperous, just as he did for your ancestors.

The Offer of Life or Death
DT 30:11-20

Now what I'm commanding you today isn't too difficult or beyond your reach. It's not up in heaven, so no one has to ascend there to bring it down. It's not beyond the sea, so no one has to cross it and bring it back. No, the word is accessible and easy to understand, so that you can obey it.

Listen, I'm setting before you today life and prosperity, death and destruction. Love the Lord your God, walk in obedience to him, and keep his commands, and then you'll live and multiply, and the Lord your God will bless you in the land you will soon possess.

But if you turn your heart away and refuse to be obedient, worshiping other gods, then I'm telling you today that you'll certainly be destroyed and you won't live long in the land. I'm calling the heavens and the earth as witnesses against you. I've set before you life and death, blessings and curses. Now choose life! Love the Lord your God, obey him, and remain faithful to him. Then you and your descendants will live a long time in the land he promised to your ancestors, Abraham, Isaac, and Jacob.

Joshua Succeeds Moses as Leader
DT 31:1-8

Then Moses said, "I'm 120 years old now and will no longer be able to lead you. The Lord said I won't cross the Jordan. Instead, the Lord your God himself will cross over ahead of you. He'll destroy those nations and you'll take possession of their land. Joshua will also lead you across, as the Lord said. And the Lord will do to those nations what he did to the Amorite kings, Sihon and Og, who he destroyed along with their land. When the Lord gives you victory, you must do to them everything I commanded. Be strong and courageous. Don't be afraid or terrified, for the Lord your God is going with you; he'll never leave you nor forsake you."

Then Moses summoned Joshua and said to him in the presence of the Israelites, "Be strong and courageous, for you must go with these people into the land that the Lord promised their ancestors. You will be the one to divide their inheritance among them. The Lord himself will lead you and be with you; he'll never leave you nor forsake you. Don't be afraid and don't be discouraged."

So Moses wrote down these laws and gave a copy to all the elders of Israel and to the priests, who carried the Lord's Ark of the Covenant. Then Moses commanded them, "Every seventh year, during the Festival of Tabernacles, in the year for canceling debts, when the Israelites are gathered at the designated place of worship, read these laws to them. Everyone, including men, women, children, and foreign residents must listen. In this way both you and your descendants will learn to fear the Lord your God and faithfully obey his laws as long as you live in the land."

The Lord said to Moses, "You will soon die, so bring Joshua to the Tabernacle and I will appoint him as Israel's leader."

When Moses and Joshua arrived, the Lord appeared in a pillar of cloud over the tent's entrance. And the Lord said to Moses, "When you die, these people will go into the land flowing with milk and honey, the land I promised their ancestors. They'll have all they want to eat and will prosper, but they will soon be unfaithful to me and worship the foreign gods there, rejecting me and breaking the covenant I made with them. I know what they're going to do even before I bring them into the land.

"And when they reject me, I will be so furious that I will reject them; I'll hide my face from them and they will be destroyed. They will face many disasters, and they will know that these disasters have come upon them because I am no longer with them. Now write down this song and teach it to the Israelites. When these disasters come upon them, they and their descendants will remember this song, and it will testify against them."

Then Lord said to Joshua son of Nun, "Be strong and courageous, for you will bring the Israelites into the land I promised them, and I myself will be with you."

After Moses finished writing in a book all the laws, from beginning to end, he said to the Levites, "Place this Book of the Law beside the Ark of the Covenant. It will remain there as a witness against the Israelites. For I know how rebellious, stubborn, and utterly corrupt they are. Since they've been rebellious against the Lord during my lifetime, they'll be even more rebellious after I die! They'll reject what I've taught them and disaster will fall upon them, because their wicked ways have aroused the Lord's anger.

"Gather all the leaders and officials of the tribes, so I can speak to them directly and call heaven and earth to testify against them."

So that same day, Moses wrote down the Lord's song. He brought Joshua son of Nun with him and taught the Israelites the words from beginning to end:

> Listen, you heavens, and I'll speak; hear, you earth, the words of my mouth. Let my teaching fall like rain and my words descend like dew, like showers on new grass, like abundant rain on tender plants. I will proclaim the name of the Lord. Oh, praise the greatness of our God! He's the Rock; his works are perfect and all his ways are just. He's a faithful God who does no wrong; he's upright and he is just.

> But you're unfaithful and unworthy to be his people, a sinful and deceitful nation. Is this the way you repay the Lord, you foolish and unwise people? Isn't he your Father, your Creator, who made you and formed you?

> Remember the days of old; consider the generations long past. Ask your father and he'll tell you; ask your elders and they'll explain to you. When the Most High gave the nations their inheritance, when he divided all mankind, he set up boundaries according to the number of the sons of Israel. For the Lord's portion is his people, Jacob his allotted inheritance. In a desert land, he found him, in a barren and howling waste. He shielded him and cared for him; he guarded him as the apple of his eye, like an eagle that stirs up its nest and hovers over its young, spreading its wings to catch them and lift them up. The Lord alone led him, without the aid of a foreign god. He made him ride on the heights of the land and fed him with the fruit of the fields. He nourished him with honey from the rock, oil from the stony ground, yogurt and milk from cattle and flock, choice meat from lambs and goats, choice rams from Bashan, and the finest kernels of wheat.

> You drank the finest wine, made from the juice of grapes. But Israel soon became fat and unruly; filled with food, they became heavy and bloated. They abandoned the God who made them and rejected the Rock, their Savior. They made him jealous with their foreign gods and angered him with

their detestable idols. They sacrificed to false gods that aren't God — gods they hadn't known, gods that only recently appeared, gods their ancestors didn't fear.

You deserted the Rock, who fathered you; you forgot the God who gave you birth. So the Lord rejected his sons and daughters because he was angered by them. "I'll hide my face from them," he said, "and see what their end will be." They're a perverse generation; they're unfaithful children. They made me jealous by a god that is no God and angered me with their worthless idols. So I'll make them jealous with a nation that's not really a nation, and make them angry with a nation that has no understanding. For a fire will be kindled by my wrath, one that burns down to the realm of the dead below. It will devour the earth and its harvests and set afire the foundations of the mountains. I'll heap disasters on them and use all my arrows against them. I'll send famine and deadly diseases against them; I'll send against them the fangs of wild beasts and the venom of vipers that glide in the dust. War will bring death in the streets and terrors will strike in the homes. Young men and women will be killed, and neither infants nor the elderly will be spared.

I would have destroyed them completely so that no one would even remember them, but I dreaded the taunt of their enemies. They'd claim the victory in defeating my people when it was I myself who destroyed them. But those nations have no sense; there is no discernment in them. If only they were wise, they would discern what their end will be! How could one soldier chase 1,000 troops, or two put 10,000 to flight? This is impossible unless their Rock had abandoned them, unless the Lord had given them up. For their rock isn't like our Rock, as even our enemies recognize. Their vine comes from the vine of Sodom and from the fields of Gomorrah. Their grapes are filled with poison, and their clusters with bitterness. Their wine is the venom of serpents, the deadly poison of cobras.

The Lord has stored up a list of their sins and locked it in his vault. Vengeance belongs to the Lord, and I will repay. In due time their foot will slip; their day of disaster is near and their doom rushes upon them. The Lord will rescue his people when he sees their strength is gone; he will have mercy on his servants when he sees no one, whether slave or free, is left.

Then the Lord will ask, "Now where are their gods, the rock they took refuge in, the gods who ate the fat of their sacrifices and drank the wine of their drink offerings? Let them rise up to help you! Let them give you shelter! See now that I myself am he! There is no god besides me. I put to death and I bring to life; I've wounded and I'll heal, and no one can deliver out of my hand. As surely as I am the Living God, I raise my hand and vow that when I sharpen my flashing sword and my hand grasps it in judgment, I'll take vengeance on my adversaries and repay those who hate me. My arrows will drip with their blood, while my sword devours flesh: the blood of the slain and the captives, the heads of the enemy leaders. Rejoice, all you nations, that the Lord has vindicated his people. He will avenge the blood of his servants; he'll take vengeance on his enemies and make atonement for both land and people.

When Moses finished reciting the song, he said, "Make sure you obey all the commands I've given you today. Repeat them to your children so they will faithfully obey the Lord's teachings."

Moses Blesses the Tribes
DT 33:1-29

Before his death Moses, the man of God, pronounced blessings on the Israelites with the following words:

The Lord came from Sinai and dawned over them from Seir; he shone forth from Mount Paran. He came with myriads of holy ones from the south, from his mountain slopes. Surely it's you who love the people; all the holy ones are in your hand. At your feet they all bow down, and from you receive instruction, the law that Moses gave us, the possession of the community of Jacob. He was king over Israel when the leaders of the people assembled, along with the tribes of Israel.

And this is what Moses said about each tribe:

Reuben: Let Reuben live and not die, nor their people be few.

Judah: Hear, Lord, the cry of Judah; bring them to their people. With their own hands, they defend their cause. Oh, be their help against their enemies!

Levi: Lord, you reveal your will by the Thummim and Urim through your faithful servants, the Levites. You tested them at Massah; you contended with them at the waters of Meribah. They showed greater loyalty to you than to their parents, siblings, or children. They watched over your word and guarded your covenant, teaching your precepts to Jacob and your law to Israel. They offer incense before you and whole burnt offerings on your altar. Bless all their skills, Lord, and be pleased with the work of their hands. Strike down their enemies, so that they rise against them no more.

Benjamin: Let the beloved of the Lord rest secure in him, for he shields them all day long and dwells in their midst.

Joseph (Ephraim and Manasseh): May the Lord bless their land with the precious dew from heaven above and with the deep waters that lie below; with the best the sun brings forth and the finest the moon can yield; with the choicest gifts of the ancient mountains and the fruitfulness of the everlasting hills. May their land be filled with the best gifts and the fullness of the earth, blessed by the Lord who appeared in the burning bush. Let all these blessings rest on the head of Joseph, on the brow of the prince among their brothers. In majesty they're like a firstborn bull; their horns are the horns of a wild ox. With them he'll gore the nations, even those at the ends of the earth. Such are the ten thousands of Ephraim; such are the thousands of Manasseh.

Zebulun and Issachar: May Zebulun be prosperous in their travels, and you, Issachar, at home in your tents. They'll summon foreigners to the mountain and offer the sacrifices of the righteous; they'll feast on the abundance of the seas, on the treasures hidden in the sand.

Gad: Blessed is he who enlarges Gad's domain! Gad lives there like a lion, tearing at arm or head. They chose the best land for themselves; the leader's portion was kept for them. When the heads of the people assembled, they carried out the Lord's righteous will and their judgments concerning Israel.

Dan: Dan is a lion's cub, leaping out from Bashan.

Naphtali: Naphtali is abounding with the favor of the Lord and is full of his blessing; they'll inherit the land south of the sea of Galilee.

Asher: Most blessed of sons is Asher; let them be favored by their brothers, and let them bathe their feet in oil. The bolts of their gates will be iron and bronze, and their strength will equal their days.

There is no one like the God of Israel, who rides across the heavens to help you and on the clouds in his majesty. The eternal God is your refuge, and underneath are his everlasting arms. He'll drive out your enemies before you and command you to destroy them! So Israel will live in safety.

Jacob will dwell securely in a land of grain and new wine, where the heavens drop dew. Blessed are you, Israel! Who is like you, a people saved by the Lord? He's your shield and helper and your glorious sword. Your enemies will cringe before you, and you'll trample upon their backs.

Moses Dies on Mount Nebo
DT 32:48-52|DT 34:1-12

Then the Lord told Moses, "Go up into the Abarim Mountain Range here in Moab opposite Jericho. Climb Mount Nebo and go to the top of Pisgah; you'll be able to see Canaan from a distance, the land I'm giving the Israelites as their own possession. There on the mountain you will die and join your ancestors in death, just as your brother Aaron died on Mount Hor. Neither of you is entering the land, because both of you were unfaithful to me at the waters of Meribah near Kadesh, in the Zin Desert. You didn't respect or honor me in the presence of the Israelites."

Then Moses climbed Mount Nebo and the Lord showed him the whole land — from Gilead to Dan; all of Naphtali; the territory of Ephraim and Manasseh; all the land of Judah as far as the Mediterranean Sea; the Negev; and the whole region that reaches from Zoar to the Valley of Jericho — known as the City of Palm trees.

Then the Lord said, "This is the land I vowed to give to Abraham, Isaac, and Jacob and their descendants. I have let you see it with your eyes, but you will not cross over to enter it."

So Moses, the Lord's servant, died there in Moab, as the Lord had said. The Lord buried him there, in the valley opposite Beth Peor, but to this day no one knows where his grave is. Moses was 120 years old when he died, yet his eyesight was still good and his strength had not diminished. The Israelites grieved for Moses in the plains of Moab for 30 days, the standard period of mourning.

Now Joshua son of Nun was filled with the spirit of wisdom because Moses had laid his hands on him. So the Israelites listened to him and did what the Lord had commanded through Moses.

Since then, no prophet has risen in Israel like Moses, whom the Lord spoke to face to face. The Lord sent him to perform miraculous signs and wonders against Egypt, Pharaoh, and his officials, things no other prophet has done before. No prophet has ever demonstrated the mighty power or terrifying things that Moses did in the sight of all Israel.

About C. Austin Tucker

C. Austin Tucker is a writer, editor, and teacher with a passion for God and his Word. She has been a Bible teacher for more than 15 years and is the founder of Route 66 Ministries, which is dedicated to helping people read and understand the Bible chronologically. She holds a Master's degree in Biblical Studies and plans to pursue a doctorate. When not writing, she's most likely indulging in old school music and sitcoms or watching superhero and time travel movies.

Connect with her at cynthia@wordtruthlifebible.com or https://www.amazon.com/author/caustintucker.

Made in the USA
Middletown, DE
23 April 2021